ON THE BASIS OF HEARSAY

by

F. J. Fishburn

Grosvenor House
Publishing Limited

This book is published by
Grosvenor House Publishing Ltd
Link House
140 The Broadway, Tolworth, Surrey, KT6 7HT.
www.grosvenorhousepublishing.co.uk

A CIP record for this book
is available from the British Library

ISBN 978-1-78623-153-6

To my wife Evi, in appreciation of sixty years of happiness, and to my ancestors who made this book possible

Acknowledgements

To my wife, Evi, for her advice and forbearance during the long gestation period of this book, to Pat Petrie for suggesting its title, to Glen Petrie for his help and suggestions, to my granddaughter Lauren Davidson for first editing it, to Kurt and Margrit Stern for their gentle persuasion to finish my book, to the Guisborough Museum and to Sharon Rose and Graeme Milton for preparing it for publication, my thanks.

Foreword

The title of my book will become clear as you read it, so don't stop here. The information it contains about my forebears is based on second- and often third-hand accounts. My grandparents died young before I was old or interested enough to ask them about their lives. At that time as my story shows, they had too many other things on their minds, to be concerned with the past. When later I tried to question my parents and other relatives I found a general reluctance to answer: "we don't talk about those days, they are of no interest" or, as my mother would say, "look forward not back."

Delving into families' histories has become popular in these quieter and less threatening days. It occurred to me, therefore, that I should make some record of my family's history and my own story as best I could, so that our descendants, our grandchildren and now great-grandchildren, of whom the first has arrived, should know something of their heritage and their origins.

It is a happy tale on the whole even with its sad moments. I hope that all who read this book will enjoy it.

Chapter 1 – Exodus

"*Schutzie wir mussen schnell gehen.* We must go quickly. I am leaving you with Frau Kupfer; be a good boy and stay quietly with her until I get back."

With these words my mother woke me around midnight a few days before Christmas 1936. She took me, still in my pyjamas, across the corridor to the apartment of the Kupfers, our neighbours, on the Landsbergerstrasse in Leipzig. I could hear some excited and worried-sounding conversation in muted tones, presumably so I shouldn't hear what was being said. I knew that my father was not at home but I had no idea of what was happening. Mrs Kupfer got me dressed and my mother quickly finished packing some suitcases which fortunately were ready and waiting. We then left very hurriedly for the *Hauptbahnhof,* where my father was waiting for us with our tickets, and took the first train to Antwerp.

My father had been arrested by the Gestapo a few hours earlier on his way home from work in one of their periodical round-ups of Jews. Nothing personal you understand, just that he seemed Jewish. As it happens he did not look particularly so, but the Nazis had a nose for such things.

My parents had no non-Jewish friends apart from their neighbours, the Kupfers. Mrs Kupfer's father was chief of, or held some high position in, the Leipzig Fire Brigade and accordingly, had to be a member of the Nazi Party. He was fortunately in a position of some authority and his good offices obtained my father's release, with the admonition however, not to wait upon the hour of our going but to leave at once.

[I called my grandparents "Opa" and "Oma", which is the German diminutive for Grandfather and Grandmother, and will, for the sake of brevity, do so in these pages.]

For some months before, I had noticed a considerable and puzzling amount of activity going on. My mother seemed to be spending most of her time at her parents' apartment rather than at the factory. Even Opa seemed too busy to pay much attention to me. There were cases and sheets and clothes laid out as if they were being packed to go away. My mother was hollowing out the legs of chairs and other furniture and filling them with what looked like coins and jewellery; all very mysterious. I had no idea what was going on, except that the normal happy routine of our lives was being destroyed.

The day when we were all assembled at the railway station came too soon, saying goodbye to Opa and Oma and my aunts Dora and Yetti. As they boarded the train, there were tears all round, particularly from Yetti who now had a serious boyfriend whom she did not want to leave. I remember her crying, "*Mein Karl, Mein Karl*, will I ever see him again?" As Opa kissed and hugged me as if he would never see me again either, he cried, which I had never seen him do, and that made me cry too.

The next few weeks seemed strangely quiet at home. We no longer went to my grandparents' apartment in the Menckestrasse and seemed hardly to venture outside. Mother kept on hollowing out furniture. The factory had closed, although Dad still went to his work, looking increasingly worried. As the warm colours of autumn were replaced by the biting winds of winter, and the trees now stripped of leaves had their branches defined by snow, our apartment became increasingly empty. Most of our possessions had been packed in large containers and sent away and it became very cold. Then one day late at night the doorbell rang. There was an urgent message for Mother delivered by hand. Our Exodus had begun.

Its planning, however, had taken some years. Opa was a nervous man, politically speaking. He did not take the view that the attacks on Jews by the Nazi Brownshirts, which became increasingly frequent from 1928, were a passing phase and in any case he was one of those Ostjuden, Jews from eastern Europe, against whom, if the German Jews were correct, they were aimed. The prosperity and optimism that the Weimar Republic had generated proved short-lived and illusory.

Ruth Gay in *The Jews of Germany* described the situation for Jews in Germany:

"By 1929 the Jews had good reasons to be nervous. Early that year a serious economic recession had begun to grip the country, imposing 2 million unemployed on the harassed German welfare system... As joblessness reached disastrous heights, sellers of nostrums – among them anti-Semitism – found ever growing numbers of adherents..."

Perhaps Opa had foreseen the rise of Nazism, or perhaps he was afraid of Communism or civil war. It was clear to him that Germany was not a safe place and he decided we should leave. It was not that Opa was particularly clever or far-sighted; he was a cynic or perhaps, more kindly, a realist – the type who believes things can only get worse. Like so many of his generation and background, Opa was comparatively uneducated in most non-Jewish matters. He was by no means illiterate; he could read and write fluently in both Hebrew and Yiddish. His German was competent but he never mastered English, though he understood it perfectly well. He was a very clever man; more than that, he was wise and it was his foresight which thankfully saved the family from the fate which befell so many other Jews.

When, towards the end of 1930, he heard that my mother was pregnant he apparently called the family together.

"*Ich habe angst.* I'm very afraid and I'm very worried," he told them. "Hitler's Brownshirts are attacking Jews everywhere, and no one is even trying to stop them. It's dangerous to go out into the street. Germany is not safe for us; we have to leave but where shall we go? There's Palestine, America or England. It will be difficult for us to get into Palestine. The English won't let us in, and in any case it would be a very hard life there; there's fighting with the Arabs and I'm too old to be a pioneer. America is a long way away, *jener eck veld,* the back of beyond, and we don't know anyone there. England seems the best chance. It's the only place in Europe which will be safe if there is a war, as, if things go on as they are, there will be.

"It's not so far away. There are opportunities there. I read in the papers that they're looking for new businesses to provide work for the unemployed, and the Government gives help to anyone starting a new business. Max, you go to England to see what you can find, and take Herman with you. I know people in the fur trade and I'll arrange for you to go there."

3

"Sigmund, you worry too much, you exaggerate," Oma argued. "They all say it will all blow over. We've already left one country and thank heaven we're doing well here. How shall we start again? We're a lot older now and with a grandchild on the way it will be very hard. I haven't the strength. How will you start a new business?"

"We Jews can't ignore what's going on. Hitler has a lot of popular support. People read *Mein Kampf* and think he's got the answers to all their problems – it's all the fault of the Jews. People cheer when his thugs break Jewish bones and windows. Here we have no status, no nationality and before long we'll have no rights at all, mark my words. I'm a simple man, *Ich bin kein grosser chochem, aber ich bin kein naar*. I'm no great sage, but I'm no fool either. I don't know anything about politics, but I see what I see and I know what I see, and what I see is bad. I see old men humiliated and women spat on. I see the words '*Juden raus*' – Jews out – everywhere. No one protests. I don't fool myself it's not happening. It's because Bertl [my mother] is going to have a child that we must go. This is no place for a Jewish child. I don't want my grandchild to be in danger. We have no choice; we must go. I've made up my mind and I don't want any arguments or long faces. Let's just get ready, but no one must know what we're doing, otherwise we might be stopped from leaving. If things here get better we can still think again, but I'm not hopeful. In the meantime you can all start learning English."

"If we go anywhere it should be Eretz Israel, that's where I want to go," said Dora, a keen Zionist.

Mother agreed with Opa: "Things look bad here. People are afraid of the Communists and support the Nazis, though I don't think the Communists would be any better for us than the Nazis. They may not pick on Jews but to them we are still the enemy. Either way it will end up bad for the Jews, it always does." Dad agreed. This was one thing he was positive about.

Uncle Max said he would do "whatever Papa says", Uncle Herman was only too willing to get away from his father's restraining hand and to seek pastures new and my Aunt Yetti was only thirteen and had no voice.

Opa was not a person who travelled blindly, and so it was that in 1932 Opa sent his sons Max and Herman to England, like Joshua's spies, to see what opportunities existed there and to learn the language. They had no easy time of it.

As Opa had read in his Yiddish papers, the world economic crisis which had caused unrest in Germany had also created a need for new industries to provide jobs in England. The North East was particularly badly affected. It seemed that the heavy industries, which drew on the local raw materials of coal and iron, were no longer needed. Government assistance and financial incentives were on offer to anyone who could provide employment.

Uncle Max, who was nothing if not diligent, found out through his enquiries and approaches to various authorities that the Council in Guisborough was looking for anyone who could provide employment for local people in light industry, so he approached them.

Guisborough was a small town in North Yorkshire with a population of about 7,000, some nine miles from Middlesbrough. Its Labour Urban District Council had been active in its efforts to attract industry and there were some premises available on the Middlesbrough Road at the western entrance to the town. These were in the shape of an old derelict L-shaped building that had been part of a disused sewage farm. Max called Opa over from Germany to see for himself.

In May 1936 the Council minutes recorded that "an enquiry" had been received "on behalf of a person, not then in the country, who was interested in opening a factory to employ 200 persons". At that time, Opa would probably have accepted anything that was offered to him because few places could have seemed less inviting than Guisborough. Home Office permission was required for the family to immigrate; representations were made to the Home Office under the auspices of the Council and two months later approval was given and the necessary visas were granted, and with my parents' and my arrival on 1 January 1937, the whole family was in England.

Opa's business, in Leipzig, had been that of a *Waschenfabrik*, a manufacturer of bed linen and similar products, including linings for coats and jackets. According to that city's records, the business, at 5 Hainstrasse, was first registered in July 1928 under Oma's name although it appears that from January 1929 until September 1933, Max was registered as proprietor. It then reverted back to Oma's name. The records show that on 4 February 1926, a Bankruptcy Order was registered, presumably against Opa, which was discharged in 1930. This would account for the business being registered in the names of his wife and son. But whatever name the business was registered in it was always very much Opa's and he ran it, as he did everything else, with great discipline; some might say a rod of iron. The files also show, presumably to record the cessation of the business:

"*Am 10.11.1936 m Ehefrau u.To. Jetti nach London*", i.e. "on 10.11.1936 with his wife and daughter Jetti [spelled thus in the official documents] to London", that being presumably the date they left for London. It is not clear why that entry did not refer to Dora, but I can only assume the reason may have been that "Jetti", known by the family as Schnucky and by me as Yetti, was still a minor, being under 21, and that Dora went under her own right.

Before leaving because their visa only became effective on 1 January 1937, my parents were to supervise and ensure the loading and safe dispatch of the containers, in which all the furniture and other items were loaded.

My father's brother, Fritz, had left Germany some time before and was working in Antwerp and we went to stay with him while we waited until we could catch the night ferry from the Hook of Holland to Harwich in Essex, about 80 miles from London, which was then the most convenient ferry route from Holland to England. Though we did not know what the future might hold, at least we were now safe. I had no idea until many years later of the lucky escape we had had.

As a postscript to our quick evacuation from Leipzig; after the war in 1945, my parents received a letter from Herr Kupfer. He had spent most of the war years as a prisoner of war in England. Though he had our address, he had made no effort to contact us lest this should cause my parents embarrassment.

6

Chapter 2 – Beginnings

I know little of my grandparents' background and ancestry. It was never easy to get accurate historical information from either side of my large and sprawling family. Both my paternal and maternal family were reluctant to discuss their roots, their ancestry or their history. This seems to have been a generational attitude as I know of many others who took a similar view of the past, namely that it was best forgotten. So I really do not know why or how most of my family came to be in Germany, and can only suggest that this was because it was the nearest place to escape from the disastrous and terrible pogroms in Russia and Poland, which occurred during the last two decades of the 19th century, and which at least then, did not discriminate against them.

After my parents married they lived in Leipzig, but Dad's parents remained in Berlin though I assume – as I have no personal memory of such events – that we visited them from time to time. Indeed, I saw very little of my father's parents. Such information as I have been able to obtain from family sources is that Opa Fischbein was born around 1864 in Odessa, the Crimea – then part of Russia – and Oma Fischbein was born around 1882 in Plotsk, Poland. There was a considerable age difference between them but I never noticed that; so far as I was concerned all grandparents were old.

It was not until they too came to England that I had any sort of relationship with them and even that was very scant. I remember that Opa Fischbein was a handsome man, tall and upright but given to a quick temper. Oma Fischbein was small and round, quiet and inoffensive and totally unable to deal with the strong characters of the Schmulewitsch clan. My father's antecedents were never spoken of, largely because my mother's family was not only large but all-consuming and little interested in the history of others.

As I grew older and began to understand more about relationships (and family ones in particular) I became aware that my maternal and paternal grandparents did not get on well. In fact, my maternal grandparents seemed not to get on well with any of their "machatonim", a useful word which means the parents of their children's spouses, for which English has no equivalent. Dad's parents were the first and for several years the only such relations.

Oma, Sarah Schmulewitsch (nee Obermann) was born on 29 October 1887 in Czestechowa, Poland, a large city perhaps best known for its "Black Madonna". Like so many Polish towns at that time it was a centre of Jewish life. A quarter of the population was Jewish. How and why Sarah came to Germany, and the circumstances of her immigration, and meeting and marrying my grandfather are also shrouded in mystery. But unlike Opa it seems she had a family, and in particular, a remarkable father who, according to family lore, married for the fourth time at the age of 80 and flew the Atlantic in 1928. (If at all it was probably in a Zeppelin such as the Hindenburg!) I merely tell the story as I heard it but I would like it to be true.

Though it was never mentioned or discussed in my presence, it seems not unreasonable to assume that my great-grandfather may have been a man of some means and helped set up my grandfather in business. My grandparents lived a very comfortable life and went regularly to the major German and neighbouring spa towns, such as Baden-Baden, Marienbad and others. As my grandfather's own business seems hardly to have been prosperous enough to support their lifestyle on its own it is reasonable to conjecture that Sarah had received a sizeable dowry and support from her father.

Opa and Oma were married in 1905 or 1906. My grandmother cannot have been more than eighteen at the time. She had three children by the age of 23. Her eldest child, Max, was born in November 1907, my mother in 1909 and her third child Herman in 1910. My mother's elder sister Dora was born in 1912 and Yetti (a.k.a. Schnucky) in 1917. Oma was only 43 when she became a grandmother on my birth. To me she always seemed old; she was constantly unwell, suffering from a variety of illnesses, including diabetes, high blood pressure and a weak heart. Opa on the other hand was always fit and well.

I was born on 21 June 1931, so I was told, which I had no reason to disbelieve, but it was not until I went to Leipzig for the first time, in the year 2000, after nearly 70 years, that I had any definite confirmation of that. My wife Evi and I went to the Wagner festival at Bayreuth, and I took the opportunity of a gap in the operas to go to Leipzig. I hadn't been back since leaving Germany but I found the offices where births and deaths were registered and, to my amazement, with typical German efficiency they were able to produce my birth certificate. Until then I had been told that there was no birth certificate in existence, but upon payment of a small sum it was delivered to me shortly afterwards.

My birth took place, apparently somewhat before schedule, at Oma and Opa's large apartment at number 5 Menckestrasse, which had big rooms, high ceilings, and corridors long and wide enough for me to be able to ride my little tricycle along them when I was old enough to do so. By all accounts my arrival, in the early hours of the morning, led to my Uncle Herman being discovered in flagrante with one of my grandmother's maids. Alarmed no doubt by the ululations usually accompanying the arrival of a grandchild, particularly the first, he fled (in disarray) the warm bed he had been enjoying, straight into his father's arms. The happiness of the occasion did not mitigate his sentence of internal exile. He was gated and put under curfew for a while but fortunately he never held this against me, indeed, he was a most loving and caring uncle and as will appear later I owe much to him, as I do to all my family. Neither the time nor the place of my birth were particularly propitious for a young Jewish boy as two years later Hitler became Chancellor of Germany, and the Nazi terror, which had already started illegally, became the law of the land.

Under German law one had to have a German name regardless of nationality; I was given the civil names of Joachim Fred. There is a Joachim in the Bible and Fred was a compromise. My mother did not wish to call me Friedrich or Fritz as these sounded too German, and I had a living relative called Fritz, my father's brother, and Jewish custom discourages naming two living family members the same. My Hebrew names were Yosef Fayvel ben Yacov, given, no doubt, in memory of some distant ancestor. I have no idea who

"Yosef Fayvel" was – I like to think that it may have been my great-grandfather who died shortly before I was born. I was always "Fredele" to my family regardless of my age, and to everyone else, except my children and grandchildren, "Freddy".

Though I was the second (and last) generation of my family to be born in Germany I did not qualify for German nationality due to the rigorous German nationality laws, nor did any of my family. We were stateless. When we left Germany we travelled to Britain on a "Nansen Pass", an identification card for displaced persons introduced on the initiative of the Norwegian explorer and humanitarian Froidtjof Nansen, a Nobel Peace Prize winner in 1922, and issued under the auspices of the League of Nations.

To my own sorrow I am an only child and I felt this more and more as I grew older. I would much rather have had a brother, or even better, a sister, not only as a companion to relieve the utter loneliness which I often felt but to share some of the responsibilities which later fell upon me and I felt inadequate to deal with sensibly alone. I once asked my mother why she had had no other children and she replied that by the time Hitler came to power in 1933 it would have been foolhardy; and by the time she came to England she had neither the time nor the strength to do so. It seems that her health was even then also a problem, though I did not know of this until much later and was clearly at that time too young to understand such things.

My parents had met through my father's brother Fritz, who met my mother's sister Dora at one of the many Zionist youth organisations in Germany. Fritz was a good-looking fellow and Dora was very lively and attractive and both loved sport. Dora and Fritz were mutually attracted and there were suggestions that they wanted to get married, but apparently Fritz was not considered to be a suitable match for Dora, who was too young in any case.

So it was that my parents were married on Christmas Day, 1929. All the Schmulewitsch girls were married at Christmas as it minimised work disruption. Opa's children were all expected to work for his business, regardless of their marital status.

My parents established their home in Leipzig, at 24 Landsbergerstrasse, an apartment in the Kroch Siedlung built in

1929/1930; very new when my parents married, an early example of enlightened town planning which became world famous later and was copied both in England and other countries around the world. I think we must have lived on the first floor; certainly we lived low enough for my mother to watch what I was doing and to call to me from the window. None of our immediate neighbours were Jewish, and they greeted each other as had become almost compulsory with raised arm and "Heil Hitler". One day in child-ish ignorance I did the same. Mother must have seen me because she immediately shouted to me to come in at once. I was never let out alone again.

My father, until we came to England, worked as an in-house accountant with his cousin Bernard Schermann, who had a large clothing business.

I have few recollections of my early days although there is one that has always remained in my memory. Chanukah, the Jewish festival of lights, usually coincides with the Christmas period and is traditionally, like Christmas, a time for gifts. Families gather together for parties and it is always a joyous occasion. On this particular Chanukah – I cannot have been more than four at the time – there was a definite feeling of excitement. I was not allowed into my bedroom and our home seemed even more full of people than usual. Though I felt something was in the air I had no idea what it was. When at last I was allowed into the darkened room the scene that met my eyes was magical, absolutely magical; I can see it to this day. Laid out on the floor was an electric train set, with all the accompanying station lights, signals and the like which my grandfather had gone to great trouble to set up, with all the love of an indulgent grandfather who loved toys himself. It was an "O" gauge model made by the famous German toy company, Marklin. It had a green motor unit, a model of the latest type of German railway engine (electric with a pantograph) and three maroon-coloured coaches, one of which was a Pullman-type dining car with tables and little lights which lit up, and people sitting in the seats. Another was a sleeping car with bunks that could be removed, also with little models occupying them. It was the very latest thing at the time and is now regarded as a classic, worth a great deal of money.

A few days after Chanukah, I was invited to the birthday party of a young disabled boy, the son of one of Mother's friends. Just as we were leaving my mother realised she had forgotten to buy a birthday present. She looked round my toys for something suitable and her eyes lit up on seeing my train set. She picked up the dining car.

"No," I cried, "You can't take that; it's Opa's present, it's part of my train, don't take that – take another carriage but not that, it's my favourite." "Hush," she replied to soothe me, "Keep calm. Just think how lucky you are; you can run and jump like a normal boy. I'll buy you another carriage tomorrow."

But, of course, she never did. I never forgave her for this, much as I loved her and good mother though she was. I have ever since refused to give away anything given to me as a present. That train set accompanied us to England and I enjoyed it for many years until it was inexplicably "mislaid" when we moved house in 1947.

Chapter 3 – England

My first sight of England was the yellow haze of the harbour lights at Harwich trying to pierce the thick freezing morning mist. It was New Year's Day 1937, very early, dark and bitterly cold. I felt wretched. I had been sick all the way over on the boat from the Hook of Holland. I could hear a lot of noise, men shouting, ships' foghorns sounding their doomful blasts, and trains clanging as they were being pushed around by busy little engines blowing steam everywhere adding to the mist and confusion. There was a long wait and then my father picked me up and carried me on to the waiting boat train. I fell fast asleep until we reached London.

England was wet and miserable and unwelcoming. I vaguely recall the boat train to London – not that I had any idea of what London was – and the smell of smoke and steam and oil. And the noise: the loud all-pervading and consuming noise; and the shouting in a strange tongue as we left the train. It was all so baffling and confusing. However, by the time the train arrived in the city I was beginning to recover and take an interest in my surroundings. We were met in London by my Uncle Herman and taken to the small flat he and his wife Ray shared with his wife's mother, Mrs Greenstein, and her brother Bernard. How they managed also to accommodate us, I do not know.

We stayed there for two or three days, just long enough, so to speak, to catch our breath, get the tickets and make arrangements for the journey north to Middlesbrough. We were to take the express train from King's Cross to Darlington, the junction for Teesside. Much smaller than the Leipzig *Hauptbahnhof*, King's Cross station was the main terminus of the London and North Eastern Railway (LNER). The station was full of noise and dirt from the black smoke and hissing steam of the huge Pacific engines panting and puffing away as they warmed up in the cold air for their long journeys to the even colder North. People were rushing around shouting and calling to each other, some were running, others just standing waiting; young couples were sadly holding hands or kissing lingeringly. Porters struggled with suitcases, guards blew whistles and waved flags. I was wide awake by now and excited by the hustle and bustle of everything around me. It was a different world. I remembered how clean and neat and tidy and quiet the railway station in Leipzig had seemed, for all its size, but I also noticed that here there were no soldiers, no policemen, no uniforms except those of the railwaymen. It seemed very informal and disorganised but friendly compared to Leipzig.

By the time we left London I was able to take in my surroundings but nothing of what I saw of London was in any way at first encouraging, nor gave any idea of the happiness to come. It all seemed dirty and noisy and smelly and there were far too many people and cars and traffic generally. As we travelled north I watched the bleak winter countryside pass by through the steamed-up train windows and could feel the cold and damp increase. At least there were some green fields, as our journey took us through pleasant countryside past small houses and towns which were often hidden by the smoke from the train's engine. I began to feel excited; we were soon to be with Opa and Oma again in a new world and our new home.

At Darlington we were collected by my Aunt Dora, who took us in a car the last 15 miles to Middlesbrough. There I was met by the amazing first sight of our new home, the Grey House, which remains one of the defining features on the landscape of my life. It was – still is – an impressive building and to a small boy it was huge. I thought it was a castle and indeed it looked like one with its great grey walls and high chimneys like crenulated towers; its broad driveway leading to steps, guarded at the top by two large stone pillars. Its large forecourt and balcony, and its huge windows were a far cry from our small apartment in Leipzig.

The address was 79 Cambridge Road, Linthorpe, a pleasant suburb of Middlesbrough. The house stands slightly above the road which gives it an added air of grandeur. I thought we were in heaven and for me it was. I had no idea how we came by this magnificent dwelling, how we could afford it, how it was paid for or the like. I never thought to ask, nor would I have been told, and the years have not diminished my ignorance although I did learn a little about the matter when Oma died in 1947.

For me this was heaven on earth, but to my family and particularly my young aunts, used to the lifestyle and cultural excitement of a major city, Middlesbrough was a profound culture shock. Leipzig was a *Weldstadt*, the "city of Bach and books" and, to many, the cultural capital of Germany, not to say Europe. It had a large and vital Jewish community and a rich Jewish life. It had cafes, restaurants, department stores, bookshops, theatres, a world-renowned opera house and orchestra (the Gewandhaus founded by Felix Mendelssohn), tourists and nightlife. No British city, other possibly than London, could offer all these and even London could not compare with the musical stature of Leipzig at that time.

Chapter 4 – Middlesbrough

Middlesbrough had the Transporter Bridge, a very fine mock-Gothic town hall and a football team, then in the First Division, but to my family, Middlesbrough was a dirty, uncivilised, cold, backward and generally unpleasant place. Looking at it just as a place, even allowing for the pleasant middle-class suburbs of Linthorpe and Acklam, I can see they were right. What it did have though, were wonderfully friendly and lovely people.

Middlesbrough, founded in 1831, was the epitome of the industrial revolution. At the mouth of the River Tees, it was a natural harbour, a port for the ships exporting the coal and ores mined in the area. Its civic badge, a lion rampant, bore the Latin motto "Erimus" – "we shall be" – on the Town Hall evidencing the founding fathers' self-confidence. Foundries and ironworks were soon established to smelt the iron ore and the ironmasters, the industrialists who established the factories, developed the town to house their workers. There was a large Irish immigration; Middlesbrough is a Catholic See. The houses were built back-to-back, *Coronation Street*-style, in rows on a grid-iron pattern, unique in British town planning at the time and the streets are named to commemorate the ironmasters, such as Bolckow – himself a German immigrant in the 1830s – Vaughan, Furness, and above all, Dorman and Long. The world famous company Dorman Long provided the iron and steel for the Sydney Bridge. Middlesbrough's redeeming features were its proximity to the seaside resorts of Redcar and Saltburn, the Cleveland Hills, and the Yorkshire Moors.

But I can, myself, remember the poverty; the children running barefoot in the streets in the cold northern winter, the dirt, the drabness. Newport Road, the port area and along the river were like similar areas everywhere, insalubrious. It was said that in certain areas policemen could only go in pairs. I cannot say how true this was but it was probably true.

Nearby were the ICI works at Billingham, Synthonia, known to locals as "the Synthetic". The eerie atmosphere created by the blue street lamps, especially when it was foggy, which it usually was, combined with the acrid chemical smells from the ICI works, and the smoke and fumes from the iron and steel works of Dorman Long, created a smelly, Stygian gloom. This was particularly bad during the long winter nights. In the daytime, when the wind was in the wrong direction (which it was more often than not), washing could not be hung out to dry for risk of damage from the chemical deposits it carried. It was a dreadful place. I believe that even today, though the town has now improved beyond recognition from those days, some parts of Middlesbrough still have the highest incidence of lung cancer and respiratory diseases in the country, according to statistics of the Health Authorities.

Yet to a young boy, not interested in operas and concerts or other attractions of a major city, it was, as I have said, paradise. There was little traffic and I could play freely in the streets of the pleasant, well-gardened suburbs where we lived. In Leipzig I had never been allowed out alone but here in Middlesbrough, living in a large house with a big garden instead of a small restricted flat, I could go out without fear. No one worried where I went or where I was. There was no need to. My parents had no need to fear roving Brownshirts looking for trouble, or offensive "Heil Hitler" greetings.

To me, it was also a liberation in other ways. I was finally able to discard the girlish clothes in which my mother had seen fit to dress me, to compensate for the fact that I was a boy; I think perhaps she would have preferred a daughter. She was wise enough to realise that the silken sailor and similar suits – all of which she made herself – although fashionable in Leipzig, were inappropriate in Middlesbrough, though she stopped dressing me up with some reluctance and no little regret.

To illustrate just how different this was from Germany, and to anticipate events just a little, by the time the factory was fully operational, I, aged 7, was able during school holidays to travel alone on two buses to take lunch to the family in the factory at Guisborough. The local bus terminal was opposite our house in

Thornaby Road. Oma would prepare and pack the cooked lunches in two or three white enamel pots held together by a handle which fitted into louvres on their sides. One of the maids – we had two – would take me across the road to the bus and put me in the charge of the conductor who would help me on and off and made sure that I arrived safely. When the bus reached its other terminus at what was known as "the Exchange", the conductor would take me across the road to wait for the red United bus to Guisborough whose conductor looked after me similarly. This stopped directly outside the factory gates. I became well known to all those regularly travelling those routes and soon managed the journey without help. One cannot imagine that happening anywhere today. Those were leisurely and friendly times.

On my frequent visits to the factory, I would be treated by the girls as some kind of pet. They made a great fuss of me and I would badger them to give me rides on their bicycles. This involved me sitting on the seat while they pushed me around, which they seemed happy enough to do. One day when I was impatiently waiting for the lunch break so I could have my rides, I took one of the girls' bikes, one without a crossbar, put my legs through, stood on one pedal and pushed and rode. That is how I learned to ride a bike. I eventually became a keen cyclist, though not without the occasional calamity.

Though, on looking back, I now realise that I spent only 17 years of my life there – only 14 if one excludes the three years at university – I still feel that Middlesbrough is where my roots are. I remember those years with great affection. They were very happy times despite the war, the illnesses, the traumas and the deaths suffered by my family. Much of my emotional heart is still in the North East, which is not to say that I would wish to live there again, because one cannot recapture the past and efforts to do so lead to disillusionment and regret. I am, however, still a fanatical – though of necessity, often philosophical – supporter of Middlesbrough FC.

The whole family, other than Herman and Ray who remained in London, now lived together in the same house. It needed to be large to accommodate us all. The front door was imposing, but rarely used as, in true Yorkshire fashion it seemed, we always came through the back door. The main door had a Victorian-style decorated window and led through a coat lobby into a large entrance hall, which in turn led on to three large reception rooms. A heavy staircase went up to the first floor and a passageway round the end room led on to the big kitchen, which had a scullery and a large pantry. This is where the back door was.

The large dining room, where we lived for most of the time, was next to and separated by two doors from the kitchen. An old-fashioned coke-fired range in the kitchen supplied the heat for the hot water. There was no central heating and efficient gas fires in every room heated the house. Gas, thanks to the proximity of the coke and chemical plants nearby, from which it was piped, was the cheapest in the country and widely used throughout the area for all purposes, including street lighting.

My grandparents' furniture was dark and heavy – it was very German! – and filled the dining room and the drawing room. The drawing room contained a large desk, several large armchairs, and a huge bookcase – at least it seemed so to me – whose main func-tion appeared to be to house a rarely used German "Backhaus" Lexicon, a cross between an encyclopaedia and a dictionary. I remember that the books were too heavy for me to handle as a child. There were several smallish rugs on the floor rather like Oriental prayer mats. One of these had a border pattern of what looked to me like swastikas, which were Indian signs. When war broke out, Opa spent several days on his hands and knees with a bottle of Indian ink carefully turning these into squares. He cannot have thought that the presence of these symbols on an Oriental carpet could have betokened any sympathy for the Nazi cause or allow the family to be suspected of being German spies, but the hatred, perfectly understandable, of anything reminiscent of the Nazis was such as to lead otherwise perfectly sensible people to lose all sense of proportion.

The first floor had a large landing, three large bedrooms and along a separate corridor, a bathroom with a toilet, set for some reason on a plinth; something like a throne. There was also a sepa-rate W.C., and at the end of the corridor was my room, a narrow room, the smallest in the house, which was only just big enough to lay out my toys. The landing had a French door which opened out onto the balcony over the front porch. Opa, who was not much given to sitting in the open, loved sitting on this balcony and he would often ask me to go down and close the front gate to stop the draught!

The top floor had four bedrooms off another landing. The living space was reduced by the sloping roofs but the bedrooms were sizeable nevertheless. This was the second-class accommodation, where the maids lived, and where visitors were usually housed.

The whole household had to cope with the one bathroom and effectively one toilet, the other being in the bathroom. Large copper boilers held the hot water. As there were no thermostats, from time to time the water in these would boil over and it would sound as if the place was about to explode. The water was the softest in the land. Before electric immersion heaters were installed, the kitchen range had to be lit in summer as well as winter, and given the Teesside climate, this rarely caused a problem. The menfolk seemed to cope reasonably well with these limited washing facilities, but the ladies' ablutions caused turmoil, particularly at the weekend when they were getting ready for a party. Dora and Yetti, who were usually quick in everything but for their toilette, sought in turn to monopolise the bathroom. At times the disputes, accompanied by language siblings use to one another on the point of murder, came to such a pitch that Opa's intervention was needed. This was short and to the point: "Out, or I break the door down!" This usually worked although I, in my room next door, secretly hoped that some day the threat would actually be carried out!

The outhouses, originally the stables with all the stalls and woodwork still there, consisted of a large laundry or washroom which had its own boiler, and a large garage which could accommodate four cars, with a loft above.

The garden was nondescript and rarely used, except by me. We had a weekly gardener, at least we seemed to have a different one every week. My family were not addicted to fresh air and the air, in Middlesbrough, rarely merited that description!

The family household consisted originally of Opa and Oma, my parents, myself, my Uncle Max and my said aunts, Dora and Yetti and there were two live-in maids. Over the next two years our number grew to include, as they were able to leave Germany, my other grandparents, Yetti's future husband Karl (who although he did not live with us seemed to be there most of the time), his parents, Uncle Herman on his visits and, very occasionally, Ray. My mother's cousin Adolph Rockman – who for obvious reasons changed his name to Peter – the son of Oma's sister Lina (who remained in Romania), also spent a considerable amount of his time there. In addition, there was a constant stream of visitors who were passing through and others who did not actually live with us, but seemed to turn up regularly at mealtimes, including the local chazen, or cantor, of the synagogue who became a close friend. Most of the time there were some fifteen or more adults and me. My grandparents were very hospitable and kept open house, which is not to say that they necessarily approved of their visitors, nor did they spare them their comments, but they never let anyone go hungry. After we left the Grey House, in 1947, it became a hotel. It had always been something like that except that while we lived there, the food and accommodation were free.

My family's arrival in Middlesbrough was not met with universal enthusiasm by the local Jewish community. We were an unknown quantity to them and some feared that our arrival might affect their position; fear of immigration is not a recent phenomenon. The enormity of what was happening in Germany had not yet been fully understood. During 1936, the year of the Berlin Olympics, with Germany in the spotlight, overt acts of Nazi anti-semitism and racialism had been toned down, at least in areas where they would be visible to visitors. At first, Germany did not prevent the exodus of Jews, provided they took no valuables or money with them. The problem was that the Jews had nowhere to go – the Yiddish song, "Wohin zoll ich gein. Where shall I go?" says it all. Many Jews were themselves afraid that an influx of Jewish refugees would produce an anti-semitic reaction in their own society, and this was the fear of some of the Jewish families in Middlesbrough.

The Jewish community in Middlesbrough consisted of about 120 families, whose make-up was probably a microcosm of the Jews of Britain, except that, so far as I know, they were all Ashkenazi, that is, of Eastern European origin. There was a family named Pinto, which is a Sephardi name, and there was the usual hierarchy; the influential families, such as the Marks, the Simons, the Nimans, and the Dobermans.

There was no kosher butcher in the town but a local non-Jewish butcher had set aside a kosher section in his shop and, once a week, a kosher butcher in Leeds would supply him with meat, although the range was limited, and he would set aside separate knives and utensils. Rose and Maurice Saville, two pillars of the community and perhaps the only strictly religious family in the town, apart from the synagogue officials, ran a delicatessen and grocery store. Unlike today, packed meats and the like were not generally available, but from them you could get sausages – wursht. The community had three clergymen: a rabbi (Miller), a cantor (Geza Wulwik) and a "shammas" or verger, who rejoiced in the name of, and was always referred to and addressed as, Mr Turtledove; he was also the "shochet", the ritual slaughterer. A large number of officials for so small a community.

Most of the elders of the community seemed to be in the furniture trade but many of my parents' generation, second or even third generation English Jews, had gone into various professions, primarily medicine and law. The firms founded by Jewish solicitors still rank among the leading practices in the area. Our family doctor was Dr Joe Israel, who was in partnership with his brother-in-law, Dr Niman. Drs Israel and Niman were, as a sideline, top-class bridge players, and the local bridge teams still play for a cup donated by them which bears their name.

Some, like Herbert and Mabel Bloom, who lived directly opposite the Grey House, were very anglicised and reserved. Others were more welcoming, but I imagine the arrival of my noisy, lively and extrovert family must have caused some to wonder what had landed in their midst. However, my family soon found a place for themselves in the community. When we first arrived the religious services were held in the Linthorpe Road Assembly Rooms while the new synagogue in Park Road South was being completed. My family became regular attenders and contributed generously to local charities. Their enthusiasm and their numbers soon meant they held an important place in the local community

Chapter 5 – Opa and Oma: My Grandparents

Opa Schmulewitsch was, I understand, brought up by an uncle and aunt and was apprenticed to a watchmaker. I do not know what other family he had; they were never mentioned or talked of. I can only imagine that he must have been sent away from Riga, then in Russia, when he was sixteen to avoid being called up for military service and proceeded to Konigsberg, then in East Prussia, now Kalinin in Russia, as an entry to Germany, and Leipzig was near the Czech border. But I have no evidence to support this.

Opa was small (about 5 feet 4 inches tall), black-haired and wiry with a forbidding moustache. He had piercing black eyes, and a look from which could silence anyone. His hair remained black until a tumour struck him, when it turned white in a matter of days. He was totally unconcerned about appearance or clothes (his or other people's). But the best thing about him was he had magic hands. His early watchmaker's training was obviously his vocation. He loved machinery and anything mechanical and was happiest lying under some machine in the factory which had gone wrong, assisted by the mechanic, Edgar Covell, identifying the fault and correcting it. When spare parts were unobtainable he made them himself. His worktop at home, to Oma's constant anguish, was the dining room table. When he was desperate for something to repair, he would dismantle the huge grandfather clock we had – which would be working perfectly – clean it and then reassemble it. He never had parts left over. He and I had great times with my train set; there was often doubt as to whose it was supposed to be.

He was the epitome of the Victorian paterfamilias, which, having regard to his background, is perhaps not the most appropriate comparison. He was a domestic tyrant who ruled his family like he did his business, with a stern hand; it always seemed to me at the time and indeed, on looking back, he was fully justified. They were a volatile crew, my family – undisciplined for all his efforts – but lively, intelligent and excitable. To me, however, he was the most affectionate and loving grandfather and one of the major influences in my early life.

I had the benefit of a favourable climate domestically. Not only was I my parents' only child, but for ten years I was in effect the only grandchild and nephew. There is an age difference of 23 years between me and my youngest cousin, Michael Selwyn. Though my eldest cousin, Judith, was born to Herman and Ray in 1937, she lived in London and "didn't count". Her mother, Ray, as I have explained, was always persona non grata with my grandparents and my aunts. When my next cousin, Geoffrey, was born in November 1940 I already had a nine-year start and there was no competition because we were in effect from different generations.

Opa hated cant and hypocrisy, and did not suffer fools gladly. Yorkshire was the right place for him; he was as outspoken and blunt as any Yorkshireman. He never mastered the English language nor, for that matter, the German. His language was Yiddish. He loved the Yiddish papers of which there were many still available and though he professed not to know English, it seemed to me that it was simply a business ploy because he had no difficulty in reading English papers and following the news on the radio during the war and in communicating with the factory staff and workers, all of whom held him in great respect and referred to him as "Mr Papa".

He was not a strictly observant Jew. Oma was; she was fanatical about keeping kashrut, the Jewish dietary laws. The big family event of the week was Friday night dinner when there was a three-line whip and all the family and guests were expected to be present. Many were the social events and friends' parties which I had to miss over the years, because they occurred on a Friday night. With all the family assembled, the ladies lit the Sabbath candles, followed by *kiddush* (the sanctification over wine) and *hamotzi*, the blessing over the bread, usually a huge *challah* imported from one of the kosher bakeries in Leeds. After dinner and *benching* (grace after meals), Opa would push back his big chair, which seemed enormous to me with its high back and wide arms, and deliberately light his cigar. He smoked nothing but Manikins, small cigars which were popular at the time, and he usually had one dangling from his mouth; I can remember the smell that would accompany him at all times. Nor would the presence of strangers, other than clergy, inhibit him. That, he would say, was his way of celebrating the Sabbath, the day of rest, which starts on Friday night. And indeed it was the only day on which he did no work. But he did go to synagogue the next morning, on Shabbat.

I do not know whether he had a sense of humour. He always appeared very stern and serious to me and there was probably little to laugh about in his life. Only Dora could get through his defences and she was able to make him smile. I think he must have felt that any show of weakness would lessen his authority.

I was, as I have said, a very good child; I had no reason to be otherwise. I was spoiled rotten and indulged, except by my mother, but for all that I doubt whether anyone would have noticed any misbehaviour, short of burning down the house. I had the Fischbein placidity not the fiery Schmulewitsch temperament. Opa's pride in me, however, had a price. I had to be top in everything at school, which somehow I often was, but not always. On these occasions he would say to me that he had been unable to leave home because he could not face the shame of people pointing to him and saying: "He is the grandfather of the boy who didn't come top!" I actually used to take him seriously, at least, at first.

Opa had three weaknesses: Oma, Dora and myself – all of whom he indulged. My Aunt Dora could always wheedle her way around him which required a very special talent. As for me, I could do no wrong in his eyes, and his greatest wish was to see my bar mitzvah, a wish that sadly he never achieved.

He was a good and devoted husband, and Oma was a very spoiled lady. She was "Salka" to him but beyond that I cannot recall any particular terms of endearment between them. There was an air of formality in all their relationships even between themselves, at least in public.

They were devoted to each other and when he died she completely lost the will to live and survived him by only three years.

Opa managed to rescue many members of the family and bring them out of Germany before the war started, some at a close call, by guaranteeing for them and providing employment in the factory. Dad's parents were brought out of Germany in 1939 and came to live with us in the Grey House. I cannot recollect how long they were there but the arrangement was not a happy one. Two Jewish housewives in one kitchen is one too many. Grandpa Fischbein did not wish to be a permanent guest at anyone's table. I remember him as a tall handsome man. Grandma Fischbein was short and stout and suffered from nosebleeds. Both were in poor health: he had diabetes and she had high blood pressure, conditions not easily treatable then. Neither party was happy with the situation and there were frequent conflicts so eventually, despite the war and the bombings, they went to live in London where they were looked after by Herman and Ray.

I cannot recall that I ever saw them again before Opa Fischbein died in 1942 and was buried in London. Oma F. then came to live with us again. By this time her nosebleeds had become serious and she had to go into a nursing home where she had an operation from which she never recovered. She died in 1944 in Middlesbrough, a month before my bar mitzvah, and is buried there.

To me, Oma always seemed old; she was constantly ill suffering from a variety of illnesses including diabetes, high blood pressure and a weak heart. She died in 1946 aged only 58. Oma seemed old in a way that Opa never was. She was about the same height as him and rather stout; her pictures always show her as a stately lady of serious aspect, and I do remember her like that but above all my memories of her are as an old and sick woman. She seemed to need gallstones removed at regular intervals and took several forms of medication daily. In my mind I always associate her with the smell of wintergreen ointment and valerian drops.

Like many of her generation she was an efficient housewife and performed economic miracles which any Chancellor of the Exchequer would have envied. In the early days in Middlesbrough there was little money and the assets which my mother had managed to smuggle out of Germany had to support not only a growing business but a large and hungry household. Economical at all times, whether by nature or of necessity, she ensured nothing was ever wasted and her oft repeated instructions to the maids in regard to any leftovers were to "put it in de small pot".

The idea of kosher was never understood by her maids, which caused confusion in the kitchen as there was a profusion of small pots and identification of their category, i.e. meat or milk, and contents, was always problematical, except to her. She was helped in her housekeeping by my mother and Dora and, when she was there, Yetti, but during the week they were all, of course, at work in the factory.

Oma never mastered the English language, or for that matter any language other than Yiddish. She had an English teacher who came regularly, a Miss Johnson, who was always known and addressed as such – no first-name terms in those days. She had an Eton crop, and like many of the ships in the port, was short with a broad beam. She wore manly clothes and we all thought she fancied Oma, but that sort of thing was a laughing matter then and people's sexual orientation was not considered of general interest. She informed me that my name "Fischbein" actually meant whalebone, which for some reason incensed me. I suppose I was ashamed at my own ignorance. I always wondered whether she was some sort of witch; it would not have surprised me to see her riding on a broom!

I communicated with my grandparents by speaking in English once I had learned it, and before that, in German; they spoke to me in Yiddish but I never noticed. I was not conscious of it at the time but I was already living in a different world from my grandparents, particularly my grandmother with whom, apart from the fact that we lived in the same house and she was responsible for my daily upbringing, I had little in common. There really was little communication between us but I don't suppose she ever noticed this. She had too much else to worry about and children were there to be fed, watered, clothed, and educated until they could fend for themselves, but not to be taken seriously. Children were very much to be seen and not heard.

The special relationship between grandparents and grandchildren usually bridges the generation gap. This is how it was with Opa and so it has been with our own grandchildren, but with Oma this somehow did not happen. Whether it is because my judgment is now clouded by the way she treated my mother I cannot say, but I do not think that I ever had any great affection for Oma. I know that she idolised me as much as she was capable of idolising anyone, and showed me much love; I greatly regret that I did not reciprocate it.

Which is not to say that I was anything other than a good and dutiful grandson. I remember when Oma was recommended to take the waters at Harrogate for one of her "conditions" which necessitated a few days' stay. We could not afford a hotel and Harrogate, like Blackpool, had a large number of boarding houses run, and usually owned, by formidable landladies who made their own rules. No one else being either dispensable or able to speak English, I was sent to accompany her. At the age of eight, my diplomatic talents were obviously inadequate to translate and mediate between an intractable English landlady, whose establishment lacked any sort of warmth or charm, who forbade any presence in her house between 10 a.m. and 6 p.m., and whose food was uneatable, and an equally formidable Jewish lady used to the grandeur of Carlsbad, Marienbad, and other fashionable European spas, also used to having her own way.

Bearing in mind that long-distance communication then was much more complicated than now, and unable to resolve the ensuing impasse and to cope with the histrionics which my grandmother was always capable of producing on demand (and which were fully justified in the present circumstances but which left the English landlady unmoved), I was forced to summon help from home and get Oma moved to less unfriendly lodgings. What strange quirk led to the choice of the first establishment remains a mystery. I suspect Miss Johnson's hand in this. She probably thought that a touch of the prison house was what Oma needed or, more charitably, that this would improve her English but I may be doing her an injustice.

One trouble with Oma was that she had no sense of humour or even of fun. She certainly took herself very seriously and did nothing to help herself with her various illnesses. I know that she secretly drank – I would often catch her going to the drinks cupboard when she thought no one was looking and she'd help herself to a large whisky or brandy. She also ate sweets and chocolates, which were totally forbidden to her as a diabetic, and she feigned heart attacks.

She had favourites among her children and played off one sibling against another. Yetti, the youngest by some years, was the most favoured, and although it might be understandable when the children are young, by the time they become adults it seems inappropriate to me to show favouritism. She sometimes made my mother's life a misery.

With hindsight, I cannot blame her for any of these things. She had had to emigrate twice in a short lifetime, first to escape the pogroms in Poland then from Germany to England. She had four children by the age of 25; she was living in a country and an environment totally foreign to her and she was a very sick woman. It probably did not occur to her that she was lucky to be alive, as we all were.

Oma had a sister, Lina, who remained in Romania, and a brother, David. Lina managed to survive the Holocaust until almost the end of the war, but was killed in 1944. The exact circumstances are not known but she was about the only member of the family who was not rescued. Her brother David came to London at some time in the late 1920s or early 1930s and married an English woman called Lily. They had a son, Joey, who although he was my mother's cousin, was a year or so younger than me. Even as a child I was aware that Lily was an unpleasant person. I met her several times at family functions and remember her as smug, spiteful, snobbish and critical of the world about her. She mercilessly bullied and humiliated her husband and son and made their lives a misery. I can only imagine that David married her for her nationality whereby he could also become English, but it was certainly a heavy price to pay.

The major influence in my early life was undoubtedly my mother. She could turn her hand to anything. Like her father, she had magic hands. Whatever she did, she did supremely well. Short in stature and stout in physique, she too suffered from ill-health, caused by high blood pressure, for which at the time there was no palliative, far less cure, which affected her heart and eventually led to her early death.

Like her father and most of the family, she had a fearsome temper. She had a very strong personality and a biting tongue when roused. She could – and I have seen her do so – reduce the strongest man to silence if not tears.

She was a good cook, and even better at baking. Though a loving and concerned mother she never really had any time for maternal activities after we came to England. She was not regarded as scholastic or academic, which I find strange as I have seen some of her school reports in which she achieved excellent grades. She was a feminist and resented the fact that she was not taken seriously simply because she was a woman, particularly by her older brother Max. Doubtless there may have been some sibling rivalry in this but the fact is that the whole business revolved around her and when she was not there to guide it, it perished.

She was fashion-conscious and always well dressed. She played cards well, as did my father. They were both good bridge players and I learned the game by watching them play. Dad preferred poker, which in a sense epitomises them. She was orderly and systematic. She preferred to play within set parameters and exercise the logic which bridge demands. My father needed the excitement of the gambling element paramount in poker; the bluffing, the assessment and taking of chances.

As a hostess, she was second to none in laying out a dinner table or preparing a party, of which there were many at the Grey House and later Brierfield in Harrow Road to which we moved after Oma's death in 1947. Brierfield had extensive grounds –

1.5 acres of garden and 200 feet of greenhouses – and there my mother became a very keen and efficient gardener. She found rest and pleasure in this at a time when her health was failing. When she could no longer work she set up a small studio in the loft above our spacious garage in which she continued to make clothes, mainly dresses for members of the family, employing a seamstress to help her.

And yet my mother cannot really be discussed outside the context of the factory. She ran the factory, and would brook no interference from anyone, least of all the management in whom she had little faith. It was her life. She devoted herself to it and sacrificed herself to it. Therein lies her tragedy and that of the family.

My father was a jolly, loveable man. About 5 feet 9 inches tall, plump, and almost bald, although what little hair he had was fair and curly; he was a good-looking rather than a handsome man. He had an engaging personality, great charm, good humour and was always smiling. He could be very stubborn and frustrating because he would not enter into any argument; instead he just clammed up. He was quite different from his wife and in-laws who were always only too ready for a shouting match, but it was difficult not to like, indeed love, him.

One Sunday, and I still do not know why I did it other than from a genuine spirit of enquiry – I tended to live in a little world of my own – I did something quite uncharacteristic. It was lunchtime and, as my father rose from his chair to reach for something, I held a very sharp pencil under him. My father was a heavy man and the consequences when he sat down can only be imagined. He shot up with a yell and made a lunge at me. I made a bolt for safety up the stairs and along the corridor to my room, my father chasing after me, Opa after him, then my mother, followed by various members of the family one after another, all screaming at the top of their voices like a scene from a *Carry On* film. Fortunately, the corridor was long and narrow and when I reached the safety of my room, I locked the door and refused to come out until Opa had negotiated a safe conduct personally guaranteed by him. Though I undoubtedly deserved severe chastisement, he ensured that I escaped it. Opa made me go to my father to apologise, which I agreed to do provided he came with me to ensure my continued safety. I went to my parents' room and there was my mother tending to Dad's very sore behind. The scene was so funny that I wept, not only with remorse, but also with laughter. I must hand it to my father that, despite the pain, he also saw the funny side and we kissed and made our peace.

Dad was popular with everyone, particularly women. He was a well-groomed man, always careful of his appearance. But he was not one's image of a Don Juan. Whether he ever took advantage of the offers available I do not know, but I doubt it, as it would have required a decision and created problems, both of which he spent most of his time trying to avoid. He was like an overgrown child. His main purpose in life appeared to be to avoid responsibility. It is hard to say whether this was a matter of cause and effect, as my mother seemed happy enough to make the decisions, but she confessed to me, later in life, that she only did so because of my father's indecisiveness.

They were a happy couple, even though – perhaps because – their characters, natures and personalities were in total contrast. They were caring and protective parents, and gave me all the love and security that one could wish for.

Dad was the supreme diplomat, which is easy when one never makes a decision. He was active in the Middlesbrough Hebrew Congregation of which he was either the President or Treasurer for some thirty years. Not to make enemies over so long a period is remarkable. When faced with a difference of opinion or asked to arbitrate a dispute he would say to each party: "Yes, I understand your point of view and you may well be right, let me think about it." He would then do nothing, hoping the trouble would disappear, which it usually did. He was the supreme exponent of the art of masterful inactivity and was considered – again outside the family – as the fount of wisdom. Thus, when he did actually make a decision it was usually accepted without demur, except of course within the family where no decision was ever so accepted.

Dad was the most obliging of men; he would do anyone a favour, and Oma took full advantage of this. He was not a good son to his parents, nor a good brother. How good a husband or father Dad was, I find it hard to judge, but there was never another son-in-law like him.

My father loved sport, not as a participant – a less athletic man never walked the earth – but as an observer, particularly if it involved gambling. He enjoyed going with me to the Boro's home matches at Ayresome Park. Above all he enjoyed racing, preferably horses, but dogs would do as well or even two flies on a wall for that matter. His great moment came when racing began to be televised. Typically, we had one of the first TV sets in Middlesbrough. He would settle down on a Saturday afternoon, his papers on his knee and his telephone at his side, with an open line to his bookie. This initially caused a dilemma as the Sabbath does not end until nightfall, but Dad settled this by declaring that in Middlesbrough, the Sabbath ended at 2 p.m. which indeed it did on the shortest day of the year. If ever he was asked whether he was up or down on his stake money he would simply answer: "Yes". When further pressed he would say that he came out "about even". On the odd occasion when he had a big win, he would spend it on some extravagance, for my mother or me, never for himself. He was a most generous man in spirit as in purse. I never heard him speak ill of anyone. He liked gossip but only for the humour of the situation.

My father was a wizard with figures, and could perform the most difficult calculations mentally, a very useful skill in the business in which he was the Finance Director, but even more useful in his racing activities. He had no difficulty in calculating the odds-on triples, accumulators, Yankees and other racing combinations in his head, an ability inherited to a limited extent by myself, but far more so by my daughters, who, however, put this talent to different uses.

He was a bon viveur. He loved to eat and to drink. He found the diabetes from which he suffered a great bore, and ignored it when not kept an eye on, with eventually fatal results.

He loved music, and opera in particular. He often spoke of the great opera singers he had heard. Richard Tauber and Benjamino Gigli were particular favourites. The Halle Orchestra under John

Barbirolli (he had not then been knighted) used to play a series of concerts at Middlesbrough Town Hall. Dad and my mother had a subscription and went regularly. On one occasion – I was about 11 at the time – my mother was ill and unable to go. My father asked me to go with him. I had no interest in music at that time, however, after some mild persuasion, and rather than let my father go alone and so as not to waste the ticket, I went. The experience was shattering and changed my life in an instant. One of the works performed was Dvorak's "New World Symphony" and, indeed, it opened a whole new world for me.

Concerts commonly contained four items: an overture, a concerto, a symphony and some other piece, possibly a tone poem or suite. I cannot recall the opening work. The concerto was Beethoven's "Emperor" – I think Clifford Curzon was the soloist – and the final item was Bizet's "L'Arlésienne Suite". This was not an exacting musical diet, but I had been to Elysium. Had I had nothing else to be grateful for to my father, that alone would have been enough.

At Dad's funeral, his cortege, which I understand was one of the largest seen in the town, stopped outside the synagogue on the way to the cemetery. There is no greater honour for a Jew and such an honour is usually reserved for a rabbi or person of great learning. Everyone, from the mayor down, was there. I always felt that my father was born at the wrong time, in the wrong place and into the wrong family; that somewhere there lurked a hidden talent waiting to be realised. The business world was not his metier. He might have made a good bank manager but he should have been born a millionaire!

Chapter 7 – Uncles...

As mentioned, my uncles Max and Herman came to England at different times. I do not know how or why but it appears that Herman came direct to London some time before Max, and he stayed with his uncle, David Oberman, Oma's brother, while Max came via Czechoslovakia as it then was. They got work with some furriers, to whom they were introduced through a contact of Opa's, whose business was in that part of the City of London where furriers then congregated known as Garlick Hill. Herman and Max were badly paid and short of money. Not far from where they worked, in the East End, was *Machzikei Hadass*, a Hassidic Synagogue and on a Friday night a meal could be had after the evening service. Herman, who had always had a religious predilection started going there regularly and one Passover he was invited by one of the congregants to join him for the seder. On this night, even more than on others, it is traditional to offer hospitality to strangers. The house where Herman was taken was that of Mrs Greenstein, who had a young daughter, Ray.

Needless to say, otherwise there would be no story, Herman and Ray fell madly in love. They wanted to marry. News of this proposed alliance was received by my grandparents with some concern and considerable disapproval. The dice were loaded against Ray, who was only 16 at the time. She was a pretty, lively and musically talented girl who sang and played the piano beautifully, but her parents were separated, a state of affairs which shocked my grandparents with their Victorian prudery. Ray came from a modest background and my grandparents always felt that Herman, a handsome and charming man, was worthy of a substantial dowry. They thought he was being lured into a totally unsuitable marriage to an apparently penniless girl with feckless parents. She was not the sort of girl they had in mind for their son. Why they should think he was any great catch, and I mean no disrespect to him, I do not know. He had no particular talent apart from being very nearly an international class swimmer, and he was certainly charming and handsome. He had no trade, however, no means of earning a living, and he was probably the least intelligent and able to look after himself member of a clever and talented family. Ray's family on the other hand may have misguidedly thought that Herman came from a family of means and would be able to offer their daughter a comfortable home.

My grandparents' theory and reasoning were understandable and, looking at the matter objectively, correct. Faced with the inevitable they came, albeit reluctantly, to the wedding and what they saw did nothing to dispel their doubts, indeed rather the contrary and they went back to Leipzig extremely unhappy and not at all reconciled to the marriage, then or ever.

On a personal level, however, they were wrong; the actual result turned out to be very fortunate for the family. Herman and Ray's marriage was a great love match which lasted until Herman died, shortly after their silver wedding. And it was Ray's British nationality which gave Herman the right of residence in England and helped to ease the way for the rest of the family to emigrate. As a family we owe a huge deal to Ray and her mother, though they were never showed any recognition of or gratitude for this.

The Schmulewitsch family always had a high opinion of themselves. It seems to me that they had ideas above their station, but perhaps it was that self-delusion which gave them the necessary confidence and panache to become successful. Ray was always treated badly by most of the family, largely due to Oma and Opa's influence. My mother was kinder than her other siblings and my father was incapable of thinking ill of, or being unpleasant to anyone. It was not until some years later, by which time my grandparents, parents and most of their generation had passed away, that my Aunt Yetti, to whom Herman had always been a loving and helping brother, and my Aunt Dora, the survivors of their generation, became reconciled (more or less in Dora's case) with Ray. I once asked Ray why she had put up with the family's rudeness and attitude and she replied: "They were a very clever and talented family, Herman loved them, and despite everything I wanted to become part of the family."

Uncle Max was a lovely man. He was very handsome, even when illness affected him later in life. He was a natural musician with a beautiful lyric tenor voice. He was a fine pianist, able to play anything by ear, a great asset at parties of which there were many at the Grey House. He could entertain an entire gathering for a whole evening. He had an impish sense of humour and was great fun. Basically a gentle and kindly person, he nevertheless had the fiery Schmulewitsch temper, and any discussion with him soon became a hearty argument, to put it mildly. He had strong opinions which, again typically of the family, were rarely carefully thought out and depended more on emotion and reaction than logic. He was intelligent but undisciplined.

When much later in life I was found to have high blood pressure and was prescribed medication, which I have taken ever since, I noticed that my own abrupt tempers virtually ceased and it occurred to me that perhaps the fiery, family temperaments may well have been due to the same cause: hypertension. My mother suffered badly from this; it caused her death and most likely was the reason for the stroke which Max suffered only a few months after she died. Herman also died young, from a heart attack at the age of only 52, perhaps this too might have been a contributory cause.

Uncle Max was a brilliant salesman; the cliché of selling refrigerators to Eskimos could have been coined for him. He was determined and his persistence usually paid off. He was generally away all week, out on the road, and was a workaholic; the business was his whole life, even after he married. He was ambitious beyond his own, and the family's, abilities.

He was also the world's worst driver. It was difficult to be a commercial representative without transport, so he and my father took driving lessons and surprisingly they both passed their tests. A Ford Ten was bought for Max and Dad had a Vauxhall 14. Those were the first cars the family had. On his first trip, out with Dad, Max was unable to negotiate the turn at the bottom of a steep hill and they finished up in a field, with the car on its side. They both had to clamber up out of the door, a somewhat undignified exit by all accounts, and the car was a write-off. Although he broke an arm and sustained some bruises, no serious damage was suffered. Max always lacked the necessary coordination and concentration to be able to drive well. His mind was always on his work and on the factory. I suppose it's difficult to drive when one needs both hands to talk!

Max married Jeanne Glick, from Leeds, on 11 January 1939 and they made their home directly across the road from the Grey House at 38 Cambridge Road. Jeanne was a big personality in every way, a real Yorkshire lass. She was tall and Junoesque, outgoing and friendly, generous to a fault, and she was fun. She hit the family like a whirlwind. My understanding was always that theirs was an arranged marriage but there was no reason to doubt the affection between them. Jeanne was no longer young by the standards of her time, and, shockingly, her younger sister had married before her, entirely against the traditions of Jewish families. Jeanne's parents were very Orthodox. She was one of 14 children, of whom 11 were still then alive, and the second youngest of six daughters. Her marriage to Max was to have an enormous influence on my life. Her elder brothers had a flourishing business in Leeds, as coal and lemonade merchants, not an obvious connection of commodities. Her brother Louis was a doctor who became a leading specialist in the Halifax area where he lived. It was he who rescued me from the Knaresborough near disaster, and took me to the Bellow family in Leeds – more on which comes later.

The wedding took place in Leeds on a Sunday, and the celebrations lasted over the weekend. My family was tiny in comparison with Jeanne's, both in numbers and in physique, but I remember it was a very jolly affair. We, the Middlesbrough contingent, stayed at the Queen's Hotel, where the reception was to take place after the synagogue ceremony on the Sunday. My mother wore a spectacular hat with a huge ostrich feather.

For some reason, women – at least those in my family – dress rather the way buildings are constructed. They start at the bottom, work their way to the top, when they "top out" by putting on their hats, and then they work their way down again. My mother had just put on her hat when she noticed a bidet in the bathroom. Strangely, she had never seen one before. It was one of those with a jet in the middle. Unsuspectingly, to find out what happened she turned the tap on, and the resultant jet hit her feather fair and square. I was too convulsed with laughter to remember how she overcame this disaster. But the wedding went ahead, feather or no.

Jeanne brought with her a sizeable dowry, most of which went straight into the business. She also brought with her many connections, and most important among these was her family. Her eldest sister Lily's husband, Abe Bellow, owned a sewing machine factory in Leeds. Jeanne from the outset took me to her very ample bosom and treated me like a son, and continued to do so even when she had four children of her own. I spent many happy times with her and her family. She was always loving and generous to me and I loved her dearly. It was at the wedding of Max and Jeanne that I met my longest-standing friend, her nephew, Neville Cohen, the elder son of her younger sister Bessie. I was seven and Neville was 18 months younger. We became, and remained until Neville's untimely death at the young age of 70, the best and closest of friends. We always referred to each other as cousins, and his parents were always Uncle Alec and Aunt Bessie; they treated me as family though there is no blood relationship, and our lives ran closely together.

Chapter 8 – ... And Aunts

My Aunt Dora was not only Opa's favourite, she was everyone's. She had an outsize personality even among the Schmulewitsch family, which specialised in them. She had strong opinions and feelings about everything and everyone and did not hesitate to express them and was never influenced by facts. She was no respecter of persons and shared her father's distaste for cant and hypocrisy, and his ability to see through a person's veneer. She did not mellow with age. Dora was attractive, slim, with a good figure and legs to make a film star jealous. She had enormous love and loyalty for her father and also for my mother, whom she revered. They were very close in all respects and worked together in the factory. Dora did not have the technical skills and abilities of my mother but she was much more worldly-wise. She was a realist and a cynic; she saw faults and was not afraid to say so.

My mother, on the other hand, for all her practical abilities did not have Opa's nose for people. Mother was an intellectual snob. She regretted her lack of a tertiary education and admired beyond the bounds of sensible judgment anyone who had a university degree, or smacked of "education". Tertiary education and university degrees were far less common than they are today, but perhaps I am somewhat biased.

During the war we had a constant stream of visitors, usually on Friday night or Saturday lunchtime when Jewish soldiers or airmen stationed locally would come to synagogue and be invited home for a meal by members of the congregation. Dad was obviously in the forefront of those who extended such invitations. One such soldier who impressed my mother with his knowledge, and became a fairly frequent visitor, was constantly held up to me as an example of an "intellectual" and what one should strive to be. I thought he was a pretentious show-off. I hated him.

Dora was my mother's right hand. In the frequent and increasingly bitter arguments which occurred in the business and indeed within the family she invariably championed my mother's cause and stood by her side.

To me, she was a second mother, certainly after my mother died, but even before that she took a great interest in anything concerning me. She was my godmother, a position which she took very seriously. When I was young she did, however, treat me as something of a personal page. "Fredele" she would say (all the family called me that, even when I was grown up), "do me a favour – go and bring me my handbag" or whatever it was she had forgotten or mislaid. But she was always there when needed, and sometimes when not! She was a major influence in and throughout my life. Her interest was not diminished when she had her own son. As will be seen she constantly reappears in this story. I find it hard to write about her without being consumed by emotion, more so than any other member of my family, including my parents; I loved her dearly. My debt to her is incalculable, and it is perhaps only now, as I look back over the years, that I can fully appreciate that, because at times she seemed to be an interfering busybody. But she was somehow always involved in the crucial decisions which shaped my life.

Dora had many interests and was good at all of them. She was very sporty and became an extremely competent golfer. She was an excellent bridge player and a good organiser and administrator.

Though Joe Menasche was not one of the original inhabitants of the Grey House, it seems appropriate to mention him here as he became Dora's husband and my uncle. I met him first when I was ill in bed with flu or something similar. Dora brought him up to my bedroom to introduce him and we became friends instantly. I use the word "friends" deliberately. While the rest of the family, understandably, treated me as a child, he treated me as a person.

Joe had left Germany very late indeed – 3 September 1939, the day war broke out – and had been involved in organisations getting Jews out of Germany, although he never spoke of it. He himself only managed to get out at the last minute.

On arriving here, Joe volunteered for army service and ended up in the Pioneer Corps from which he was eventually invalided out. The Pioneer Corps was regarded by the rest of the army as the dregs: the lowest of the low; the depository for those soldiers unfit for any other sector of the army. Its principal function was to do all the army's dirty work, in a quite literal sense: to dig latrines and trenches, to prepare the foundations for roads and bridges, to lay out barbed wire where required and generally carry out whatever unpleasant tasks no one else was willing to do. In the early years of the war, however, it probably had the highest level of intelligence, culture, and knowledge of foreign languages (few could even speak English properly) in the army, because all those refugees and aliens – many of whom had been interned, through one of Winston Churchill's dafter ideas, and wished to serve in some military capacity – were sent to the Pioneer Corps. Many of them were soon transferred to the Intelligence Corps and played a significant part in the war effort.

Joe was very quietly spoken, not, as one can appreciate, a characteristic of my family. When he did speak, it was to good effect, and as to hear him required silence from his audience, his involvement reduced the noise level. He was very intelligent and in his quiet way had many of the qualities of Opa. He and Dora were married – in the Schmulewitsch tradition – at Christmas in 1941.

Joe was an excellent chess player. When I was about five, Opa started to play chess with me and taught me the rudiments of the game. I had an aptitude for it and soon beat him regularly, though I suspect that there may have been some grandfatherly tolerance in this. My father also played with me and I continued to improve. Uncle Max was a very competent player; Uncle Herman even more so and I honed my game with them though rarely had the opportunity to play Herman. I was soon regularly beating them all. When Joe arrived, however, I met my match. He was in a different league altogether and, unlike the rest of my family, did not exercise patronising charity to me. It was a long time before I beat him and I was never able to do so regularly, even when I reached County standard.

He took as much interest in my welfare as Dora did and what they did for me, they did together. This does not imply that there was always unanimity between them on the subject.

Yetti, the youngest of my mother's siblings, was only 14 years older than me – the same age difference as between me and her son, my cousin Harold. I cite this exciting statistic simply to demonstrate the generation gap which effectively exists between me and my cousins. She was called "Schnucky" by all but me; I thought it a silly name for a grown-up. She was tall and beautiful and was much in demand by the unmarried Jewish men in the area. She had, however, fallen madly – and I do not use this word as a cliché (she was besotted) – in love with Karl Katz whom she had met in Germany, again through the accidental offices of Dora at a Zionist organisation to which they both belonged. Looking at a photograph of him it is easy to see why; he had film-star looks and his sexual attraction is obvious even in an old picture. He remained a handsome man into his old age. Though my grandparents disapproved of Karl – and time proved them right – Opa also helped Karl and his parents to leave Germany and his father came to work in the factory.

Karl had an outgoing, extrovert personality, but he lacked finesse; he was no "gentleman". He came from a small German village called Neselroden and although he was a German Jew, he was more German than Jewish. He had German nationality (until Hitler took that away) and was not an Ostjude like us. His parents had been born in Germany; his father, Wilhelm, had served with the German cavalry in the First World War and been awarded an Iron Cross. Karl was uneducated, and boorish. He enjoyed practical jokes and had a schoolboy sense of humour – and a German one at that.

Karl was very much a man's man, an outdoor type. He was great fun and loved children, with whom he had a much better rapport than with adults. He would put me on the crossbar of his bicycle and take me for rides, and he loved to tell of the time a policeman stopped him and berated him for putting his "son" at risk. He was always kind and affectionate to me and I was always made welcome by him; I was very fond of him as a child.

Yet he very nearly killed me. He was an excellent but very fast driver, and owned a very powerful car: a Triumph Dolomite. One day, on the way back from Leeds where he had collected Max's fiancee, Jeanne Glick, for his engagement party to Yetti (the alliance having finally been sanctioned), he crossed swords, or more accurately roads, with a lorry. The car was totally wrecked; he and Jeanne sustained severe head injuries. Fortunately, I was in the back. On the way to Leeds I had sat in the front, but for the return journey, despite my protests, I was made to sit in the back. When the collision occurred, I was thrown forward but only on to the floor, sustaining no more than a bruised knee. Karl's recklessness caused the collision but his skill and speedy reflexes averted a more severe outcome. We all ended up in hospital. I was lucky, I only had a bruised knee.

I used to wear *tzitzes*, a sort of miniature prayer shawl but for some unaccountable reason had not done so on that day. I felt that I had had a warning from the Almighty. I continued to wear them until well after I was married, despite curious glances and inquiries throughout my time at school, army and university. So superstitions arise.

Karl was a person of strong contrasts. He could be kind and generous at one moment and greedy and mean-spirited the next. He certainly had charisma and it was easy to understand why my aunt – and indeed many women – fell for him. He also had a cruel streak and a fearsome temper. Max and Karl had a mutual antagonism and it went further than that. Max, to put it simply, hated Karl. Bearing in mind the fiery Schmulewitsch temperament it is not difficult to understand the powder keg their joint presence created.

To my grandparents' disgust and annoyance, Yetti seemed to spend more time with Karl than with the family, and in an intimacy which was not considered fitting for a Jewish girl. This deeply offended my grandparents' sense of morality. Yetti had always been indulged as a child and was headstrong. Effectively, she took matters into her own hands and went to live with Karl in West Hartlepool, a few miles from Middlesbrough. This forced my grandparents' hand and despite my grandfather's reservations, and the flouting of the Jewish tradition that daughters married in order of their age, she and Karl were married in 1939 – at Christmas, of course. Apart from the fact that she babysat for me – as she told me when asking me to repay the compliment by doing the same for her children – I had little contact with her. She was young and beautiful and had her own agenda. However, she came to play an important part later in my life.

It is difficult as a child to understand the strong sexual attraction which people may feel for each other. Yetti and Karl had this initially, but unfortunately, that waned over the years. Their life was economically difficult. Karl never benefited from the financial success enjoyed by the family and felt – and was made to feel – an outcast. However, he had the last laugh. Late in life he became successful and sold the business he had struggled so long to build up for a very large sum. Sadly, by then his relationship with his wife had effectively ended and they never together enjoyed the happiness in old age for which she, at least, had so long waited. But my grandparents were right; they should not have married. It was never a happy marriage.

The only place in the Grey House that was free from the smells of either Opa's Manikins or Oma's wintergreen ointment (I don't know what good it did but its smell pervaded the house) was the kitchen; probably because Opa entered it only for the purpose of passage. The kitchen had its own brands of perfume, usually chicken soup which seemed to be constantly on the stove.

To cater for so large an establishment, which usually doubled in size at Passover, required considerable logistical skills. Our staple meat diet was chicken. During the war, meat was rationed and in any event hard to get, but one could rear one's own chickens, which my mother did. We thus always had a plentiful supply of eggs and birds. Reverend Turtledove, the beadle, was also the "shochet" – the slaughterer – trained in the art of the ritual methods required by the laws of kashrut. My father would buy the chickens or turkeys when in season from the farm – he had his favourite sources which no one ever knew – bring them home in a crate and Mr Turtledove would come and cut their necks in the wash house which was used for that purpose. I could not bear to see him doing this, and hated the grotesque sight of chickens running around headless.

The average toll was about a dozen chickens per week. They all had to be plucked and cleaned, and apart from the feathers, nothing was wasted. What could not actually be eaten made very good stock, and my grandmother's chicken soup attained heights of perfection. It was the original Jewish penicillin; it cured everything. She also made all her own challahs, plaiting the bread for the Friday night blessing; her own *lockschen* (noodles); and all the traditional trappings to be included in the chicken soup. For starters, there was usually her own home-made gefilte fish. With the main course there were the usual potatoes, *tzimmes* (a sweet form of carrots), and any other fattening food she had the time to prepare. Salads were a rarity. A hungry family which has been working all week needs proper food, which is not to infer by any means that they starved during the week! It was little wonder that by the time the Friday meal came to be served she was embarking on her regular weekly heart attack!

The usual Friday chaos was exponentially increased at festivals. Passover was the worst for my grandmother. We would always have two seder nights, and of course, the central part of the celebration is the meal, which is preceded and followed by prayers. Opa liked to have all his family around him. Friends and strangers who are not able to make their own seder or attend one are traditionally invited and there would rarely be less than thirty people at the table for the seder nights – both of them. By the time of the first seder my grandmother was on her "third heart attack", as opposed to the one she had on the usual Friday.

Being the object of so much love and attention in a family like mine also had its disadvantages. Every decision regarding my upbringing, my education or anything else affecting me, became a matter for debate by committee and the committee consisted of the whole family. Because of my mother's strength of character, whatever the debate, she insisted that the decisions were made by her and my father and in this respect at least, my parents were of one mind, usually hers.

In fact, my life and that of my family ran on quite separate lines. I was growing up culturally divorced from them, a division that became greater the older I got. I doubt whether I was aware of, or appreciated, the great sea of love and affection on which I floated. I tended to resent, even when quite young, any interference in my life. To me, I suppose it must have been instinctive, as I doubt whether I had the ability to rationalise it. I strove to establish my independence from this all-embracing octopus of a family, which would smother and extinguish one, if not resisted. It may sound ungrateful, but every coin has its obverse side, even love.

There is a possessive element in most families; in mine it was particularly strong. Not as regards my parents, because they did bring me up to be self-reliant. Though she never articulated any such suggestion, perhaps my mother had a sense that she might die young. My parents may have felt that even in England security was not guaranteed. They understood, I think, that my world would be very different from theirs, and not one that they could understand, far less share. They were very conscious of their immigrant status and wished to ensure that I would not be prejudiced by it. They wanted me to become an Englishman – even an English gentleman. There was no discussion with my parents on these lines – one did not discuss such matters with, far less consult, one's children – but all their conduct supports these suppositions.

Maybe they felt that being the only child in this noisy, argumentative and domineering family was unhealthy, but I doubt whether they realised that despite all the love and affection showered on me, I was very lonely. I had no one to talk to, no one who had time to do things with me, except Opa, who always managed to have some quality time with me, mainly at weekends. As previously mentioned, I would dearly have liked a brother or sister, and often in the years which followed regretted not having a sibling. I resolved not to repeat the error when I married and had a family. But I was not unhappy, far from it. I came to terms with my loneliness; I even enjoyed it, and still have no great need of companionship. I like people, but I learned to manage perfectly well on my own.

Chapter 10 – Social Life

We regularly had parties at the Grey House. My family's numbers were sufficient to ensure a lively do even without guests, but seemingly no one refused an invitation. There were singing and dancing parties, card parties, tea parties, dinner parties, parties where games were played, and parties where the Cantor, Geza Wulwik, entertained everyone with a wide range of songs. There were even parties where I was allowed to stay up and listen to him singing. Not only did he have a glorious voice, but he had a great sense of fun, and was an entertainment in himself. He was a refugee from Czechoslovakia, and though he did not formally live with us, he seemed to be in our house most of the time until he married.

Everyone smoked in those days and the house was never free from the smell of stale cigarettes and cigars. It's a smell which now seems very evocative of the past as it is now so unacceptable. Dora and Joe were very heavy smokers, as were my parents. Only Yetti and Oma (and I) did not smoke. Jews tend not to drink much, but we eat a lot. The tables in the Grey House would groan with home-baked cakes, biscuits, trifles, jellies and sweetmeats of all sorts, and even though they wouldn't be drunk, a full range of alcoholic and other beverages would always be available.

And then there were the really big parties: the weddings. Yetti and Karl's, at Christmas 1939 and Dora and Joe's in 1941. For the first of these the war had not yet made an impact, and Oma had saved up provisions for some time. I was a very reluctant page, forced once again to wear ridiculous clothing, doubtless made by my talented mother. The young daughter of another refugee German family, Susie Stern, was the bridesmaid. I was eight and she was much younger and very pretty. She looked the part; I felt silly.

By the time Dora and Joe were married, war had begun in earnest; things were more difficult, but they did not seem to disturb the happiness of the occasion. This time I somehow managed to avoid any formal involvement.

It was not just our family who celebrated weddings at the Grey House. Opa and Oma also made the house available for the marriages of the rabbi's two daughters, Ruth and Naomi, as there was no other house of suitable size whose *kashrut* could be guaranteed. All the catering was done at home by Oma and her cohorts and even the brides were not exempted from helping with the preparations. They were all happy occasions, but I know that the toasts to absent friends had particular poignancy during those difficult times.

Chapter 11 – First Schools

For many years I thought that I had started school in Leipzig. I certainly remember being given a *Zuckertorte* – a sort of cornucopia shaped like a dunce's hat and filled with sweets and chocolates, given to children when they start school – together with a school satchel. There are even photographs to prove I had one. Apparently, as I learned when making a reparations claim for broken schooling after the war, what I thought was a school must only have been a kindergarten, as children start school in Germany at the age of six, not five as here. So in fact, my first school was in England.

Finding a school for me was difficult. I spoke no English and the state schools would not accept me. How different it is today, when English is virtually a second language in some schools. I was eventually accepted by the excellent Mrs Relph at her junior school, The Priory, some ten minutes walk away from home. My father was introduced to her through the good offices of a young female member of the synagogue who was a teacher at the school, and who undertook to teach me English. Mrs Relph was a small, compact, roundish lady, with white hair tied back in a bun. She was a kindly person though in the nature of schoolmistresses of her time, a disciplinarian, but tempered with mercy.

I have the fondest memories of that small school. I have no particular capacity for languages, at least not when it comes to speaking them, but I soon learned English, with a strong Teesside accent of which more than a trace remains to this day. The teaching methods were traditional: we learned to write by copying out, in copperplate handwriting, wise old apothegms of which my favourite – not that I understood what it meant – was "all is not gold that glisters". I never managed to cope with this and my handwriting was ruined from the start. The three Rs were taught on basic principles. Tables were learned by rote. Perhaps I'm old fashioned but I have always been grateful for this basic training and can see nothing wrong with it.

Mrs Relph was a Roman Catholic. All the pupils would attend services at the Catholic Church, which was almost opposite the school (directly opposite the school, by the bus stop, fortuitously was a sweet shop!) – and I was not excused. My parents could not understand why on Ash Wednesday I came home with dirt on my forehead. But as truly religious people do, Mrs Relph not only had great respect for my religion, but encouraged its strict observance.

My great friend from that school was Peter Unwin, who in later life joined the Foreign Office and became an ambassador to Denmark. He had a Hornby train set of the same gauge as mine and we combined our resources to create a very fine layout. His parents would often invite me to their home and take me on many outings, so I saw much of the surrounding countryside long before my family did. I made many friends at school and soon had a social life quite separate from that of the family.

I stayed at The Priory for over two years. I must have made great progress because I began to bring home excellent reports, and reached the top of the class. Competitiveness was thought beneficial and encouraged, and I have never been able to understand the educational doctrine which seeks to avoid the fact that some children are more able or talented than others.

I do not know why my parents decided to move me to another school, but in 1939 I was sent to The Firs School in Nunthorpe, a village halfway between Middlesbrough and Guisborough. My parents used to drop me off at school on the way to the factory.

By then my father had his own car: a silver-grey Vauxhall 14 (registration number XG 6298 for those interested in such minutiae).

The Firs took weekly boarders as well as day pupils. The owner and headmistress was Mrs Malyon, whose two sons, Keith and Neil, were pupils at the school. She was a formidable woman, with blonde hair turning to grey, tall, and well built. She wore glasses and had a slight squint which caused her to tilt her head and gave her a somewhat lopsided appearance. I had liked Mrs Relph; I did not like Mrs Malyon. In so far as Mrs Malyon thought about it at all, which is improbable, I doubt whether she liked me either.

No doubt the change of schools was dictated by the fact that, despite Neville Chamberlain's "piece of paper" to which no one in my family attached any credibility any more than the politicians did, war was inevitable and my parents wanted me out of the way. Middlesbrough was a key port; there was an RAF aerodrome at Thornaby no more than two miles from our house, and we were surrounded by iron and steel works, shipyards and heavy industries, all likely targets for enemy bombers. Transport was going to be problematical and although we had a car, petrol would be virtually unavailable, driving in the blackout would be dangerous, and there would be a factory to run. All these assumptions proved correct.

Chapter 12 – The Factory

The factory, aka the Guisborough Shirt & Underwear Company Limited, was how we were able to escape from Germany. The company was formed in 1937 and, as its title indicates, it had been intended to manufacture both shirts and underwear; it managed shirts and pyjamas but it never made underwear. It provided the wherewithal for the needs of the family – and they were great – although it was later to become a god who demanded sacrifices.

I do not know why Guisborough was chosen originally; other immigrants in similar circumstances founded businesses in nearby Darlington, or bigger cities like Newcastle or Leeds. Perhaps it was pure chance that Guisborough Council had been active in its efforts to attract light industry to provide employment in a heavily depressed area but, while from a larger perspective it seemed an odd place, it served very well and I cannot imagine that I could have been happier anywhere else.

The factory was on the site of a derelict sewage farm on the Middlesbrough Road at the western entrance to the town. A five-year lease had been granted on the empty buildings at an unbelievable £52 per annum. A family continued to live in the house fronting the road and the yard became the entrance to the factory and the car park, though it would be more correct to call it the bicycle park, because all the girls left their bikes there. Opa, my father, Uncle Max and Joe Menasche (after he married Dora) were the directors. There was also one outside director, Alfred Edwards, then Labour MP for Middlesbrough West. It will be noted that none of the daughters was made a director. As the business expanded, offices were taken in Fountain Street, opposite the railway station, at the other end of the town, and those premises were also used as a warehouse.

Mr Edwards was hardly the typical Labour member and in due course, after the war, crossed the floor of the House of Commons. He was a handsome man, silver-haired, beautifully dressed; very much my family's image of an English gentleman. He was suave, well-spoken, wealthy, with his own car and chauffeur whom he would not allow to exceed a speed of 40 m.p.h. (perhaps a wise precaution in the light of the roads at that time). He was the company's spokesman, when the need arose, but Opa did not trust him. Opa trusted few people and being a relative – even a child – was no guarantee of trust. He was rarely wrong in his judgment, harsh as it may have appeared at the time.

The factory, as I shall continue to call it, had little meaning for me at first. It was where my parents and other members of the family spent the day; where I would take their lunches and where I would play in the car park or the surrounding fields.

Before the factory could produce a single garment all the girls had to be trained and this was my mother's responsibility. The Schmulewitsch girls were talented; they were very skilful with their hands, particularly at sewing and dressmaking. My mother was the eldest and had the most experience. She could take any garment to pieces, indeed any textile item, and recreate it. She could work out exactly how it had been made and how its manufacture could be improved, and just from a picture or photograph of say a dress or a coat, could work out how to make it. She could walk round a factory which made clothes and, from memory, replicate the processes to the extent that when competitors realised this they would no longer let her into their factories. The men were welcome but not my mother.

In Germany, Opa's business had been mainly making linings for fur coats, bedclothes, linens and the like, but not shirts. I do not know why they chose shirts. Perhaps Max had identified a possible market, or there was no market for the items which they made in Germany, where their particular experience lay, so they had to start from scratch.

The local potential workforce was totally unskilled; the raw material did not look promising. Apart from the language barrier, there were many cultural difficulties to overcome, or at least to understand. My family, used to the medical and social care programmes taken for granted in Germany, then as they are here today, found incomprehensible (indeed disgusting) the practice, common even among young girls in their early twenties, of having all their teeth removed at the first sign of dental trouble and replacing them with dentures.

The local girls had neither the ingrained discipline or work ethic of the German girls my mother was used to. Nor did they have the sophistication of city girls. It was a long way from Leipzig to Guisborough. She trained a few girls, who then trained others. Foremost among these was one named Emily Thomson, who became my mother's deputy and eventually took over from her as factory manageress. She gave the business many years of loyal service.

At first, all the samples of the shirts the factory hoped to sell were made by my mother. Max, the supreme salesman, would hawk them round the clothes shops and stores, such as Binns the local department store and wider afield. It was hard going and the early days were exhausting. Indeed, I cannot remember any time when the demands of the factory were not exhausting but, as it came later to prosper, my parents could take some holidays. Max's persistence and perseverance eventually brought success and the company numbered Marks & Spencer among its customers. Actually, the war brought relief in that the company obtained contracts from the Government to make shirts, first for officers and then for soldiers and airmen generally.

My mother took full charge of the running of the factory itself, that is the manufacturing part. In this she was closely helped by Dora – known to all as "Miss Dora", which did not change when she married – and, until Karl took her over, Yetti. The business part – the finances, the sales, and policy generally – was left to the menfolk, a policy which ultimately was to prove disastrous, but this is to anticipate.

My mother ran the factory as her personal fiefdom – totally dictatorially. When approached to allow union representation, she flatly refused, strongly supported by Opa. She told the union that they could not represent her workers half as well as she did herself, and in this she was right. She would, when she disagreed strongly with management decisions, ban the management from entering the workshop. She fought bitterly for her girls and if she was baulked by the management she would call the girls out on strike herself, usually by way of a sit-in, which was more comfortable. She was a formidable lady. She appreciated that without the workforce there was no business at all and she realised that, even though unemployment in the area was high, her girls were not easily replaced. They had been well trained; some became highly specialised and extremely skilful. Much time and effort had gone into their training and setting up the operating procedures, and she was not going to allow some management whim to endanger this.

My mother was as strict with her girls as she was with the management. Though she often appeared arbitrary, she was also very fair, and on one occasion astonished me by her humanity. I then understood why "her girls" so respected – nay, worshipped – her. My mother would listen to any genuine complaint or request, but she would not tolerate insubordination (even from me). It was also her principle not to rehire anyone who had been sacked.

I happened one day to be in the outer office to the factory. A very angry woman arrived asking to speak to my mother. Knowing my mother's own fiery temperament I was prepared for fireworks, but I decided to stay and see what happened. My mother came out: she was assailed by the good lady, who wanted to know why her daughter, aged 16, had been peremptorily dismissed. Mother, to my surprise, because in my experience that was not her way, listened very calmly to all that the girl's mother had to say. When the tirade was ended and the woman had run out of steam, I expected an explosion from my mother. But no; to my astonishment, Mother said, very quietly:

"Mrs Smith, how many children do you have?"

"Six," was the reply.

"Do you let them do as they like?"

"No, I do not."

"I have three hundred in there. Should I let them do as they like?"

A moment's silence, then the woman burst into tears: "No; you're quite right. I'm sorry I spoke like I did. But we need her money, and I don't know how I can manage without it. She won't find another job easily. Please take her back."

"I never on principle take back anyone I've sacked, but if you will promise me to deal with her yourself and that she'll behave herself in future, I'll make an exception this once, but no further chances."

They then both went for a cup of tea in the works canteen.

Chapter 13 – War

The day Neville Chamberlain, the Prime Minister, addressed the nation over the radio at noon on Sunday, 3 September 1939, my whole family was gathered round the dining room table listening; nervous and worried. I was lying prone on the floor reading. To me it all seemed very exciting. We were going to bash Hitler and all would soon be well. The rest of the family, naturally, had very different emotions. Though glad that some resistance was at last being offered by the rest of Europe to Hitler's progress and hoping that this would at least ease the plight of German Jewry, little could anyone have imagined what was to come. I do not think there were any illusions about the difficulties ahead; my family had seen at first hand evidence of Hitler's power and the support he had in Germany. It was a sombre gathering, one which must have been mirrored countless times round the country. Everything that had been built up over the previous two years, and had not yet been consolidated, was threatened.

I, of course, was oblivious to all this. I continued to live in my own small world. I knew nothing of their problems except what I gathered from overhearing conversations which I was not supposed to hear. Indeed, all the family shared in this conspiracy of silence. If I entered a room while they were talking about something which they considered unfit for my ears, they would stop talking and tell me to "go away and play". Such topics ranged from scandalous matters to jokes involving sexual innuendoes – not that I would have understood them.

The first immediately visible impact of the war was the blackout. The Grey House had very large windows and these needed to be covered by black material which allowed no light to escape. Wooden frames were made for the large flat windows in the kitchen, over which blackout material was stretched. They were then lifted into place at dusk and removed in the morning. They were very effective. Curtains had to be lined with the same sort of material and windows had to be criss-crossed with tape to avoid the glass splintering in case of damage by bombs.

Rationing was introduced and shortages soon became apparent. The young men began to disappear. I remember witnessing one particularly tearful farewell between one of the maids – a small, chunky and very pretty girl – and her fiancé in his army uniform off to war. Did she ever see him again, I wonder?

Chapter 14 – Evacuation

My parents decided to send me away to school so that I would avoid the bombing which they expected, as Middlesbrough was a likely target. I became, to my chagrin, a full-time boarder at The Firs. After a few months, my school was evacuated to the Lake District, to a pretty little village called Newbiggin-on-Lune. The River Lune, which is, I think, a tributary of the River Ribble, seemed to run along the high street. After a short time, we moved to Grayrigg, not far away, a small hamlet. I do not know why. Children were informed on a need-to-know basis, if at all.

At Grayrigg we were accommodated in a large country house, the sort which is now popular as a country house hotel. The house and gardens were extensive and pleasant. To my delight, a cart track ran from the end of the garden to a level crossing on the main Euston to Glasgow line, then the old LMS (London Midland and Scottish) railway.

There was a signal box at the level crossing and, as I have always been fascinated by trains, I became friendly with the signalman and would run down to the signal box whenever I had the chance. The signal box was of traditional design. The impending arrival of trains was announced by a telegraph bell and for a few minutes all would be action: levers had to be shifted to move the signals whilst those ahead of the train had to be opened and those behind closed. The "road" ahead had to be checked; the next box had to be alerted as the trains passed from our section to his. All was hustle and bustle and then the train would go noisily by in a moment, ignorant of the efforts made to ensure its safe progress, spewing black smoke from its stack, and steam from every orifice: at speed if an express; more leisurely if a freight train. This was romance, energy, excitement, life. The sense of power was almost unbearable.

I would have given anything to be the driver of one of those trains. In the few minutes before the next train was due, my friend the signalman would pour me out a cup of tea from his flask and occasionally I would be allowed to hold the levers while he pulled them.

Because of the war, few passenger trains ran, and those which did were usually double-headed, that is, pulled by two engines, and were much longer than usual, often up to some twenty carriages. Also, as the trains were approaching Shap, the highest point of the railway system in England, there was often an extra engine attached at the back, to help the train up the steep incline.

I was thrilled at seeing the great trains go by. My day was full if I was lucky enough to catch sight of one of the great streamlined Coronation type 4-6-2 expresses with their streamlined red or blue livery, the latest thing of their day. I experienced the glamour and fascination of these wonderful steam engines, and the hard-working older engines drawing their heavily laden goods trains, puffing and panting, like smoking dragons, with their clanking wheels and rhythmic carriages, at close quarters. They may have been dirty and smelly and inefficient compared with today's bland self-satisfied looking trains but each one of those engines had its own character and personality. I was totally captivated by them, and still am.

I was very unhappy at this school. My move to it, followed by my evacuation with it, had not gone without vociferous objection by me, Opa and my Aunt Dora, who took her duties as my god-mother very seriously and was a guardian angel to me all her life.

To me, that school was a prison house. I was very lonely, not because I needed company, of which there was more than enough, but because I was denied the privacy and independence to which I had become accustomed. There was a strict routine for everything. What we ate was regulated; we had to go to the toilet every morning and our stools were inspected. If we were unable to produce any, we were given some mixture called California Syrup of Figs – which was sweet, and actually quite nice. Our hair was constantly inspected for lice. We were given all sorts of unpleasant medicines, for whatever illness was suspected, whether or not we were unwell.

We had to eat whatever food was served. I remember one of my fellow pupils, John Outhwaite, could not abide onions. When

he refused to eat them he was not allowed to leave the table until
he had. So he threw them on the floor. He was red-haired and had
the temper to match. There was a great struggle of wills. He stood
his ground for a long time and eventually had to give way, but he
was not served onions again! I was very upset and disgusted at the
whole episode. I had a much easier way of dealing with any
similar problem. I would merely say, that I was very sorry, but I
was not allowed that food on religious grounds. As I was the only
Jewish boy in the school this could not be checked. There would
generally be an element of truth in this, as there were not many
things I could eat.

We had to write home weekly. Our letters were checked and
censored, and those we received were opened and read. The occasional visitor had no doubt taken back reports that I was wasting
away. My family, well aware that the fare at an English boarding
school, at any time, and even more so in wartime, would be inadequate and uneatable, would, in good Jewish tradition, send me
food parcels. These parcels were opened and shared out. When
Dora learned of this she was furious and was convinced that the
Head and the Matron, Mrs Newton, had kept the best for themselves. There is no evidence either to support or refute this allegation, but then the evidence would have been consumed. In all
fairness, I must say that all food parcels were shared out, but as
mine were the biggest and best, I probably lost out the most.

Chapter 15 – First Love

It was at that school that I first fell in love. Like Priory House, The Firs was a mixed school. Unusually, I made few friends, in fact among the boys only one: John, the son of the Matron. Among the girls there were two Norwegian sisters, Meta was my own age, her sister Inge a little younger. Meta had true Nordic colouring; glorious long golden hair – usually plaited during the day, but radiant when she combed it out at night – blue eyes and very fair skin. We were among the older children and therefore the last to go to bed, so we were alone together every evening, chatting over our Ovaltine or Horlicks. I cannot say that at the age of eight or nine I had any sexual arousal, but she was very pretty and I loved her, so I kissed her on the cheek rather tentatively and, when she did not object, I kissed her again. Experience later showed me that this usually worked with girls.

After some time Mrs Malyon found out – someone had snitched, no doubt the odious Keith. She treated the matter as if I had committed some capital offence. All that had happened was that one eight-year-old boy had kissed one eight-year-old girl, because she was exceedingly pretty and he was very lonely. She gave me the strap, a painful hit across the hand with a shortened dog strap. I was no coward and took my punishment even though I had never had any physical punishment inflicted on me before, nor have I since, and I deplore its use. I was not physically hurt very much, but I was deeply affronted. The hurt to my pride and self-esteem was deep. But I was not going to let Mrs Malyon see me cry or derive any satisfaction from the incident, although that is not to say that I did not cry in my bed. I made up my mind to get away from that school as soon as possible.

Escape was the only solution, but this was not made easier by events at home. The Government, fearing an influx of German spies among Jewish refugees, decided, under the Defence of the Realm Acts (a relic of the first First World War updated for the occasion), to intern all alleged enemy aliens. It was Churchill's idea to "collar the lot" but this was not one of his finest hours. Though none of the family (except Karl and he was not "family") had any, let alone German, nationality, Opa, my father, Max, Herman and Karl were all interned on the Isle of Man. For Opa, and others like him, this was terrible. To have fled Hitler's Germany, to have been given visas to settle here, to have established a business providing employment where it was needed – ironically on war work at the time, making uniform shirts for the army – and then to be arrested and imprisoned like a criminal, was unconscionable.

Opa was released within a month and Dad, Max and Herman within three months. To Yetti's distress, her "poor Karl", as she would speak of him, was not released for a year, but then he had German nationality – indeed (as I have said) his father had been awarded the Iron Cross for services to the Kaiser in the First World War.

My unhappiness at school was made greater by the fact that I had no visitors. The other children seemed to have regular visits from their parents, some of whom taking pity on me would invite me to join them on their outings. I felt like an orphan. Eventually, shortly after Dad had returned from the Isle of Man, my parents wrote to say they were coming for a few days. It was spring and the weather was fine. They came and stayed at a nearby farm which offered bed and breakfast and on the first day of their visit we went for a walk. The Lake District is covered by drystone walls, and footpaths run between them, through them, and sometimes over them. My father was not noted for his agility or athleticism. Indeed I cannot recall any activity or interest of his which was not essentially sedentary. The only exercise I ever knew him take was horse riding on the sands at Coatham after the war, and that is also pretty sedentary! Trying to negotiate a stile which had caused me and my mother no trouble, my father decided for some reason to jump off. He was a heavy man, as I have said, and he fell and broke his ankle. Somehow we got him back to where he could see a doctor, who put him in plaster and he had to return home. My disappointment was immense. That, in a strange way, typified my relationship with my parents. Though they were there in the background and I never went short of material things, they were never there in person – physically – when I needed them. So, I learned to fend for myself.

Two things made life tolerable. The first was reading. I was an avid reader. Here, again, my father had been the catalyst, though somewhat unwittingly. Keen to ensure the moral and literary improvement of his son he asked Herman to bring me, from London, a book on Oliver Cromwell. Why Oliver Cromwell? Dad had heard of Oliver Cromwell as a sort of hero figure to the Jews of England as he had been responsible for their return to this country, some 350 years after their expulsion in 1290. Why from London? It may be that Dad doubted there were any bookshops in Middlesbrough, not an unreasonable assumption though actually unfair. More probably he felt his own command of the English language, in which Herman was fluent, was not up to the purchase of such a volume. Herman's English may have been fluent but his history was not. What he actually brought was *Oliver Twist*. He said that he had not been able to find any books on Oliver Cromwell and trusted this would do as well. It did for me but Dad was horrified at first; he had no idea who Oliver Twist was, nor, of course had I. I seized on it, devoured it, and called for more. I became a Dickens addict. I also read all the *Just William* books, *The Scarlet Pimpernel*, John Buchan – whose chauvinism and anti-semitism I did not then understand – Biggles, Dornford Yates – see under Buchan – whatever I could get my hands on. The volume which Herman kindly (and mistakenly) presented to me was the first in my library. It was published by Collins in their Library of Classics series, and came with a hard, slip cover.

The second item was Meccano. We were allowed to bring some toys and games with us from home and I brought my Meccano set. Meccano was a construction kit, made of metal, with bars, rods, plates, wheels, nuts and bolts. One could make the most exciting things with it; cars, bridges, cranes, almost anything.

There were occasional outings from the school, but one day we – that is the senior pupils – were promised a very special treat: an evening outing. To someone used to going to bed, so it seemed, at dusk, this was a terribly exciting prospect, and when we learned that the treat was to include a cinematographic performance, the anticipation was scarcely bearable. I had been to the cinema only once before, when I was with my parents in Belgium visiting Uncle Fritz – I think it must have been Ostend. There was a children's matinee, some cartoon show, at a local cinema. My family was punctual to a fault; they were always afraid to miss anything. Being virtually first in the queue at the cinema, I rushed to get the best seat – and headed for the front row. I saw nothing. What I heard was a jumbled noise. I made a mental note not to make the same mistake this time.

The breathlessly expected evening duly arrived. We walked to the village hall and took our places. We were then treated to a documentary film, in streaky black and white, with wobbling frames, all about lifeboats. A worthy film, I'm sure, with some exciting episodes, but not *The Arabian Nights* or even *Tarzan*. But it was only a loss-leader. We were then shown a second film about the evils of drink, offered some milk or chocolate and biscuits, and asked to "take the pledge", that is, to forswear intoxicating liquor for ever. Our hosts for the evening were the Band of Hope, a temperance society dedicated to the suppression of alcohol. It was doubtless a good cause, but I regarded it, young as I was, as a serious case of misrepresentation, if not downright deceit, and swore off temperance for ever. To me, it was simply typical of the school.

Getting home for holidays was difficult. Though the distance from the Lake District was not great, only about 60 miles, due to the shortage of petrol and the effect of the war generally, travel was slow and circuitous. Sometimes parents of other children would give me a lift; at other times it was usually Dora who collected me, and it was she who visited me from time to time. When Karl was released from internment, he and Yetti came to see me and I had an enjoyable day with them, but my parents never came again and my grandparents did not travel.

The only release from my own internment, as I regarded it, was to go to another school. Because my parents were now living in Guisborough, I was eligible for the excellent grammar school there. This school was reputedly the best in the area but entrance could, apparently, only be achieved by passing the Scholarship, as the 11+ exam was then known. I do not know how it was arranged. I suspect Dora's influence, but my parents must have appreciated just how miserable I was and agreed to it.

I am not quite sure how it happened. From the snippets of information I collected – I would remind my readers of the title of this book – an almighty row developed at home after one of Dora's visits.

Apparently she said something like: "That boy is terribly unhappy. You can't leave him in that *goyishe* anti-semitic school. They steal his food parcels, his toys and his clothes. They don't feed him properly and they don't teach him anything. You're destroying him." Dora was never one to minimise a situation. "You've got to get him out of there."

Opa then intervened: "Bring him home at once!" went the command.

I am sure that the bit about not being adequately fed was the catalyst. No one ever challenged Opa's orders. My parents had heard about the local school, Guisborough Grammar School just up the road, so to speak.

Driven by Dora to take action, never an easy thing for my father to do, Dad went to see Mr Routh the headmaster and explained the problem to him.

According to reports, the matter went something like this:

"My son is at a private boarding school, where he is very unhappy and I don't think he is getting the education he needs. Your school has been highly recommended and from what I hear would suit him very well and I am sure he would be a credit to you. Would you take him?"

"Is he bright?"

Mr Routh was obviously unaware that to their parents, all Jewish children are geniuses, but my father had by now learned enough about English attitudes not to go overboard.

"Well he appears to be. He beats us all at chess and he is an avid reader. He started with *Oliver Twist* when he was seven."

"This is a Scholarship school. He would have to pass an examination. If he did we would obviously accept him. How old is he?"

"Nine."

"Nine did you say? Well, the Scholarship examination is usually taken at the age of 11, so your son is still a little young."

"But what if he took the exam and passed it; there would be no reason for you not to accept him. Would you allow him to sit the examination and take him in if he passed it?" argued my father. "We do have to get him away from that school and I think he is quite clever."

"Well, it would be unusual but so are the circumstances; I see no reason why not. I will see what can be arranged."

And so it was that in the spring of 1941 I took the Scholarship exam and being the only way out of purgatory I had no alternative but to pass it. Because we'd been evacuated and due to the problems of travel, I could not take the exam at the grammar school itself and arrangements were accordingly made for me to take it at the vicarage in Kirby Stephen, a nearby market town. The vicar himself would invigilate. In all fairness to her, Mrs Malyon must have cooperated in making the necessary arrangements, and ensuring that I was taken to the examination, because no one in my family would have known what to do.

The vicar was charming, and made me feel very much at home. I took the examination in his study. Not only did he invigilate, but he ensured that I had a constant supply of tea and biscuits. I cannot think of pleasanter surroundings in which to take an exam. I wish I could remember more of that occasion, but apart from the tea and biscuits, it is lost to my memory. For the next two or three weeks, every minute of which hope mingled with anxiety, life seemed poised on the point of a needle. Then suddenly Mrs Malyon called me to her study – I wondered what great sin I had committed now – to tell me that I had passed the Scholarship exam. I received the tidings with great relief and joy. Though the school year had not yet ended there was no purpose in my remaining there, so I went home, without regret, except for leaving my little Norwegian friend. I did not see her again until many years later when we met at the home of a mutual friend on one of my rare visits to Middlesbrough.

Dora came to collect me. She shared my dislike for Mrs Malyon and rather unfairly I thought, despised Mrs Newton, the Matron.

Dora did not hesitate to hide her feelings. She also tended to be protectively paranoid and was convinced that I was the victim of envy, not to say anti-semitism. There may have been some substance in the first, but I am quite sure that there was none in the second allegation. She had asked Mrs Newton to prepare some sandwiches for the train journey home, as it would take some four hours and require four separate trains and three changes, though it was only around 60 miles away. The school had duly provided beetroot sandwiches on the cheapest plain white bread of the cardboard variety.

Dora, however, had stayed overnight at the same local farmhouse as my parents had done on their aborted visit. There the farmer's wife had given her, with typical country generosity and without charge, some food for the journey; – "The lad'll need this" – some large sandwiches well-filled with meat and chicken, some apples and biscuits, and a flask of tea – fare fit for a king. Dora was not as conscientious in her observance of the laws of *kashrus* as were her parents but in any case, this was wartime and feeding me was a matter of urgency, of life and death, as it were, for the sake of which even God's rules could be suspended. Despite the war and rationing, Dora threw the school's measly beetroot sandwiches out of the train window in disgust. With them went my childhood. I was nine years old.

Oma was horrified when I returned home. It was only about eighteen months since she had last seen me and I was undoubtedly thin, though probably as fit as I had ever been. Whatever the gastronomic deficiencies of the boarding school diet, it was well balanced and healthy. I had never been fat but to a Jewish grandmother of her generation thinness was a sign of starvation, of poverty, of ill health. It was a condition which required immediate treatment. It was, above all, a challenge. Oma determined to fatten me up and started me on a regime of thick soups, potatoes, bread and butter (culled from the rations of other members of the family); anything that would ensure weight gain. A sumo wrestler would have approved. The diet worked well; I have had a weight problem ever since.

Chapter 16 – Guisborough Grammar School

The new school had some 200 pupils and twelve teachers; a high teacher-pupil ratio. It copied certain public school characteristics; for instance, it had a tuck shop; it stood in its own grounds and had its own sports facilities within those grounds. There was a distinctive school badge, a pointed double oval with a late mediaeval icon of Jesus in an inner oval and the words "Schola Grammaticalis Jesu de Guisborough" forming a border in the outer. We had a school magazine, *The Gisborian*, of which, in the fullness of time, I became editor. It did have an air of distinction about it and it seems to me a matter of great regret that by an act of political vandalism it was at some later stage, long after I had left, turned into Prior Pursglove's Sixth Form College.

Guisborough Priory was one of the ruins that, in the words of the old music hall song, "Cromwell knocked about a bit". It had been an impressive building and one of its offshoots was the grammar school founded in 1561. The late Victorian buildings stood in the old Priory grounds. By this time it had come under the control of the Local Education Authority but maintained its traditions. Previous headmasters had all been clergymen and the then current headmaster, Mr J. R. Routh, was a lay reader.

My family, particularly Oma, urbanites to the core, hated Guisborough. If the move from Leipzig to Middlesbrough had been a culture shock, then that to Guisborough was even more so. Middlesbrough had few pretensions to culture, but it had plenty of places of entertainment: three large cinemas, including an Odeon (recently built in late 1930s art deco style), the Elite, the Gaumont, formerly the "Opera House" (though how much opera it had ever seen was questionable), and a number of smaller cinemas – there were about eleven in all. There was a variety theatre, the Empire, where all the best variety acts appeared, as they did before television made it unnecessary, a lively amateur

Little Theatre – where, incidentally, some years later I saw the best Mercutio I have ever seen, played by one of the local Jewish members, Jack Adler – and periodical concerts in the ornate Gothic town hall, the grandest building in the town, by the Halle and other orchestras as well as regular visits from solo performers, such as Myra Hess and Moiseiwitch.

Guisborough, in contrast, had only its flea-pit cinema, where every Saturday morning for the princely price of one penny you could watch weekly instalments, in glorious black-and-white grain (uninterrupted if you were lucky), of the *Mark of Zorro* or the *Perils of Pauline*, each episode ending with the hero or heroine about to die, hanging off the edge of a cliff or tied to railway lines with a fast approaching express, or similar predicament. Somehow by the following week he or she had survived. I often wondered what they did during the week; nor was the solution to their immediate problem always explained. One had to take much for granted.

The family had taken a house at 31 Park Lane. This was the only detached house in the road, but it only had three bedrooms and the population emigrating from the Grey House, though much reduced, was still large. I do not know how we all fitted into it. Immediately opposite the house were fields, inhabited by cattle, who looked at us over their fence. Oma would introduce visitors rather bitterly: "Meet the cows, my neighbours," she would say.

I was due to start at Guisborough Grammar School in October 1941. The first term of the year always started on a Thursday, which gave time to settle down in one's class, meet one's future friends, get one's books and gear together, and generally prepare so that work could start in earnest on the following Monday. Unfortunately, as has often happened, the start of the academic year coincided with the Jewish New Year, *Rosh Hashanah*. I had to miss the first two days of my new school and when I duly arrived on the Monday morning I got lost. Not knowing the way in to the school – I had never been there before – I committed the heinous solecism of entering by the front gate, a right reserved for staff and sixth-formers.

Fortunately, someone saw me wandering around and took pity on me. I was shown into the headmaster's study, something generally reserved for a special reward, or more usually, punishment. An invitation to the Head's study was not usually welcomed, but Mr Routh, very much a no-nonsense person, was kindness itself. As a deeply religious man, he respected the faith of others, and throughout my many years at that school I had no problems over absences for Jewish festivals or activities which conflicted with the Sabbath. Indeed, Mr Routh was more insistent on meticulous observance of these than I was.

Not only did I miss the first two days, I then had to miss further days for Yom Kippur and then Succoth, the Feast of Tabernacles. It was some four weeks before I completed a full week at the school, and my classmates already envied the number of holidays I enjoyed. Though we lived in Guisborough, we went back to the Grey House for the Holy Days, when we all went to synagogue, war notwithstanding.

The school was divided into three houses, colour-coded, namely Challoner (green), Pursglove (yellow) and Bruce (blue). These names all had some particular historical significance to the school. House points were awarded both for scholastic and sporting success. I was allocated to Challoner, which at that time was the most successful house. The headmaster took me to the storeroom and fitted me out with sports kits, in Challoner colours – football shirt, shorts, socks and boots; gym shirt, shorts and shoes – and a kit bag to carry them in. I was then provided with all necessary school books, exercise books, pencils and the like. These were all free. Though clothes were rationed, and one needed coupons to buy them, I believe that no coupons were required for these.

School uniform consisting of cap, blazer, tie, short grey trousers (until age fourteen when long trousers could be worn), white shirt and grey knee-length socks, was obligatory. The uniform was not free and required an expenditure of clothes coupons. The ban on long trousers before the age of fourteen did not make allowance for the disparate growth rate of different boys. I was big for my age, and looked more than my years. At fourteen, I and others even taller, looked ridiculous in short trousers with knee-length stockings.

Duly fitted out I was then taken to my form room to meet my form master, Mr Spedding, and my new schoolmates.

"What's your name?" he asked me.

"Freddy," I replied causing great mirth, and "Freddy" I was ever afterwards to all in the school, from youngest boy to the Head, except on formal occasions. I didn't know I should have answered, "Fischbein". At that time I had never heard of anyone being called by his surname.

The school day started at 9.15 a.m. with assembly, at which daily prayers were said and announcements made. The headmaster and staff all wore gowns for this and for teaching. At special services, sports days and public occasions, they wore their full coloured university gowns and mortar boards. All this was new to me. Male teachers were called "Sir", and women, regardless of their age or status, "Miss". We stood up whenever a teacher entered or left a classroom.

The Head had some difficulty with my name. The "Fisch" part was easy. The problem was with the "bein". In German this is pronounced to rhyme with "wine". He pronounced it as "bane". In the end he unilaterally decided my name should be Fishburn, which happened to coincide with a nearby locality, and so it became, well before it was accorded official recognition. My parents found the change convenient. It was not too different from the original and they were happy to shed a name which was recognisably German. They had no allegiance to Germany and did not wish to be identified with it in any way, so they adopted the name. I note that even in the USA, my uncle dropped the "c" and became Fishbein.

I started in form 1B. Forms were sensibly numbered in the Grammar School. We had no incomprehensible denominations such as "Remove" and "Transition". We started at the first and, barring accidents, ended in the sixth form. There was a lower sixth and an upper sixth, but that was reserved for the gods, to whose ranks I acceded in due course.

There were two streams: A and B. No one was concerned at the possible harm to the psyche by being put in a B form. We were obviously made of sterner stuff than the modern pupil, or perhaps, with a war on, there were more important things to worry about. Form 1A consisted of the "scholarship boys". Form 1B consisted of the others, boys who had passed the school entrance exam but not the Scholarship. I did not understand the distinction and doubt whether anyone gave it much thought. Those who were expected to do better academically were in the A stream. It later transpired that though I was a "scholarship boy" I was put in the B stream because of my extreme youth – I was the youngest boy in the school for two years and even when I was in the third form some of the new boys entering the school were older than I was – and it was felt that I would need time to catch up with the older boys. There were about fourteen boys in my class and eighteen in 1A.

Also, for the third consecutive time, I was the only Jewish child in the school. I believe that I was the first Jew the school had had. This is not as remarkable as it sounds, as there were few Jews in the area, and they were mainly based in Middlesbrough. The early market traders and pedlars who made their rounds in the district had no pretensions to a grammar school education for their sons.

My new colleagues mainly came from the surrounding towns and villages: Loftus, Lingdale, Skinningrove, Carlin How, Boosbeck, Brotton and other localities with similarly wonderful names. They came in on school buses, cycled or walked. They were nearly all the sons of artisans, farmers, steelworkers, miners and small shop-keepers. I was one of the few representatives of the *bourgeoisie,* if I could be counted as anything. The Grammar School boys were the local intellectual elite, and their parents were proud of the fact. Many of them had made great sacrifices to send their sons to that school, not only forgoing the income they might have produced, but in having to support them. However free education was, keeping a boy at school was still a big financial burden. But these parents valued education and appreciated that it would ensure their children a better life than they had had.

Though I had started school a few days late, after most had established their places and started to form their friendships, I had no difficulty in feeling accepted and making friends. My first "best friend" was Tommy Dalton, a farmer's son from Lingdale. He was small, fair-haired and very handsome. He had the warm red col-ouring of an autumn apple. After I moved up a form and into the "A" stream, where Tommy unfortunately did not join me, I made new friends in my new class and these I maintained for the rest of my time at school.

Chief among them was Peter Radford, who was my main chal-lenger for top place; between us, throughout our school careers, it was for most of the time turn and turn about. Not only was he at least as good academically as I was, but he was beyond my reach on the football field. About 6' 2" tall, well built and agile, he was a superlative goalkeeper; part of an incredibly good school team. He was good enough to have become a professional, and he did in fact play for Oxford and also for Pegasus, the leading amateur soccer team of the day, made up of Oxbridge men.

Other close friends were John Brettle, with whom I travelled to and from school on the train, the Spa crowd, and above all, because it was a friendship which outlasted all the others, George Read. He is the only one of those friends with whom I have kept in touch all these years. Peter Radford went to Keble College, Oxford, originally intending to enter the priesthood but went into the police force instead. I saw Tommy Dalton some time after my story appeared in the *Middlesbrough Evening Gazette*, as a result of which I was invited to address a ladies' luncheon club, and had the opportunity to renew my acquaintance with the area. I have from time to time heard from others but they are spread, I think, far and wide, and being older than me started on their respective careers somewhat before I did.

Though I suppose I was something of an outsider, coming from a different background, culture and class from my companions, I never felt this, nor was I ever made to feel it. There was only one instance of anything which could be taken as an anti-semitic remark. I was no angel, and I gave some cheek to the head boy, the son of Mr Thomas the history master – who riposted that he was "…not going to take any cheek from a little Jew-Boy". To his credit, he immediately apologised – not an easy thing for the school captain to do in public to a snotty first former.

There were sensitive moments too: such as when the pictures of the concentration camps came to be released, and when by contrast, in what was still Palestine, the King David Hotel was blown up and the British Army sergeants were hanged by Menachem Beigin's Irgun. Neither the overt sympathy for the former, nor the lack of it for the other, which I shared, affected our relationship. There was an innate and intelligent mutual respect for the rights and opinions of others on delicate subjects.

Because most of my friends lived on the other side of Guisborough from Middlesbrough, the only opportunities for any social contact out of school were at the weekend. I saw a lot of John Brettle during the week and we often compared homework notes. To meet the others was difficult and the Spa, a local dance hall, provided an ideal place for this, as well, of course, as being a place to meet girls, in whom by the age of sixteen I was more than interested.

Wherever I went, I was warmly welcomed. I would sometimes stay over the Christmas and New Year period with Peter Radford. His mother was a large, affectionate woman, who made the most delicious Yorkshire puddings. His father was highly intelligent, and we had long discussions on all sorts of matters. I could only marvel at the comparison between the small working-class house full of books, and the opulent houses of English Jews where not a book was to be seen, other than perhaps the latest bestselling novel.

These were surroundings where I felt at home. Here were real people, who had had to work and fight hard for any improvement they had achieved, and who were at last able to realise (through their children) the ambitions which they had been denied. The Christmases and New Years I spent with Peter and his family were very happy times. The walks, the pubs, the girls we danced with, the food we ate, the turkeys, the sides of beef, the Yorkshire puddings – above all the Yorkshire puddings, each as big as a plate and filled with the most delicious gravy which I can still taste even as I write about it – and the whole atmosphere were just immensely pleasurable.

For my part, I was pleased when I was able to reciprocate, after we moved to Brierfield following Oma's death in 1947. I never invited them to the Grey House. I was probably conscious of the great divide between my friends and my grandparents, and felt that neither would feel comfortable with each other. My parents, who were the most hospitable of people and did their best to make all my friends very welcome, could not relate to them in the way that, for example, Peter's parents did to me. This may have been a shyness on my parents' part about their foreign accent, but I think it was more than that.

The contrast in lifestyles, not so much between my friends and myself as between our respective families, did not seem to matter to us, but I think my parents may have been self-conscious about it, whether due to the perpetual Jewish fear of causing anti-semitism or because of some latent social conscience, I do not know. Though my family all had strong left-wing views, I doubt whether their reasons were in any sense political. The matter was never discussed with my parents. Very few things of importance were ever discussed. As far as my parents were concerned, it was my home and I could, within reason, bring home anyone I wished.

At Guisborough Grammar School, I was part of a serious, disciplined and efficient regime for the first time. So far as human nature could prevent it, there was no favouritism, nor victimisation. Effort was rewarded, idleness punished, directly or indirectly. There was a strong work ethic. The emphasis was on education, which meant learning the basics and mastering them. I came into contact with Latin (not Greek) and French. Kennedy's *Shorter Latin Primer* (usually turned into the Shortbread Eating Primer by the addition of a few strokes) was one of my bibles for some years.

Because most of the young male teachers had been called up, the school had to recruit older – some very old – retired teachers, and even worse, believe it or not, women teachers, to deal with the deficiency. One of the teachers recalled from retirement to teach French was a Dr Hartog, who I suspected was a co-religionist. It is a mystery what he was doing there because he was a gentle, kindly old soul, used to the cloistered atmosphere of a university, where he had been a lecturer (or more). He was completely unable to handle a classroom of unruly kids and made little effort to do so. His idea of teaching was to give the class something to read and retire to his *Times* crossword. He didn't last long.

The Second Master, Mr Thomas had no such problem. He was a Welshman of military bearing; his presence and demeanour demanded respect. He was a strict, old-school disciplinarian. He was a stickler for good manners and proper behaviour about which he constantly lectured us. He considered even the mildest display of the female figure, in other than full dress, pornography. In short, he was somewhat old-fashioned, even at that time, but it did no harm to be subject to an anti-libertarian philosophy. Whatever view one might take of his attitudes, he did instil some measure of self-discipline in us, and he did care. He was a most conscientious teacher, but he was not a good one.

He was also the games master, of which he was a much better teacher than he was history. He had fertile soil to plough. My year provided some of the best footballers the school had known. As we grew older, we produced a soccer Xl which could take on and best all-comers of equal age.

My first form master was Ken Spedding, a small but lively man, who was also a sports and music master. He exuded energy and enthusiasm, and you felt – at least I did – that you had to put the same effort into learning as he did into teaching, if only not to let him down. He seemed to spot in me an ability to write very early on. We had been set an exercise to write a description of a subject of our choosing. Remembering the excitement I always felt at railway stations, I chose to describe the scene at one, thinking of my departure from Kings Cross. My essay took three quarters of a page, a brevity which I have never since matched. He marked it "A", and read it out in class. My reputation was established. The problem, however, with a reputation is that it creates the pressure to live up to it. This is not to say that I did not have the odd brush with authority. Made arrogant by success, I thought that with my Jewish knowledge of Psalm 24, I would have no difficulty in learning it and that a brief and cursory scanning would suffice to satisfy the weekly exercise which was to recite it by heart. Unfortunately, the version chosen was that in the King James version of the Bible, with which I was not familiar. I was a disaster, but was able to rectify the matter by the next day as I have an almost photographic memory which was put to use on this occasion.

The Latin master was Jack Sherrill, a tall lean man of 55 who looked 35. He was another enthusiast. His trousers were always a little short, and he always appeared to be in a hurry, his gown flowing behind him as he rushed across the quad from one class to another. He managed to infuse his subject with enthusiasm, and made Latin live. He was unmarried when I started school, but then a new, very pretty, blonde French teacher arrived called Mary.

She must have been much younger than Jack, but he swept her off her feet and we were soon in need of another French teacher.

The enthusiasm shown by nearly all the teachers for their subject created an atmosphere where though learning was taken seriously, it was also made pleasurable. I for one, was carried along by this enthusiasm, this love of learning. Guisborough Grammar was quite a remarkable school, and much of the credit must be given to the headmaster.

Our progress was carefully monitored. We had weekly marks, and weekly positions. These were shown on cards which we were supposed to take home to show our parents. I never did, nor would they have understood them. After the first year these became monthly cards. They did not displace the usual end of term reports, which I did show my parents.

At the end of my first week I was fourteenth in the class; the second week I was ninth; the third week I came top. Thereafter, as long as I remained in that form I was regularly top, or near top, of the class. After the first year I was moved into the "A" stream, where the competition was much harder. Though I came top in various subjects from time to time, I was on average about fifth, until it came to the end-of-year examinations, when I was usually in the top three.

I had a knack with exams, possibly helped by the photographic memory I inherited from my mother. I seemed to have an instinctive skill for coping with being tested. I was never nervous. I was usually able to identify the point of a question and keep my replies succinct (they had to be, as there was not all that much knowledge to display). I also seemed to have a talent for spotting the likely questions, though I did not entirely rely on this, and was generally able to time myself in exams. I occasionally came unstuck, for example in physics when some manual dexterity was needed in carrying out experiments. For instance, I never mastered the Wheatstone Bridge, whatever that may be, but as long as my answers had to be written I was in good shape.

Any artistic tendency I may have had was stifled at birth by the arts mistress at the school, known as Granny Hood – who was one of the retired teachers called in to fill the gaps caused by the call-up of the younger masters. She found it difficult enough to control an unruly mob of schoolboys without having to devote time and attention to one, in her eyes, totally without talent. Art in all its forms was, for me, a void which lasted until well after I was married and my wife taught me to appreciate its beauties. I had a similar experience with singing. The singing teacher, one Gavin Kaye, came weekly from Middlesbrough. He was not a member of the staff. He ran through a few of the common songs – "John Peel", "Glorious Devon", "Hearts of Oak"– a few psalms, that sort of thing. If you could sing, all well and good; I was told to mime!

As I had no wish to participate in the prayers, I asked for permission to miss morning assembly. It seemed a good time to finish my homework. Mr Routh, however, anticipated me. He had no objection, he said, to my not attending prayers, but not so that I could use the time to catch up on my homework. He required me to get my Hebrew teacher, Rabbi Miller, to set me work to do and allowed me to use his study. There could be heard for many years, particularly those before my bar mitzvah, the sounds of Jewish ritual chanting issuing from the private rooms of the headmaster of Guisborough Grammar School. What any passer-by who heard it made of it, or what reaction the graves of the long-deceased Priors of Guisborough Abbey had we shall never know, but no one in the school gave it the slightest thought.

Mr Routh's own subject was RI (religious instruction) which was compulsory in schools in those days, and having regard to the school's religious connection, entirely appropriate. There was a strong feeling among Jews that their children should not be subject to any teaching of Christianity.

While Mr Routh did not seek to overcome my objections to attending RI classes, which he assumed reflected my parents' views (though they were probably oblivious of the matter) and made me study Hebrew instead, he saw no reason why I should not go to the lessons he gave on the history of Christianity. He was absolutely right in this, as he was in most things, and I am grateful to him for his insistence. I learned much that I think would have been denied to most Jewish children which, like anything else learned in youth, informed my views in later life. I have many reasons to be grateful to Mr Routh and his school.

Term always ended with an assembly at which the head boy read the last few paragraphs of Ecclesiastes, closing with the words "Remember now thy Creator in the days of thy youth". Ecclesiastes is the one book of the Bible which speaks to me. Its wisdom and philosophy have had a great influence on me.

"Vanity of vanities saith the Preacher, vanity of vanities; all is vanity", in other words, all is futile. "There is a time to die and a time to live". Nothing better expresses how little control we actually have over our lives. As this was from the Old Testament I saw no objection in attending the end of term assemblies. It was also when term prizes were handed out, and as I was often a recipient, it would have been churlish not to be there.

Chapter 17 – Sexual Awakening

The sheltered existence I had led before grammar school left me totally ignorant about life in general and sex in particular. It was a subject not discussed by my family, at least not in my presence. Dora was noted for her risqué jokes and repartee, but the rest of the family, and certainly my parents and grandparents, were somewhat puritanical. I was not unaware of the female form as, on a hall table of the Grey House, there was a bronze, art deco-style statuette, about twelve-inches high, of a nude woman with arms upraised and perfectly shaped breasts and legs. When older and alone, I would lovingly run my hands over it. I cannot imagine how my grandparents came to own such an object. But I did not know what there was between the legs or how children were made. I suspected that female genitalia differed from mine but not having sisters did not know in what way. I knew no "bad language"; no one in my family used deletable expletives, not in English, or in my presence, anyway and probably knew none. (Apart from Karl, who in true German style learned the language from the bottom up, that is, the swear words first.) The worst word I knew was "bloody". I had much to learn, and the knowledge was not long in coming.

Many of my contemporaries came from "rough" neighbourhoods and nearly all had siblings and were conscious of the opposite sex. They were mostly older than I was; at the age of ten the extra year or two makes a great difference. Intellectual precocity does not imply social maturity or equal physical development. Being with a much older group can have its disadvantages. I was very young, and very innocent in sexual matters. Puberty was, so to speak, afoot; sex was becoming an active issue for my colleagues long before it became so with me. But I did not wish to display my ignorance: I had already entered by the wrong gate once when I started school, passing through the one reserved for masters and sixth formers instead of the main entrance used by the hoi polloi. Being the youngest member of the group increases peer pressure.

Magazines, if they showed the female nude, did so with the discretion – though not the art – of the classical painters. There was always the equivalent of a fig leaf, and from the photographs no one could have suspected that pubic hair existed. Our source of wonder over and information about the female body was the naturist journal *Health & Efficiency*, whose front cover was usually adorned by pictures of healthy young ladies sporting their naked breasts, engaged in some energetic exercise which enabled their attributes to be most effectively demonstrated. Needless to say, when Mr Thomas caught a boy with the magazine in his possession – usually an old and tattered copy – he came down very heavily on him, and gave us a long lecture on pornography and the wickedness of the sexual depravity evidenced by these lewd pictures. (He should be living at this hour!)

However, my ignorance was dissipated in the fullness of time but when I discovered what I was supposed to have been missing I must confess to a feeling of disappointment – "is this what all the fuss is about?" was my reaction.

I should have liked to end this chapter with a lyrical, or perhaps passionate, description of that supposed seminal, climactic, cataclysmic moment in a boy's life when he loses his virginity and becomes a man. Unfortunately, life is not always perfect. Though my recollection of much of my early life is clear in my mind, I have none of that event; how, when, where and with whom it occurred, and why my memory is blank on the matter, I cannot say. Unfortunately, I had no Rosie to bring me cider on an idyllic hot autumn day in the Cotswolds.

Chapter 18 – Sports And Games

Other activities I discovered at the Grammar School, completely new to me, were football, cricket and most other sports. I had never seen either a football or a cricket ball before. These were not items within my family's experience and were not in the curriculum at either Priory House or The Firs. When I was first given my football boots at school, I was uncertain as to their purpose, but forbore to ask lest I display my ignorance and bring ridicule on my head. Sunderland won the FA Cup for the first time in 1937 and football was a religion "Up North". I had instinct enough to keep quiet.

Games took place on Wednesday afternoons. Football is not a difficult game to understand and I soon got the idea, but was not always sure which way I was supposed to kick. At break and lunchtimes, virtually the whole school would disgorge on to the playing fields, which were in the school grounds, for a kickabout and such skills as I was able to acquire were developed there. I soon became an aficionado.

Football was played on the Continent, and some of my family had actually heard of the game. Cricket was another matter. I had not seen it played and knew nothing of the rules. Mr Thomas had given us a rudimentary lesson on the rules of football – soccer and rugby – but cricket was outwith his concern. I literally did not know one end of a bat from the other.

After the rules had been briefly explained to me, I was sent in to bat. When I received my first ball, which seemed to come rather high, I was not sure what to do with the bat – rather like some English teams – and fielded the ball, so to speak, with my chest, whereafter I fell to the ground somewhat injured and turned over, like, my friends said, a turtle, thus earning me the nickname of "Turt". In time, this was another game whose mysteries I eventually mastered, not so much as a player, though I did become keen, but as a theoretician. It was a game I could not explain to my family.

On the last Wednesday of every spring term came the one event of the year which I hated and dreaded: the school cross-country. This was a five-mile course over muddy local roads and country lanes and invariably it seemed to take place in rainy or windy conditions. Spring in Cleveland is not what Browning had in mind. It always seemed to be won by the same boy, a good friend of mine, Maurice Oversby, in about 17 minutes, by which time I had just about reached quarter of the way. By the time I got back most of the field had gone home. The stitch generally hit me after about 100 yards and thereafter it was pure purgatory. Fortunately, just as there was usually someone a little better than I in those matters which I considered my speciality, there was always someone fatter or more maladroit, or slower, in those fields in which I was doomed to failure, and my saviour from being last in the cross-country race was often one Derek Wilkes, bless him.

I could cope with gym, which we had twice a week, except for the boxing which Mr Thomas also thought fit to introduce. When I came to the school, though no coward, I was, by the lights of my colleagues, a sissy. I had no experience of games or sports involving physical contact. Though the primary schools I had attended were described as mixed, they were essentially girls' schools, and had none of the games that boys play. I found the idea of fighting repugnant. I could see no purpose so far as I was concerned, in the noble art of self-defence. Anyone wishing to attack me would hardly resort to the Queensberry Rules. I could have understood being taught judo, but boxing seemed a harmful waste of time. Happily, the whole idea was soon dropped.

In fact, I could never really see much purpose in any sport not involving a ball, but that may have been due to my own incapacity for sustained momentum over any distance. I therefore generally took up positions which minimised the need to run. I could be quite fast over ten yards, enough to beat an oncoming forward to the ball, but five miles, indeed, even 100 yards, was quite beyond me. I became a fairly proficient goalkeeper and wicket keeper, sufficient to play for my house and in later life, my college. I suppose one could say that with time I became a very keen, though not very competent, sportsman.

The school also had its own Scout Hut and troop which I joined, and I soon became an enthusiastic member of the Scouting movement. This club was run by the physics master, Mr Savage, another wild enthusiast, who knew as much about Scouting as about his own subject. Being in the Scouts gave the opportunity to mix and make friends with boys in other years, whom you would not usually get to know, as each school year, indeed each form, tends to be its own enclave. The Cleveland Hills was a beautiful area in which to go camping which we did several times a year. I felt very proud in my Scout uniform which still included the old South African-style hat. As a Scout I think I mainly learned how to tie knots: reef knots, sheep shanks, bowlines and the like. My first proficiency badge was, typically, for the care of the inner man – cooking.

At the end of my first term at the Grammar School my parents gave me – I imagine it was for Chanukah – a full grown-up bicycle. I was tall for my age and its size presented no problem. It was a black Raleigh with low, racing handlebars and Sturmey-Archer gears. It was the best present my parents ever gave me. I loved that bike and rode it everywhere. I would have taken it to bed with me if allowed. I cared for it lovingly; cleaning it after every ride, and overhauling it thoroughly at the weekend, a little like Opa with his clock. When we moved back to Middlesbrough, I would often ride it to and from Guisborough, not daily for school as that would have been too exhausting and taken too long, but in the school holidays. That bicycle gave me the freedom to roam.

The factory, which had been only peripheral to my life, began to feature much more after our move to Guisborough, if only because of its proximity. The Fountain Street office was only a few minutes walk from the school and it became convenient to pop in there to see my father from time to time. The outbreak of war, which could have been ruinous, helped the factory as it became a supplier to the War Office. Government orders were not simply for the asking. They had to be tendered for and inspectors were sent initially to inspect the factory premises, to satisfy themselves that the orders (if given) could be met and that conditions were satisfactory. Once the orders had been placed there would be regular inspections to control quality. The Ministry determined the price of, and supplied, or arranged the supply from its own suppliers, the necessary materials. The specifications were set out in great detail and there was no scope for variation. Fortunately for us the samples, made by my mother to these specifications, were considered satisfactory, and the orders placed.

At first, the orders were for RAF officers' shirts, which were no problem at all as the materials were top quality poplin, grist to the mill, and army shirts for other ranks, which were a different matter. The khaki material was thick and hard to work with as the existing machinery was designed to take much thinner material. By all accounts it was Opa's and my mother's combined skill and ingenuity that eventually overcame the difficulty, but never entirely satisfactorily. The ultimate consumers of these garments unfortunately had more important matters to concern them than the fit of their shirts.

When the menfolk were interned, as previously mentioned, the factory had already started on Government contracts but fortunately one or two senior personnel remained to run the office. I remember particularly Mr Peacock, who suffered from consumption and smoked for his condition – unbelievable today – some strange herbal cigarettes. His condition precluded his being called up for military service. He knew sufficient of the administration to keep things going, and it was not necessary to go out and get orders. Auntie Jeanne, though pregnant, came in to help. She was a good administrator and between them the business was kept afloat. There was also another refugee who had been taken into the business, a Mr Seidler, who was a loyal servant for many years.

In retrospect, I see that in the local area our family business provided necessary employment – in some cases for whole families. Not only was Edgar Covell employed as mechanic, his wife Marjorie came and cleaned for the family, his father was night watchman and his daughter Olive and her three siblings all worked in the factory in one capacity or another. In a very short time the factory became an important and integral part of the life of the town, and was known to all as "The Factory".

Chapter 19 – Taxi!

As the war progressed and it seemed that Teesside, though it had some serious air raids, and was often subject to hit and run raids by one or two enemy aircraft, had not been chosen as a major target by the enemy, it was decided we should all return to Middlesbrough. To some extent we had already done so at the weekends. The problem at that time was transport. Petrol was scarce, and though a small ration was available for anyone on war work or government contracts, driving at night in winter – and in the North East the winter nights are long – with masked head-lights was not for the drivers produced by my family.

Opa decided to create his own air-raid shelter within the Grey House and had built a reinforced false ceiling in the passageway behind the dining room. This would have been strong enough to protect us in case of a direct hit on the house, but I do not know how we would have fared had the walls caved in. Fortunately, this was never put to the test.

The travel problem was more or less overcome by a one-man taxi service, owned and operated by one Bob Hodgkinson. Taxis had a special petrol allocation. The use of this for private purposes was an offence for which the local magistrates invariably handed out the severest punishment permitted to them. Bob ran a Morris 14, which was rather a pleasant car. He was supposed to come at 8 a.m. every day to take those family members working in the business to Guisborough. Punctuality was not his strong point.

Bob had a strange private life. He was a short, skinny, unpre-possessing man. His face was thin, with a long nose; he was not quite ugly but made a fair stab at it. He was about 45 years old. He had a wife and three children, but would, more often than not, turn up with a very pleasant-looking young woman aged about 22 or 23. Apparently, she had some titled connection. Whether it was through birth or marriage was never quite clear, but she came from the very opposite end of the social ladder to Bob. No doubt she was responsible for his usual late arrival. What she saw in him no one could understand. He was a very skilful driver, but though a pleasant enough fellow he had few other obvious qualities, either intellectual or personal. She on the other hand was very personable and did not appear to be unintelligent. They were certainly an odd match. He can only have had some extraordinary sexual attraction for her. When they turned up together, he would somehow fit her into the gap between the front seats. This did not please my family, but he kept on doing this. This arrangement lasted for some years, but one day he appeared alone and we heard, although not from him, that she had returned to her own family.

Dora and Joe remained in Guisborough. They later moved to Redcar, noted for its wonderful beaches, and its racecourse, which of course became a favourite haunt of Dad's. Joe wished to stay as far away from the family as practicable. He felt that being with them all day in the factory was enough.

I remained at the Grammar School despite the return to Middlesbrough. There was usually no room for me in the car and Bob was far too unreliable. In any event, I preferred to go on my own, and because of my fondness for trains, I generally travelled that way. I was the only commuter at first but was later joined by John Brettle whose family also moved to Middlesbrough. John and I became very good friends. At first, he was considerably smaller than I was, but between the ages of 14 and 16 he grew extraordinarily rapidly and finished half a head taller than me. Until I learned to drive I made my own way to school from Middlesbrough. My independent means of travel typified how my life was separate and distinct from – one might almost say outside – the family. Our lives touched at points, but from Monday to Friday I might have been a lodger, so little did I see of any of the family. We assembled on Friday night. During the week, my daily routine was breakfast on my own, the P bus to the station, train to Guisborough, five minutes' walk to school, back home, high tea or supper, usually alone, as the family ate when they came home, homework, bed.

My father and Joe, occasionally with Mother and Dora, and Max when he was not on his travels, usually had lunch at the restaurant in the Fox Inn only a few minutes' walk from the school and around the corner from the office. It was owned by the parents of one of my school friends, Hilton Armstrong. I would sometimes join the family for lunch as this was often the only time of the day that I had the chance to be with them. The food was quite good – certainly better than school lunches. As we were concerned with the progress of the war, the radio would always be on for the one o'clock news, which was read by newsreaders with the neutral accents proselytised by the BBC as the correct pronunciation. The announcer would always state his name: "This is the one o'clock news and this is Alvar Liddell reading it." One day, we heard the announcement being transmitted in a broad Yorkshire accent: "This is the one o'clock news and this is Wilfred Pickles reading it." We thought it was a joke at first, and even in a North Yorkshire hostelry, the diners, after recovering from their initial shock, were all convulsed with laughter. The experiment of having newsreaders with regional accents did not last long.

Opa had never been ill. He was always sprightly and active, with jet-black hair. He had a magnetic presence. Though small, he made his presence felt, and heard. He had never, even to me, been an old man. His 61st birthday was on 28 June 1943 and he was, so we all thought, fit and well. By 28 July, one month later, he was dead.

His fatal illness struck suddenly. He collapsed, and a tumour on the brain was diagnosed. There was no treatment in those days. No chemotherapy was available, but even had there been, it would not have helped. It was too late. Unfortunately, in some ways, Opa was a fighter. He had no wish to die. His greatest desire had been to see my bar mitzvah, which was due to take place on 1 July 1944. His struggles were in vain. There was no resisting the tumour's rapid growth.

My family, in their usual overprotective way, tried to shield me from what was happening, but the crisis, the comings and goings of medical men, the anguish, the tears and the despair could not be hidden. A sense of deep gloom pervaded the house, the factory, the very air. Everything conceivable was done. More and more specialists were consulted. Prayers were said in the synagogue; Opa, in accordance with Jewish tradition was given a new name: Chaim, which means life. Nothing helped. His deterioration was rapid and heartrending. I was not allowed to see him, until very near the end, when he asked to see me. I was taken in to his bedroom and can remember how horrified I was at what I saw.

My grandfather was propped up by several pillows in his huge bed and was hardly visible. His black hair had turned completely white, his face was haggard, his jaw hung loose; he could barely talk. At first I wanted to run away, but I was paralysed. I could not move; I could not speak; I could not cry; I could do nothing. I looked at him for what seemed ages, but probably was no more than a few seconds He looked at me out of his rolling eyes, and said, in Yiddish, in a barely audible voice:

"Kim, Freddele, Kim zur mir." "Come to me."

I went to him and he held me close; he kissed me and I could not, would not, let him go. I was numb with shock. This wonderful man, whom I so adored, and who so loved me, was dying and soon would be no more and nothing could be done about it. He died a few hours later.

In accordance with Jewish tradition he was buried within 24 hours. An immense crowd attended the funeral. This was followed by the traditional *shiva*. On their return from the funeral, the mourners, Oma, and her children put on old clothes, and shoes without leather, as a mark of mourning and had an old garment ritually cut and torn. This is a particularly dramatic and, for some, traumatic moment. It has a great emotional impact. It seems to emphasise the cutting of the life line, or the connection between the dead and the survivors. What tears are spared at the funeral are shed at this moment.

During the next seven days, a stream of people came to the house to bring comfort to the mourners, who except on the Sabbath sat on uncomfortable, low chairs as part of the mourning ritual. The mourners are not permitted to leave the house except to go to synagogue. Prayers are said morning and evening, when a full *minyan*, a quorum of ten Jewish men above the age of 13, has to be present, to enable the male mourners to say *Kaddish*, the prayer for the dead.

The rabbi usually delivers a eulogy on the first or last night, or sometimes both and others too may have their say. Traditionally, visitors are supposed to bring food and sustenance for the mourners who are not allowed to prepare food or do any work at all, but in reality they expect sustenance to be provided for them in the form of tea or coffee, and cakes. Often the *shiva* week is more like a week-long coffee morning/afternoon.

The *shiva* serves a useful purpose. It provides the opportunity for friends and acquaintances to pay their respects to the family. Though the greatest crowd usually arrives for the evening prayers, there are visitors throughout the day. Usually they stand around chatting among themselves while waiting to shake hands with the mourners and wish them "a long life". Watching them can provide much amusement. When they have all gone home, an informal head count is made, to see whether "business" has been good that day. Dora, always trenchant, would give a running commentary on the well-wishers, not always as *sotto voce* as might have been desirable. A watchful eye and careful ear can reveal much; who are having discreet, and sometimes not so discreet, affairs; who are not talking to one another; who is saying what about whom; the budding romance; the budding divorce; and gossip generally. Any disorder in the dress is revealed; the hanging thread, the unintentionally dropped hem, the unseen ladder, the hole in the sock, are all evident to the sitting mourners. Any shortcoming provides material for subsequent dissection. Any incongruity causes mirth. One caller, in a surfeit of emotion, disgorges his false teeth; another has failed to do his trousers up properly. There is little to do, during quiet periods, but to pick everyone to pieces.

The *shiva* has much to commend it, however. Mourners are given time, indeed are required, to mourn and desist from all routine work and mundane matters. It is cathartic, and gives a kick-start to the healing process which time alone can finish. You know you have to mourn so you may as well get on with it. But it also provides the opportunity for members of a family to scratch each others' eyes out, and go back to their respective homes, more at loggerheads, or worse, than before. This is also a catharsis. Mourners' spouses do not sit *shiva*, but stay around, and if they are not actually the cause of the family in-fighting, they soon get caught up in it. As a result, relations are often at a low ebb by the end of the week, and the family unity and goodwill, and reconciliation, which the death appeared to have effected is shown to be, what in reality it always was, evanescent. This is exacerbated when the deceased has left a will not dealing fairly – not necessarily equally – between his children.

Herman and Ray came up from London. All out-of-town visitors who had to stay over had to be accommodated, and somehow were. It seemed at times, and this was one of them, that the Grey House had extendable walls. As the women of the family were debarred from doing any work, much responsibility fell on the in-laws and the maids. Auntie Jeanne proved indispensable as an organiser. She ensured that no one went hungry.

Being a grandchild I did not sit *shiva*, but my sorrow was no less on that account. They were sad days. I felt Opa's loss deeply, more so than I at first realised because he and I had been very close. We were good friends. Whatever the exigencies of the time, his day always had in it a space for me. He had few ambitions; seeing me have my bar mitzvah had been one.

Sadder still, however, were the ramifications of Opa's death. The struggle for power within the family began. Oma was immediately appointed Managing Director of the company. This was obviously an appointment of convenience. I doubt whether she had ever been to the factory except when we lived in Guisborough, and probably not even then. It was not the first time, however, that she had been a figurehead. In Leipzig, when the business had been in her name, Opa had still been in control and was able to keep his family in check. Oma was totally incapable of doing so, and was subjected to pressure from all sides. As she had no business knowledge or experience, she was incapable of making an informed decision, and acted on prejudice, favouritism and whim and was easily manipulated. Fortunately, she had no real power and a deadlock position, where her casting vote might be decisive, was avoided.

Opa's death left Oma totally disconsolate and inconsolable. She let herself go completely as regards her health, and lost the will to live. Except for the few months Opa spent in internment, and her holidays in the continental spa resorts before the war, when she had gone to take the medicinal waters, they had never been apart. She was lost without him. She had no wish to take his place as head of the family.

In his will, dated 23 July 1943, only five days before his death, Opa left everything to his wife, "Salka Schmulewitsch", and appointed her as his sole executrix. He was not able to sign his will, except by an "X", and the will states: "... the contents having been first read over and explained to him, he being unable to write and having affixed his mark hereto...". The witnesses were "Harry Simon solicitor" (the family solicitor), and my father.

How much Opa knew what was going on is questionable. Probate of the will was granted on 30 August 1943, just a month after the death, which is unusually quick. I note with interest that in signing the will for the probate application, Oma spelled her name "Schmulewitz", which was not the same as in the will, and wonder why the Probate Registry did not point this out. The gross value of the estate is stated to be £1,263.18s. (£1,263.90), the net value £376.16s.6d. and estate duty £3.15s.4d. This was not the estate of a wealthy man. I do not believe that Opa had any idea of what he was signing, nor do I understand why it should have been thought imperative to get him to make a will, as intestacy would have had the same practical effect, though perhaps not as quick.

I am no believer in ghosts or apparitions, and am an agnostic as regards life in the hereafter, but shortly after Opa's death I had a strange experience. I had gone into my grandparents' bedroom to fetch something for Oma, and stood for a moment to look at myself in the large full-length mirror which was their wardrobe door. I saw Opa standing close behind me. He looked as he had always looked. He was quite distinct.

"Look after Oma!" he said.

When I turned round there was nothing to be seen. I was not afraid. I had no need to fear my Opa. I told no one; there was no point. I would either have been disbelieved, or someone would have had hysterics. I recount here, for the first time, the event as it occurred. This was not a figment of my imagination, though, doubtless, that will be the general consensus. I do not seek to give any explanation. I tell it as it was.

Eleven months later, on 31 May 1944, Oma Fischbein died, aged 62. She had been ill for some time. She suffered from severe nose bleeding for which she underwent an operation that stopped the bleeding, but she seemed worse after it than before. She was in and out of hospital, which was only a few minutes' walk from the Grey House, but failed to recover. She was a sweet, inoffensive old lady, whom I hardly knew. Her death came just a month before my bar mitzvah.

Chapter 21 – Bar Mitzvah

My bar mitzvah, on 1 July 1944, was a muted affair. Bar mitzvahs are usually an occasion of great rejoicing and parties to mark a boy's religious coming of age. I could now be counted for the ten men required for a *minyan*. This is sometimes a doubtful privilege as I was liable to be called out to make up a *minyan* when I would have preferred to be doing something else, like staying in a warm bed on a cold morning.

I read the week's scheduled extracts from the Torah and the Haftorah – the excerpt from the Prophets which concludes the Reading of the Law – on the Sabbath morning, in a voice which was just beginning to break. For that reason, Gavin Kaye's admonition in school singing lessons – "Mime, Fishburn, mime" – might well have been echoed by many of those in the synagogue on that day.

On the other hand, I was well-taught and knew my portion. In fact, I still do. I had been prepared for the event for over a year by Rabbi Miller, who must have suffered much during this period, but regardless of the quality of my voice, I did him credit, and hope he felt the effort well-rewarded.

The party which my parents gave, and to which the whole community was invited – in Middlesbrough, not to invite anyone would have been a slight and totally out of keeping with my parents' nature, not to mention my father's leading position in the community as an officer of the synagogue, which he had been for many years in one capacity or another – was as lavish as wartime and the unfortunate circumstances allowed. But there was no dancing or music, and try as one might, the shadow of the death of my grandparents could not be avoided.

I had to give the usual speech expected of the bar mitzvah boy. My father had asked the rabbi to draft this but I discarded his offering and wrote my own, which rather dwelt on the close relationship I had with Opa, and the personal tragedy for me, of his untimely death. I think everyone would have been in tears in any case, but I helped them on their way, and found it very hard to deliver. It must have been a good speech, because I have since had a reputation as a good speaker, and there have been few family occasions on which I was not called upon to speak. I enjoyed doing so.

The subject matter of the Torah reading on that day was a strange one. It concerned the laws relating to the red heifer – *pora adomah*. This creature had to be pure and unblemished, and the strict definition of what that meant made it virtually impossible to find such a beast. The animal had to be burned, and its ashes, and nothing else, could purify a person after certain transgressions, but at the same time, those ashes would defile anyone else. The Jewish sages and rabbis over the centuries have not been able to explain this or provide a satisfactory exegesis. It remains one of the mysteries of the Torah. Personally, I did not see anything particularly odd in this apparent paradox; there are many antidotes and medicines which will cure the sick and make the healthy unwell. This was, to me, simply an early example. Far stranger to me was the nature of the animal – why a heifer, why a red one? But then, what do I know?

I received the usual quota of fountain pens, propelling pencils, and the like. I was grateful for the sentiments behind them. It was wartime; luxuries were hard to find. One particular gift intrigued me: an electric razor. As it would be some years before I needed to use it, this seemed to me to be forward planning carried too far. My favourite and most appreciated present came from Dora and Joe: a gold Accurist watch, which I wore for many years, and which kept perfect time. But no gifts could have compensated for the losses suffered that year.

My parents had wanted me, after my bar mitzvah, to go to Clifton College, a public school which had a Jewish house – Pollacks. I was not usually consulted in such matters. It was a little like the army; I received my orders and went. I got wind of this intention, and having already experienced boarding school, flatly refused to go. When the matter was first mooted, Opa and

Oma – no doubt afraid to see me once more emaciated – were similarly opposed to the idea, and though their views were usually not taken account of, after Opa's death the matter was quietly, and to my intense relief, dropped.

Chapter 22 – A Sad Tale

Herman and Ray, my London uncle and aunt, came up – a rare event – three times that year: for Opa (Schmulewitsch) and Oma Fischbein's funerals, and my bar mitzvah, with my cousin Judith, their first child born in 1938. Ray was very much persona non grata with the family and Herman was hardly more welcome. The reasons for their semi-banishment have been detailed above. However, families are families, and they were never excluded from family events such as funerals and simchas such as weddings and bar mitzvahs. Herman's very presence seemed to create hostility and inevitably precipitated, for whatever reason, a family row.

He was never accorded an equal seat, as it were, at the family table. When London had been subject to heavy bombing and other families encouraged their London relatives to come and stay in a safer location, no such invitation was extended to Herman or his family. Opa was not a cruel man; he tended to be unforgiving but not to the extent of putting a life at risk.

While Herman was barely tolerated, Ray was effectively ignored. Herman had been no less instrumental than Max in preparing the ground for the family exodus from Germany. Ray and her family had provided food and shelter for members of the family, and my parents and I had stayed with them between arriving in England and moving up to Middlesbrough. They had taken in my paternal grandparents and cared for them, when there was nowhere else for them to go. At the age of 23, Herman had contracted meningitis, a killer illness even today despite all our modern medicines. His chance of survival was given as slim. He did survive, though much weakened. He was very handsome, quite differently from Max, with the Oberman genes dominant: tall, broad-shouldered, very athletic, and a wonderful swimmer. Among his achievements was winning the 50 metres breaststroke event at the competition for all the High Schools in Leipzig six months after he had won the 100 metres at the Bar-Kochba sports in that city in 1 minute 32 seconds. Bar Kochba was an organisation for Jewish youth, akin to the Maccabi idea. His illness had left him weakened physically and with a permanently damaged heart; he also became emotionally much more volatile than before. That he survived at all was due to his strong physique.

I cannot say that I was actually discouraged from associating with Herman and Ray when they came up north, and they certainly made a great fuss of me, largely perhaps because I was the only member of the family to talk to them. Though kept away from any unpleasantness as I was, and protected from things I shouldn't know about, I could not help but be aware of the estrangement between Herman and Ray and the rest of the family but I did not understand the real underlying reason for this. I had heard remarks to the effect that "that woman had sent a policeman" and had threatened the deportation of the family. "That woman" was, it transpired, not Ray, but her mother, Mrs Greenstein, and between her and my grandparents, it was hate at first sight.

It was many years before I could obtain anything approaching a coherent account of the reason for this. It was a taboo subject. From what I can gather, it seems that when Herman and Max first came to London, they tried their hand in the fur trade, while looking for opportunities elsewhere as already described. When the factory was established, whether for economic or family reasons or at whose behest, I do not know, Herman remained in London. He was effectively excluded from the family business, given the job nominally as an agent, a "rep", but that would not have produced a living income as there was as yet nothing to sell so he had to try his hand at other things. Together with his mother-in-law it appears that he tried to do business as a general agent, which involved buying goods and selling them for a profit. Goods were often bought on approval or on a sale-or-return basis. It was alleged that in the course of this trading he took certain goods on approval and sold them without accounting to the original seller for the price. It seems that he was charged by the owner of the goods and prosecuted for theft.

Mrs Greenstein, a doughty fighter, determined and streetwise, decided desperate remedies were needed. She went to see Norman

Birkett Q.C., one of the outstanding barristers of his day, who was to feature prominently in the Nurenberg trials after the war. She insisted on seeing him, despite his clerk repeatedly telling her that she had first to see a solicitor. Apparently she waited outside counsel's chambers for several days until Birkett noticed her, and after being told her story by his clerk, he agreed to see her. He listened to her tale of woe and told her that he could not take the case himself, but would help her to get appropriate legal representation. In the course of the preparation of Herman's defence it seems that advice was given that Max, my father and Opa should be asked to give evidence for Herman. Apparently one leg of the defence was to assert that he was acting on the instructions of members of the family and in the course of the family business. I find this hard to understand as it can hardly be helpful to assert that a wrongdoing was at the instigation of another; this merely adds to that the crime (and for that matter the tort) of conspiracy. However, the outcome was that as none of the family was willing to give evidence for Herman, and wanted to have nothing to do with the matter – the very idea that any other member of the family should be involved was anathema and unthinkable – subpoenas were issued against them to appear in court, and Ray was sent to serve them herself.

She accordingly turned up at the Grey House, with a policeman, to serve the subpoenas, and in the course of the row which inevitably followed, she is alleged to have threatened that if they did not appear in court in accordance with the subpoenas, they – Max, Dad and Opa, and the whole family – would be deported. That their evidence might have been damaging to Herman's case – as it would have been – did not seem to occur to Ray.

Looking back some decades after that event, and always accepting the accuracy of the account, it seems to me that someone must have taken leave of their senses. Under duress and when their loved ones are threatened, people do strange things, but what were the lawyers thinking about? What evidence could have been given that would have helped Herman? The plea that he had committed the alleged offence at their request, on their behalf, or had been in cahoots with them, would not have absolved him.

In the event Max and Dad did go to give evidence, which was of no assistance to the court. They simply denied all knowledge of the matter. I suspect that the real motive of the threat was to obtain funds from the family to pay for the goods. In the event Herman was acquitted. I do not know on what grounds or what arguments were submitted on his behalf, but I have no reason to suppose that justice was not done.

No thought could have been given to the effect that the appearance of a policeman would have on a middle-class immigrant Jewish family insecure of their position, afraid of anyone in uniform, not accustomed to the idea of the friendly English bobby, to whom the police were oppressors, not liberators, agents of a hostile state, and whose very name inspired fear. To link this with the threat of deportation must have been intensely distressing, and it is not difficult to understand why this was regarded by the rest of the family as unforgivable. Even for someone living in a culture where the policeman was regarded as a friend, it should not have required a great exercise of the imagination to understand the emotions that the appearance of a policeman would arouse, to say nothing of the accompanying threat. The kindest interpretation that can be put on this is that there was a clash of cultures.

One of the strangest of Jewish characteristics is the speed with which Jews adapt to their surroundings. Jews are cultural chameleons, even while keeping their religious identity. This is true of myself. Although young and still living at home, I was already no longer part of the family's culture. I was English, which none of them ever fully became. Ray and her mother thought like London Jews, and had no real understanding of how a refugee German Jewish family would react.

Herman and Ray made every effort to seek reconciliation, and though there was a partial restoration of diplomatic relations after my grandparents died, the damage was never quite undone. Dora, in particular, who had a long memory and unforgiving nature, took a long time to effect any sort of reconciliation with Ray, which she eventually did, on the grounds that Herman and Ray had been very good to Yetti when she was in distress, but I do not think she ever actually forgave her.

Chapter 23 – Wartime

My bar mitzvah came at a time when the Germans, in desperation, having lost the war in the air, developed the buzz bomb, the V1. This was no more than a bomb with wings and an engine and once the engine cut out, the bomb would fall to the ground. There was usually sufficient warning for people to take cover, and RAF pilots developed a way of intercepting these bombs in flight and tipping them over with their wing tips. The buzz bombs were later followed by a much more dangerous weapon, the V2 rocket, which came without notice. These caused considerable damage and casualties. Militarily by then as the Germans were everywhere in retreat, they were of no consequence; their object was to shake morale. Bombing never seems to have had this effect, but many who had returned to London after evacuation decided it was time to seek some safer spot.

Auntie Jeanne's sister Bessie Cohen, her husband Alec, and their four children – the youngest just three months old – all came up for the bar mitzvah, and stayed for several months until the danger was over, and Neville and I became very close and remained so for the rest of our lives. The Cohen family, except Neville who stayed with us, lived with Jeanne but effectively lived at the Grey House, which had the room to accommodate them. Neville could not get into Guisborough Grammar School, as he was not in the right catchment area, but during his stay he went instead to Middlesbrough High School, which probably came as something of a shock to him after the City of London School.

Neville and I did our homework, and spent most of our time, together. He was the nearest thing I had to a brother of my own age. Our respective parents got on well, particularly our mothers, who had many qualities in common. In the fullness of time Neville and his family more than reciprocated my parents' hospitality.

It is strange, looking back, how little the war appeared to affect our daily life, or perhaps more accurately, how quickly people adapted to wartime conditions, so that they assumed the guise of normality. One could not escape the war; the newspaper headlines daily recorded our defeats and losses. Reading them now, it is interesting to see how they dealt with some of the major disasters, such as the loss of Singapore or Tobruk, or the sinking of major ships. It was not that they presented these as a victory; it was more that they held out hope of survival when there appeared to be none. On the other hand, they also treated good news rather cautiously, as if not quite believing it.

Opa, from the outbreak of the war until his death, kept a close watch on events. He had a huge map on the dining room wall, showing the centres of operations. When these moved from Europe, after Dunkirk, to Africa, he rolled up the map of Europe and replaced it with a map of Africa. When the war returned to the mainland of Europe, with the German invasion of Russia, he had two maps. He plotted progress with coloured pins, and needless to say, I became as involved with this as he was. For this purpose he had no difficulty in understanding the news broadcasts and reading the newspapers. We anticipated every move the Germans and their allies would make, with the same measure of success, or possibly greater, as the Allied High Command. Every German advance across the desert in the direction of Egypt, and the potential threat to what was then still Palestine, caused alarm and despondency, and every counter-attack by the English army produced corresponding cheers.

Opa limited himself to those centres of operations, and an enemy, he could understand. He had no interest in the war in the Far East. That could as well have been on the moon, and he resented what he considered the wasted effort which it involved. The soldiers, airmen and warships would have been better employed fighting the Germans. Looking at the singular lack of success in the war against the Japanese, the loss of Singapore, Malaya, the sinking of the battleships in Singapore harbour, and disaster everywhere until the Americans led the fightback, who can say his strategy was wrong?

Unfortunately, Opa did not live long enough to lead his armies to victory. Against that he was spared seeing the horrors of the Holocaust.

Our part of the North East did not suffer the destruction inflicted on London and the Midlands. There were air raids, some causing considerable damage, although many attacks were simply "hit and run" raids which caused more alarm than damage. The local papers would refer to a "town in the North East" suffering air raids, as if the Germans were unaware of their targets. The enemy would immediately identify the town or area in question, whereafter the papers would say: "It can now be revealed..." In fact, more damage was caused by some youths who set fire to and burned down the Binns department store in the town centre than by the enemy.

There were bad nights when we would sit cowering in Opa's homemade air-raid shelter. It was hard to know whether the noise came from our anti-aircraft fire, or from enemy action. It was probably both, but the house rattled. Opa, not one for sitting still, got himself made an air raid warden, despite his alleged lack of English. He would put on his tin hat and insist on patrolling outside during air raids, despite Oma's wailing. There is no more alarming sound than that of the air raid warning siren with its undulating whine, a sound designed to send your stomach plummeting to your boots, and none more welcome than that of the "all clear". I think we were more worried about Opa's pretensions as an air raid warden than we were about any harm to ourselves, because we did feel protected. Sitting in an air-raid shelter at any time, under any circumstances, is unpleasant. We were lucky; we were spared the experience of really heavy bombing. We were all issued with gas masks and took them with us everywhere at first, as it was an offence to go out without them, but this habit soon fell into desuetude, and before long one would have had difficulty in finding one's gas mask.

The fighting itself was far away, and to us in the North, even the threat of invasion had no immediate impact. We saw little of the war as war, but I did witness one war "incident" early in 1942. There was an army exercise in Guisborough. Civilian traffic was supposed to have been banned from the roads on that day. It was all very realistic and exciting, with smoke, bullets, bombs and the like. Suddenly, a civilian motorcyclist who should not have been there appeared through the smoke. Blinded, he rode straight into a Bren gun carrier and suffered fatal injuries.

One memorable event was when a plane crashed very near to our home. The Grey House was only about five miles from Thornaby Aerodrome, about 30 seconds flying time, and directly under one of the approaches to the airfield. Returning badly damaged from one mission, and trying to land, one of the Wellington bombers suddenly lost power. It brushed the trees of our house and dived into the house immediately opposite 25 yards away. It could as easily have hit the Grey House.

The papers contained daily reports of people being fined for absenteeism from work or from fire-watching duties: there were prosecutions for rationing offences, particularly clothing coupon trading. In the local papers, increasing column inches were devoted to military casualties. But the war, despite rationing, the blackout, the grim headlines at times, and the absence of young men, seemed far away and life went on. Damaged buildings were repaired or rebuilt. No one went hungry – indeed many had never been so well and so healthily fed. There was little to spend money on, so one could not avoid saving. Most commodities were subject not only to rationing but to price controls, and black marketeering and profiteering were severely dealt with by the courts. The magistrates had a field day protecting the integrity, as they saw it, of society and punishing traitors. Middlesbrough was not a place where there was sufficient prosperity to create an active underworld.

The factory was busy with war work, and enjoying a period of comparative quiet and prosperity. Travel was difficult, so one stayed at home. Local authorities devised various "holiday at home" entertainments. There was a spirit of unity and common purpose, but this did not inhibit miners and factory workers from striking for more pay or better conditions.

At a time when victory appeared finally to be within the Allies' grasp, the Germans, almost as a last fling, developed the V2 rocket which was aimed at London. It came without warning and there appeared to be no defence against it. It caused more damage than the Government was prepared to admit although we in the North only read about it or heard about it on the news and were not directly affected. We were, of course, concerned at the risk to family living in the range but fortunately the bases from which the rockets were launched were soon overrun.

VE day, 6 June 1945, came shortly before my fourteenth birthday. It was then that the horrific pictures of the concentration camps began to come through. I remember that there was a sense of disbelief. The joy of victory was abated by the pain of the tragedy, the scale of which became more apparent day by day. There was a feeling of "there but for the grace of God...". The family, more than ever, had to be grateful for my grandfather's misgivings and foresight. We were incredibly fortunate as the immediate family escaped unscathed. Only Oma's sister perished, but her son, Adolph Rockman, who was in England throughout the war, survived. My father's brother Fritz, also survived the war. He was living in hiding in Belgium, during which time he actually married and had two children there.

It was many years before things returned to any semblance of pre-war normality. There was still a war on in Japan. It was a relief to be free of the blackout restrictions, and other petty and annoying nuisances of a siege economy, but rationing continued, the young men were still away, and further horrors were still to be reported.

I am indebted to Mr Andrew Clarke, a local historian for the following report, except for the words in brackets:

"Disaster came on 22 March 1945 when the whole factory went up in flames destroying not only the buildings but all the sewing machines and stocks of garments. Concern had been expressed at the time about the delay in fighting the fire and in his report to the Council, which was responsible for the fire brigade at the time, the chairman said that the outbreak was first discovered at approximately 3 a.m. by Mr Barr who lived in the House at the end of the former Sewage Farm which was now the factory. He called on Mr Norminton a council official [with whose son Colin I was very friendly], who lived at the West End (about 100 yards from the factory) and in the meantime Mr Covell, the night watchman [the father of the aforementioned Edgar] went into town to summon the Fire Brigade. Shortly after 5.30 a.m. three firemen and a trailer arrived on the scene, found they had no pump and returned to the station for it. When finally the pump was brought, it was found to be out of order. A call was put through for the Redcar Fire Brigade at 5.59 a.m. and on arrival at 6.15 a.m. they were first to have water through. The fire was soon under control, but the whole of the factory was gutted and only a shell remained, with rows and rows of charred skeleton frameworks of the sewing machines.

"Over the weekend, emergency plans were put into operation to continue production by renting alternative premises. Machines were installed in the Challoner Hall, New Road and in the Priory Hall, Westgate. Employment for the girls was saved."

That these Keystone Cops antics of the local fire fighters should have occurred in the war, when emergency services were supposed at all times to be in a high state of readiness, beggars belief and makes one wonder what would have happened had lives been at risk. From a practical aspect, it was better for the factory to be totally gutted than partially damaged, but some of the machinery might have been saved, had there been a semblance of efficiency.

There was great weeping, and distress, understandably, as financial disaster loomed. As it happened, the bulk of the stock of materials required for making up garments was stored in the warehouse in Fountain Street. Only that needed for the immediate production schedules was in the factory at the time. Stock would have been difficult to replace. With the resilience typical of my family, which they were to show time and again, they set to work to recover the loss. My mother's and Dora's organisational skills were fully tested. New machinery was hard to find in wartime, but the family connection with the Bellow Machine Company in Leeds resulted in the supply of new machines and equipment, and the business was soon operating again, albeit in a somewhat reduced state. Within a short time, the factory was rebuilt, expanded and improved.

The new building was purpose-built, more or less square, on two floors and was a great improvement on the old one. It provided room for a modern layout of machinery, and better facilities for the workforce. It did not take long for the phoenix to rise from the ashes, but it did take a great expenditure of energy by those involved, and the price they paid in distress and ill-health was great.

As the war came to an end, Government contracts ceased, though these continued for a time supplying shirts for soldiers being demobilised. Each soldier was given civilian clothing – demob suits – to start them back in "civvy street".

New customers had to be found, and at a time of great shortages of civilian clothes and consumer goods, this was not difficult. For a time, anything sold, so great was the demand.

Chapter 25 – The Collector

I have always been a collector, an Autolycus, a gatherer of unconsidered trifles. I amass things, and I have had too many hobbies and interests to list here. My train set and my Meccano were my first great loves, but they soon reached a stage where space prohibited further expansion. Though I have long yearned to build another railway layout, I appreciate that it is an ambition now unlikely to be realised.

From the moment I read my first Dickens I tried to find as many books of the same edition as I could afford. This was Collins' "Library of Classics". They were small books and I see from one of them that they cost 4s.6d. – about 22.5p. I did not limit my purchases to this edition, and my books became one of my great pleasures.

I acquired another hobby. It was all Aunty Jeanne's fault, in a way. She asked me to do some shopping which involved a visit to the local newsagent, and told me to buy myself something out of the change. She had done this before. I usually bought a bar of chocolate or something similar for 1d (an old penny). This time, a large packet containing 1000 stamps from all over the world caught my eye. It cost 6d. There was also a small stamp album and stamp hinges at the same price. I was something of a goody-goody, and rarely, if ever, took liberties. I was too well-brought-up for that, but on this occasion something went wrong. I yielded to temptation and bought the packet. As there was no point in having the stamps without an album to put them in, I bought that as well: total outlay, one shilling. Technically, I had not transgressed because no limit had been put on my pourboire but I knew, in my heart, that I had overstepped the mark. My parents were appalled and insisted I take the lot back to the shop at once. Aunty Jeanne, however, would not hear of it. She was always generous to a fault, indeed, and sometimes without discretion. She thought it was very amusing and forgave me with one of her big, bear-like hugs and a kiss. She enjoyed retelling the tale. And thus, aged nine, I became a philatelist.

Once I had caught the music bug, I had to have records. These were still the old 78s and hard to get hold of during the war, but by dint of searching record shops, antique, or more accurately, bric-a-brac shops, and getting relatives and friends to look in their attics, I was soon able to get hold of some very fine recordings. Records, if one could get them at all, were expensive.

In the isolation of my room, in the village of Guisborough, I would listen to the old HMV Black Label recordings of the Sextet from *Lucia di Lammermoor*, or the Quartet from *Rigoletto*, with great tenors such as Caruso, Martinelli, Gigli, Tito Schipa, Jussi Bjorling and sopranos such as Dame Nellie Melba, Tetrazzini, Licia Albanese, some of whom were no longer singing or even alive, and others whom one had no chance of hearing in the flesh.

Having said that, in fact I did get to hear Gigli and Schipa, at their several farewell concerts at Leeds Town Hall. I saw quite recently Jussi Bjorling, now very old, in a Covent Garden production of *Palestrina*. I had a very good friend in Middlesbrough – Arnold Brechner – one of my few friends who was not from school. He was one of those people who was generally better at anything than I was. He was my only contemporary who could regularly beat me at chess, and he was even more obsessive with any interest he took up – and he was not always selective. He was able to find records, or source them, when no one else could. We spent hours comparing recordings or discussing the relative merits of one singer over another – was Tito Schipa a greater singer than Gigli?

I collected virtually every recording made by Gigli, who was my great operatic hero. His acting style, for lack of a better term, might not gladden the heart of a modern producer, but he acted with his voice, and in my opinion still has few equals as a singer.

There was also a whole esoteric world of record labels. HMV dominated the market, but there were Columbia, Parlophone and others. HMV itself had a wide variety of labels – white, black, red, plum and so on. White labels were the older expensive ones, no longer being produced, black labels had replaced them; red were the standard issues, plum, popular music. When the Al Jolson films appeared I became a Jolson devotee and collected all his records.

Chapter 26 – Other Interests

I also became interested in photography; I think this was Neville Cohen's influence. I acquired various cameras, and, needless to say, had to develop my own films, so I appropriated some unused corner of the house (there weren't many) and made it into a dark-room. It had been a linen room, under the stairs, so it was very small but big enough to accommodate the necessary equipment, including an enlarger. Mathers, a local photographer and purveyor of photographic equipment, was my supplier. I was a good customer. I do not think that my skills as a photographer would have kept the wolf from the door, but I enjoyed the process of developing the photographs more than taking them – the scientist rather than the artist.

My passion for trains led me to trainspotting, that is to say, collecting railway engine numbers. There is a magic about steam engines. They were the fastest, cheapest, most comfortable and effective means of long-distance public transport in Britain for over 100 years. Every engine had its own characteristics. They were infinitely various, ranging from the Mallard, the record-breaking Pacific 4-6-2, one of the Gresley Streamliners, the Flying Scotsman, or the Coronation Scot, on the London to Scotland main line which I had so enjoyed seeing while I was evacuated to the Lake District, to the modest little 0-4-4 tank engine which pulled and pushed the Guisborough train.

Ian Allan published books listing all steam trains according to the railway company which ran them – LNER, LMS, GWR and Southern were the operating companies before nationalisation. Middlesbrough was not on the main line and it was rare to see any of the "big" engines there, though there were one or two spotted during the war heading troop trains, but we were only 30 minutes from Darlington and an hour from York and Newcastle, all major railway centres. Stephenson's "Locomotion" was on constant display at Darlington where, of course, it all began in 1825, with the Darlington and Stockton Railway. I would often go there and stand on the platform with my notebook recording the numbers, and where they had them, the names of engines rushing through or stopping at the station. This was one of my less expensive hobbies. I was also fascinated by modelling and when they became available I would buy and assemble kits of aircraft, ships, cars, buses, whatever was going, and painstakingly spend hours painting them.

In my boyhood those were the chief non-competitive and sedentary activities which occupied my spare time. They were all costly activities: how could I, a mere schoolboy, "nobbut a lad" in the local vernacular, afford them? I often wonder that myself. I had a generous father, and there were frequent little gifts, all gratefully received, from other members of the family. I had half a crown (2/6d) a week pocket money, a large sum at the time, which was increased annually. I was frugal, in that I spent my money carefully, and saved up for what I wanted. There was not much to spend on. Sweets and chocolates were rationed during the war. Comics cost one or two pennies. Most goods were subject to price controls. My travel and food for school were all provided. A little did go a long way then, but when I needed extra funds for a special purchase, Dad was open-handed. Mother did not at all approve. She thought like Mr Micawber. She believed in financial discipline. Dad would say: "Don't tell your mother," when helping me out. I would reply: "I won't if you don't." But somehow my mother was always aware of what was going on. It was not possible to keep secrets from her. For a person as forthright and frank – as in a "free and frank discussion" – she could be unexpectedly diplomatic and hold her peace. But in her mind she recorded it all. It was difficult to fault the nature of the expenditure, which, apart perhaps for the stamps, was all on cultural and uplifting interests.

Chapter 27 – Hebrew Studies

When we first came to Middlesbrough there was an active B'Nei Akivah, an association of Jewish youth dedicated to Jewish education and activities. Essentially, it is a religious group, though that aspect was not treated too seriously in Middlesbrough. They would come and collect me every Saturday, as I was one of the youngest children. Most activities were centred around the synagogue but many others took place in people's homes or outdoors. This was not quite my first introduction to Jewish education as the kindergarten I went to in Leipzig was a Jewish one, part of Dr Carlebach's educational establishments, which were well known.

I did not go to the Cheder, the religious classes run by the synagogue. My parents thought it better for me to have private lessons. I do not know why. My first lessons were with Mr Solomon who lived close by. He was a small, stocky man, and an excellent teacher. My Hebrew tuition was soon suspended, however, when I went away to school. The Solomon family moved to London. (No one would have guessed then that Harry, the kid brother, would become a very successful solicitor, chairman of a public company, and be knighted for charitable services.)

When I returned from evacuation, my family were living in Guisborough, and Hebrew lessons would have necessitated a journey to Middlesbrough. Travel, unlike in the pre-war days was not easy for a youngster, particularly in blackout conditions, and it was not until we returned to Middlesbrough that my lessons could be resumed. By that time we were approaching my bar mitzvah.

I would go to Rabbi Miller at his home, every Tuesday and Thursday, on the way back from school. His wife, Bessie, would ensure that I had a cup of tea and a biscuit. It was a hard regime, because after the lesson, which would last between one and one and a half hours I had to get home, have supper, and do my homework. I would usually not arrive home until about 7 p.m., which meant an 11-hour day since leaving in the morning. There was quite a bit of walking involved as the rabbi did not live on a direct bus route. This was not too bad in the long summer days, but in winter, when the days were very short, and often bitterly cold, it was tiring.

Although Rabbi Miller was a learned man, he was not a good teacher – he was too impatient – but I have to acknowledge that he had a great influence on my life. He gave me the idea of becoming a lawyer. I could never accept absolutist principles. The case always had to be proved to me. Because of this, in another context, I had the greatest difficulty in accepting theorems in geometry. I had no difficulty in understanding the logic which followed from the given posits, but how did they come to be, was my problem, and why should one accept them? We were taught, even after it was known not to be true, that the atom could not be split, and that matter can neither be created nor destroyed. I was sceptical, however. I needed to be convinced.

I would argue at length with Rabbi Miller, who was of the old school. He was a sincerely religious man and intolerant of the peccadilloes of his congregation. In fact, he was totally out of sympathy with it, and was unsuited to be its rabbi. The early settlers in the town who had founded the Middlesbrough community were observant Jews, but after they died, as is the way with outlying communities, their descendants tended to leave the town, and those who stayed became increasingly secular. This was due to their lack of religious education and the needs of their businesses. There were many in the community who could barely read Hebrew and had difficulty in following the services, and Rabbi Miller's erudite and recondite sermons were incomprehensible to them. He could not cope with this.

He was a deeply unhappy man. During the time I had lessons with him, I had the impression that he was becoming increasingly embittered. He seemed sad. Whether he would have been happy in other surroundings, one cannot know. The modesty of his home and standard of living, which his emoluments from the community permitted, were a sad reflection of his relationship with his congregants and out of keeping with their own comparative affluence. He had fallen out with the doyen of the congregation, its oldest, wealthiest and most influential member. Rabbi Miller would address his sermons away from the side of the synagogue where the offending congregant had his seat. I once asked him why he did this. He replied: "Who is there on that side to talk to?" But this was symptomatic of his disaffection with his congregation.

Rabbi Miller had ample compensation at home for his troubles with his congregation, because the Rebbetzin, Mrs Miller, although a tiny woman in stature, was a giant in every other way. She was always cheerful, lively, active in the community, well respected, much admired and liked. They had two sons and two daughters, all highly intelligent.

Many boys' Hebrew studies came to an end with their bar mitzvah, but I continued mine long after that, as long as I remained at school. My headmaster had some influence in this, as absence from school prayers was contingent upon my studying Hebrew, for which, as I have described, he made his study available to me. I cannot say that my Hebrew studies expanded and developed as they should have done. I seemed to do the same things year after year, basically learning the week's portion of the Law. There was some Midrash, but not sufficient to arouse my interest, and to me it all rather smacked – and often still does – of arguing how many angels can dance on the point of a needle. Being an Orthodox Jew does not necessitate faith or belief, but observance – practice. Much later in life I once asked our rabbi, Rabbi Bernstein, a very learned man, to explain this. His answer was that belief follows practice; observance leads to faith. I have difficulty with this concept. I can understand that a club has its rules and members must abide by them, but who makes the rules and who can change them? I cannot pretend that I got much out of these lessons, but perhaps Rabbi Miller obtained some benefit from the additional income they produced.

Chapter 28 – School Friends

As I reached the sixth form, I became friendly with some of those who, being in a higher form, had seemed out of reach and they were in school terms considerably older than me. I treated them with the respect their seniority deserved, and was happy to sit at their feet when appropriate. Tony Hearn was one of these. He was academically brilliant. Not only was he invariably top of his form, and gained subject prizes galore, distinctions in his exams, and an open scholarship to Oxford, he was also Victor Ludorum at the sports days. He was a complete all-rounder. I know that he had an ill mother and there was very little money in his home. She had had to make sacrifices for his education. This left him, understandably perhaps, very angry with society, the world, and life in general. He was like a coiled spring and this made him difficult to get on with at times. He was extremely left-wing in his views. I remember that Max unwisely chose to have a political discussion with Tony once at our house and thought him a dangerous communist – but having regard to his background it would have been more remarkable had he not had left-wing views. He was later to do me a good turn for which I have always been grateful.

Sport, particularly our sometimes misguided allegiance to Middlesbrough FC and, more rewardingly, to Yorkshire County cricket, was another common factor with my friends. The Boro' drew support from a large catchment area and locals have to support their team, rather than some far off successful glamour side. We hated Arsenal and Sunderland, names which to this day I have difficulty in getting past my lips. We would watch the Boro' from the Boy's or the "Bob" end (because admission was only one shilling – a bob). Having often agonisingly watched the Boro' play on the Saturday, we would play the match all over again on the Monday morning. It was not always doom and gloom. As long as Mannion was playing there was something to cheer. The Boro' at one time had a winger named Linacre whose legs were like matchsticks and he was always getting them broken, but he had marvellous ball control and the sight of Linacre and Mannion exchanging passes and running rings round defences was worth a bob of anyone's money.

League and cup football resumed after the war in 1946. Middlesbrough FC were in the First Division, and had one of their best ever teams. Apart from Wilf Mannion they had George Hardwick, their captain and captain of England, at full back. Mannion and Hardwick played for England against the rest of the world. As the maximum wage for footballers at that time was £21 per week, the larger teams – Manchester United, Arsenal, Spurs – could not entice players to join them with large financial incentives like they do today, and while in effect this restrictive practice made a mockery of the idea of freedom of contract, it did mean that some of the smaller teams were able to retain their star players.

Middlesbrough reached the 6th round of the FA Cup in 1947. This was as far as they had ever been. They were drawn at home against Burnley, which was then a leading club. If Boro' won they would reach the semi-finals for the first time. The excitement was immense. Everyone who could get into the match did so. The Boro's ground was at Ayresome Park, only about ten minutes walk from home. Over 50,000 people packed into the ground. I was among them, with my mates from school. The crush was reminiscent of that at Wembley in 1923, and we too had our mounted police. But the crowd was in benevolent mood. No one doubted the outcome. The game was a typical cup tie: keenly fought, which means that the players kicked hell out of each other, no prisoners were taken. Burnley players were dirty – ours were all saints. With ten minutes to go, the scores were level at 1-1. Then Johnny Spuhler, our right winger, beat his defender and scored. Absolute pandemonium broke out, everyone was cheering. Suddenly, we noticed a linesman's flag was raised: an infringement – offside. Offside against whom? Not Spuhler, he had beaten his man. This was a mystery only the referee could explain, and he had to be smuggled out of the ground later under heavy guard. We lost the replay 1-0. And it was more than 50 years before the Boro' got into the semi-finals, but when they did, they also reached the final.

Cricket was no less important to us. There was great excitement at the first post-war Ashes tour by the Australians. Several of us from school went to Headingley on the first day of the Test. We got there about 3 hours before the match was due to start, which meant a very early departure from home, as the journey to Leeds was over two hours. England had one of their finest teams: Hutton and Washbrook to open the batting, Compton and Edrich to follow. The Australians, captained by Bradman, included Keith Miller, the world's greatest all-rounder and Ray Lindwall, the best fast bowler. It was a memorable occasion; Len Hutton was due to open the batting on his home ground.

England had won the toss and elected to bat. The fielding side came out and took their places. Amid tumultuous applause, and great expectations, Hutton walked slowly out to the crease, took guard, and looked around the field. He indicated he was ready. The crowd became quiet. We all waited with great excitement, memories of Hutton's record 364 against the same opponents at the Oval in 1938 still fresh in our minds, confident of a repeat performance. Lindwall walks back, it seems like 100 miles, and marks the start of his run. He limbers up and starts to run, slowly speeding up as he jumps to deliver his first ball; Hutton plays, misses, and is out, clean bowled: complete silence from the crowd. The disbelief was palpable. I, and the rest of my mates, just sat there stunned.

The rest of the day was meaningless for us. For the record, Australia scored 304 for 3 in the last innings, also a record, to win the match. I have had disappointments as a follower of sport, but this ranks among the greatest.

Chapter 29 – The Rovers' Return

The war was over. Labour had won the general election, and Clement Attlee was now prime minister. My family were looking forward to a return to normality. But what was normality? For my generation, normality was rationing, blackouts, shortages, fatherless families, makeshift teachers, and yet with all that there was a sense of common purpose, of pride in victory. It was clear even to a school-boy that a new era had started, if for no other reason than the result of the general election. As, I suppose, did most schools, we held a mock election, and – surprise – the Labour candidate won. But there was also a Communist candidate who was runner-up. Russia was still our friend, and communism was not yet a dirty word.

The Guisborough Shirt & Underwear Co. Ltd. celebrated the victory by holding a "Victory Dance, Whist Drive and Cabaret" on Monday, 4 March 1946 at the Coatham Hotel, Redcar. The dinner menu was traditional English: oxtail soup, roast beef, lamb or pork, Brussels sprouts, green peas, creamed or baked potatoes. This was followed by trifle or mocha sponge and custard, coffee and biscuits. There was little provision for vegetarians or indeed for any of my family who did not eat unkosher meat, but doubt-less special provision was made for the top table. The dance pro-gramme contained 16 items including quicksteps, foxtrots, waltzes, military two-steps and medleys, with the odd schottische thrown in. A good time was had by all.

The end of the war brought back our teachers. One Monday morning our classroom door burst open and in came a new master. The first words he said, and they remain in my memory, were: "Glory be to God for dappled things..." No introduction, no self-identification. "Anyone know who wrote this?" he asked. We sat blankly. "Gerard Manley Hopkins," he told us. Such was our introduction to Geoff Farringdon, our new sixth-form master.

Just back from the war, he was a charismatic and colourful figure. I immediately established an excellent rapport with him. He introduced concepts which were entirely new to us. He changed our way of looking at things, and taught us to think differently. He introduced us to poets and writers we had never heard of – Gerard Manley Hopkins being one. He opened up a whole new world and came just in time for me.

Geoff had been with the RAF in India and had developed a contempt for the Hindus, who would not fight, and an admiration for the Muslims, who would, but that was a soldier's viewpoint. On the whole, teachers kept off politics. He was a good cricketer, noted for his bowling, and for many years he played for one or other of the local teams.

Geoff Farringdon, who taught English, and Philip Cooper, the French master had a particular influence on me. By this time I was in the sixth form, having taken my School Certificate examination two years ahead of time. Having struggled in third to fifth place in the fifth form throughout the year, I came top in the exams.

Being a sixth-former – albeit lower sixth – was to rank with the gods. I could now legally enter school through the front gate. I no longer had to wear a school cap, and we no longer had desks in a classroom. The sixth form room was a common room, with tables and chairs. There were free periods, and the number of subjects was now limited to four, depending on which one was taking in the next major examination, the Higher School Certificate. I had obtained distinctions in six subjects, a credit in one (physics) and a pass in the last (art). I could have chosen either sciences or arts for the HSC. It was not possible then to combine them. Having already decided that I wanted to become a lawyer, I had to take arts subjects; English, History, French and Latin.

Similar comments apply to Philip Cooper, the new French master, but he was much more cosmopolitan and bohemian. French was one subject where we had been comparatively well-taught during the war, but under his tutelage I came to be able to read and write the language as well as I could English. But not to speak it, which is not to say that I couldn't, simply that I could not master the accent. My French had a broad Teesside accent, and the French being French, professed not to understand what I was saying. Perhaps they didn't. Though I got alphas in all my written work, my orals usually got a "D". Fortunately, they counted for little in the final result.

Philip broadened our range of French literature. He introduced us to writers of whom perhaps we should have known but didn't – Alphonse Daudet, Anatole France, Chevallier: the lighter side as well as the serious stuff. He was a francophile and had a way of infecting us with his own enthusiasm. After their surrender in 1940 and due to the actions of the Vichy government during the war, which was considered collaborationist, the French had not had a very good press, and were not highly thought of, at least by the sixth form of Guisborough Grammar School. He made us think again. He was not dogmatic, just persuasive. He argued with the Gallic logic he was so fond of explaining to us.

Among other signs of return to peacetime conditions was the revival of the Gilbert and Sullivan operas, which the school had regularly performed before the war, a tradition established by Mr Routh, and my affection for them was born. All the school was in involved in one way or another and the performances, usually three, were all open to a paying public. We were fortunate in having Mr Arnatt, and Eric Garrett, one of our colleagues, a tall handsome lad with a wonderful baritone voice. Mr Arnatt, a post-war addition to the teaching staff, was an excellent actor, light on his feet and with a great sense of fun. He could do the patter songs, such as the "very model of a modern Major General" with an aplomb that any professional would have admired. Eric went on to become a member of staff of the Royal Opera at Covent Garden, where he has sung in countless performances, and I have seen him on the stage on many occasions over four decades.

The scenery and props and many of the costumes were all made in the school. There was an unofficial offstage chorus to augment that on the stage. The girls – "the cousins and the sisters and the aunts" – were boys, and very pretty they looked, made up and dressed as girls. I would have loved to have been in the chorus on stage but my singing talent was such as to limit me to the very fringes of the "unofficial" chorus. The finished product was excellent and the enthusiastic applause which followed each performance, not always entirely objective as most present had some personal interest in what was happening onstage, reflected the enthusiasm which had gone into the production.

It was through Philip Cooper that we had our first taste of France. In 1946, just a year after the war had ended, he organised a trip to Paris. The cost was £21 per head, for the coach trip, channel crossing and seven days in Paris. By that time, with Philip's influence on us, we were all dying to go. We, as a form, had just seen our first French film – *Les Enfants du Paradis* – and realised what we had been missing: what a good film was. It still brings tears to my eyes whenever I see it. Arletty set all hearts trembling. Here was a real woman, not one of the artificial glamour queens from Hollywood, over whom we had hitherto drooled. The impact was immense, and there was not one of us who would not have sold our grandmothers to take that trip to Paris. And we would have been right to have done so, as it remains one of the great experiences of my life.

Paris in 1946 was a pathetic image of the city it was to become and presumably had been. Though it was declared an open city early in the war and thus escaped bombing, at least by the Germans, it had suffered massively during the occupation and from some hand-to-hand fighting in its liberation. It was grey and unkempt, but it was still beautiful. It was hard not to think with sadness of the words of the song "The Last Time I Saw Paris". Its "grandes allees", the tree-lined streets (then still free from the traffic congestion which later threatened to ruin the city), its buildings, the Seine, exceeded all one's expectations. Many places do not live up to their reputations, or one's expectations of them. Paris exceeded them, and still does every visit. Now I think in terms of the Cole Porter song: "I love Paris in the springtime, I love Paris in the fall..."

We travelled to Paris by coach, taking the Newhaven-Dieppe ferry, because that was the cheapest route. The journey to Newhaven took some 11 hours. There were no motorways then, and coaches were not as well equipped as those of today. In reality, they were primitive, cold and uncomfortable. Cross-channel ferries similarly were old-fashioned and stabilisers were unknown. The crossing took four and a half hours, and the last stage of the journey a similar time. In short, it took us nearly a day to get there.

We put up in a small and rather decrepit looking hotel in the Montmartre district. It was the sort of place where, as one of my colleagues put it, the customers "lived on the fruits of love and threw the skins out of the window"; the sort of place where, when my wife as a young woman in Paris, tried to book into for three days, the concierge said: "Pour trois heures peut-etre, mademoiselle, mais trois jours... Je regrette..." with a French shrug of the shoulders.

Food was, to our surprise, in short supply. There seemed to be no fresh eggs, only hard-boiled. Coffee consisted of chicory. There was no fresh milk, fruit or vegetables and we did not find any of the famous French croissants we had heard so much about. Our general impression was that we were, from that aspect, better off at home. Still, we managed to survive mainly on a diet of potato crisps, hard-boiled eggs, and dried milk but hardly noticed the dietary deficiencies in our excitement at just being there.

This was romance; this was "Abroad". And one of my great love affairs started. I still get withdrawal symptoms if I have not been to Paris for any length of time. Fortunately, this is a love affair my wife shares with me. I must admit that my fidelity is tested from time to time by the city's inconstancy. Carefully worked out routes are frustrated by new road systems. If you want to go by bus, you find that the route(s) don't operate on that particular day; the art gallery will inevitably not be open, or the part you want to see is closed – just like London in fact. But the sun just has to give the city its shining smile, and all is forgiven.

I did not come home with my colleagues. My mother was by this time becoming increasingly ill, and needed an operation. Before the operation, however, she had to lose a considerable amount of weight, and get fit. The Bircher-Brenner clinic in Zurich specialised in the treatment she needed, and she went there for some weeks. The arrangement was that I would join my parents in Zurich and that we would then go on to somewhere in the Alps. This was in June.

I accordingly took the train from Paris to Zurich alone which pleased me. The train stopped for a time in Bern and I had time to get out and wander round the station, which seemed to be full of shops. I could not believe my eyes. After the rationing at home, and the scarcity in Paris, here was a cornucopia. There was an unbelievable abundance of food and merchandise of all descriptions; it was like a gastronomic Aladdin's cave. I had never seen so many chocolates, sweets, cakes, breads, croissants and the like; meats, sausages, cheeses, dairy products. It is hard to describe the effect of the enormous contrast. I have seen great contrasts between poverty and wealth in adjoining streets in Rio de Janeiro and in Mexico City, indeed, in almost any large South American city, but this was a contrast between war and peace, not social disparity. In the middle of a continent ravaged by a war of unprecedented carnage and cruelty there was something almost indecent in this display of opulence and plenty.

Zurich emphasised the contrast in a different way. Here was a well-organised, rich, spotlessly clean city. I recall that my mother, out walking one day, tripped and fell to the pavement. She was wearing a white suit but she was able to get up, give a slight brush with her hands, and walk on without any mark on her. The city was white and beautiful with its lakeside frontage – and soulless. There was a great hum of early morning traffic – no petrol rationing here – the rush hour being from 6 to 8 a.m., by which time everyone was at work. By 6 p.m. they were all in bed, or so it seemed. My parents stayed at the Baur-au-Lac, one of the finest hotels in the city. I stayed nearby at a more modest establishment, the Dolder. My parents did not believe in indulging me in luxurious surroundings. Both hotels, in true Swiss style, were well appointed and immaculately clean. Dad thought he would take the opportunity also to have some massages and treatments. It was decided that I should take tennis lessons to keep me occupied while Mother was having her treatment. I did so with enthusiasm, and so started another of my favourite activities.

After a week in Zurich, when my mother's treatments were over for the moment, we went on to Engelberg, a typically Swiss alpine town, more noted for winter sports than summer activities.

There were fine walks and more tennis. We stayed in a modest Jewish hotel. A family called Mohl was staying at the same hotel. The elder daughter, Eva, was slightly younger than me. She was very beautiful: with blue eyes, blonde hair and a light, peaches-and-cream complexion. She tended to wear blue which showed her fair hair to perfection. It would be hard to picture anyone more Aryan-looking. It transpired that it was her looks that had saved the family. When they crossed from Germany into Switzerland she was the first to go through the immigration process and no one suspected that she, and hence the rest of the family, was Jewish, and they were not turned back as many Jews, with perfectly satisfactory documentation, had been. Her family were, in fact, strictly Orthodox Jews. Needless to say, I fell head over heels in love with her. In the two weeks we had together in Engelberg, however, we seemed never to be alone.

This was the first time, and so far as I can recall the only time, since we came to England that I had been on holiday with my parents. There were many occasions later when we went to London together for a weekend or so, but there were no family holidays. We flew back to London. It was my first flight. The air-craft was a DC3, a Dakota, recently converted to civilian from military use, and very basic. There were no in-flight comforts like there are today. We landed at Northolt, which was still an RAF station. The buildings were glorified Nissen huts, with few passenger facilities. Air travel was still primitive but at least there was no hanging about waiting for luggage or queues at the customs or passport desks. It was uncomfortable, but quick.

My parents had made friends in Engelberg with a Swiss family who lived in Zurich; they invited me to come and stay with them the following year. I flew out alone from Northolt. My main purpose was to see Eva again. Her family were near neighbours of my hosts. I saw Eva nearly every day, but never alone, because wherever we went her little sister came too. It suddenly dawned on me, as it had not the previous year, that we were being chaperoned. An unmarried Jewish girl from a religious family is never allowed out alone with a man. It did not spoil my enjoyment of being with Eva, but it was more than somewhat inhibiting. I suppose that I was privileged even to be allowed out with her at all but I still wonder why I was encouraged to go to see her. Her parents must have consented, indeed been party to, my invitation. My parents must have acquiesced. They did not usually send me off abroad alone. In Orthodox Jewish families people marry young, and marriages are often arranged. Nothing was ever said to me, but perhaps someone had marriage on their mind. It certainly wasn't me.

That romance soon ended because Eva and her family moved to the United States shortly afterwards and, though we corresponded for a little while, I did not see her, or hear of her again. I am not a good correspondent, and I admit with regret that any relationship which is dependent on my writing letters will soon perish. Email facilitates matters but even so I am not good at maintaining long-distance contacts.

Chapter 31 – Another Death

While Opa was still alive, Oma made some effort to live by the rules and accept the diet laid down for her by her doctors. On one occasion she had been advised that her condition could only be helped by a particular regimen which included ham. Jews have a special aversion to the pig and to many the idea of eating pig in any form is anathema. A Jew who eats pork is considered a lost soul, so this piece of medical advice caused great consternation. However, Judaism, for all its strict observances, is nothing if not pragmatic. To save a life, almost anything is permitted. Oma was persuaded against all her beliefs and superstitions to accept the advice. Ham could not be allowed into a kosher house; therefore, the wash house, the scene of the weekly ritual butchery of the chickens, was thoroughly cleaned, and provided with a table and chair, cutlery and plates for Oma to eat her ham. I do not know whether it did her any good, but I think she came to enjoy it. The plates and cutlery had to be thrown away when Oma finished her diet.

After Opa's death, Oma ceased to take any account of her condition. As previously mentioned, she would eat sweets and chocolates which, because she was a diabetic, had been absolutely forbidden, and became a secret drinker. I would often catch her taking a surreptitious drink of whisky as I was myself going to make a clandestine telephone call to a young lady who lived nearby, and was the object of my passion at the time.

There was a surrealist incongruity in the sight of a stout, middle-aged, white-haired matriarch taking a secret swig from a whisky bottle. And when Oma had the inevitable reaction to her dietary misdemeanours, which came in the various forms of gall-stone attacks, or liver or abdominal pains it was my mother, who was herself not well, who had to get up in the night and deal with a difficult and uncooperative patient, and then go to work the next day.

Oma had several attacks which caused her doctors and the family much concern. It seems that Ruthin Castle in Wales, now a nursing home, had specialist treatment suitable for her needs.

She was taken there urgently one Christmas. All the family went there, leaving Aunty Jeanne and myself alone at home. She had prepared a huge turkey for the whole big family and she and I ate that entire turkey ourselves over a period of three days. We ate it for breakfast, lunch and dinner. We had turkey hot, turkey cold, turkey schnitzels, turkey stuffed, turkey neat, turkey salad. And when Aunty Jeanne had exhausted all other possibilities, turkey sandwiches. We were quite proud of ourselves, and our heroic efforts remain part of family lore to this day, quite overshadowing the reason for our self-sacrifice.

Oma's serious heart condition worsened in the autumn of 1946. She was again taken for treatment to Ruthin Castle but she had lost the will to live. She died there on 17 November 1946. She might have lived longer had she taken any care of herself or heeded her doctors. As one might expect, her funeral was well attended and the mourning heartfelt. My aunts and uncles, even Herman – despite the severity with which he had been treated – had great love, as well as respect, for their parents. The *shiva* followed the pattern of that when Opa died. Oma's death was a relief in many ways, not least for my mother, who had had the burden of looking after her and receiving very little appreciation for her efforts.

Oma's death marked the end not only of a generation, but an era. My grandparents had all had to emigrate twice in their comparatively short lifetimes and readjust to new countries, new cultures, new languages, new ways. I was the only grandchild old enough to know and appreciate Oma and Opa. I was also the only one of my generation, on my mother's side of the family, not to have been born in England. In fact, I was the only one of all my generation to have been born in Germany as my cousins on my father's side were born in Belgium.

Oma's death had more serious consequences for the business and for my immediate family than that of Opa. By this time only my parents and I still lived with my grandparents, and the number of inhabitants of the Grey House had fallen. Yetti and Karl lived in West Hartlepool and Dora and Joe in Redcar. My parents had lived in the Grey House and paid their proportion of its upkeep and maintenance in order that my grandparents should not have to live on their own, and the house remained in the name of my grandparents. My mother was very unhappy about this but Dad, always anxious to avoid any form of controversy or unpleasantness, saw no problem in this arrangement. No doubt my parents felt that to raise the issue of their being included on the title deeds as owners might be taken as a sign of lack of confidence but they were sure that the family could be trusted to do the "right thing". It would not have been possible to mention the matter to Opa. Any approach to Oma on the subject would have resulted in an immediate heart attack.

Oma had made a new will on 7 June 1946, five months before she died. She went, not to the family's usual solicitor or any of the other Jewish solicitors in the town but to a non-Jewish firm of solicitors, unknown to the family. The solicitor had been recommended to her by the maleficent Miss Johnson, who accompanied her there. This is self-evident from the fact that in the will the only name spelled correctly, including that of the testatrix, was my mother's. Oma's will caused my parents great distress. She slighted my mother not only by not appointing her, the eldest daughter who had looked after her since coming to England, as an executrix, and appointing Max and Dora, but by naming her children, to whom after certain specific gifts she left everything in equal shares, in the following order: 1. Yetti, the youngest; 2. Dora; 3. Max; 4. My mother; and 5. (last) Herman. It was quite unnecessary, in fact, to name them at all. A gift to all her "children living at her death in equal shares" would have been enough.

These dispositions may seem to have been fair on the face of the matter, but this ignored the fact that the Grey House was our home, and that my parents had an equitable interest in the house by reason of their contributions to its purchase, maintenance and upkeep. It is clear that Oma went to the solicitors recommended by Miss Johnson because none of the Jewish solicitors in the town would have allowed her to make a will on these terms. It is also clear that Miss Johnson went with her because Oma's English, despite the many years of Miss Johnson's tutelage, was quite unequal to deal with such matters as giving instructions for a will. No doubt she acted on one of the many fits of pique she directed at my mother. It was a sad example of posthumous malevolence by a spiteful woman.

The specific gifts included one thousand shares in "the Guisborough Shirt Company Limited" to "Yetti, and a similar number to her grandchildren living at the date of her death in equal shares". By the time of her death there were several grandchildren. I, for one, was until very recently quite unaware of this gift. It may have been worth something at the time, if the company had been sold, but not otherwise. The gift to Yetti also caused great trouble, as it risked involving Karl in the business, which would have been totally unacceptable. Shares in private companies are valueless, as the directors are usually not bound to recognise transfers to third parties, and the best that can be achieved is for the executors of the will to hold the shares in trust for the beneficiary, but even if the transfer is registered, the shares unless they confer control, have no value in themselves until they come to be sold. Karl, needless to say, saw this as an opportunity to claim a one-fifth interest in the business. Disregarding the inaccuracy of his arithmetic, I believe that the matter was settled by a cash payment.

The family reactions were unexpected. Dora and Herman, not usually allies, were aghast and expressed themselves ready to forgo any interest they may have had in the proceeds of the sale of the house. Max, on the other hand, spurred on by Jeanne felt that the wishes of the testatrix could not be disregarded. As for Yetti, she needed the money. Karl's plastic doll business was hardly providing enough for their living and she was regularly subsidised by Oma and my mother. Despite this, she did not wish the house to be sold. She was quite happy to take the same view as Dora and Herman.

My mother was understandably very hurt and upset by the whole episode. She decided that she did not wish to remain in the Grey House. It was entirely her decision. My father wanted no part in the matter. He was, unusually for him, disgusted at the whole business. I, of course, knew nothing of this at the time. In the event, it proved a blessing in disguise. My parents soon found another house, inestimably better than the Grey House. This was Brierfield, in Harrow Road, only about 200 yards away. For the first time since coming to England my parents and I were alone in our own home; the Grey House would always have been regarded by the family, understandably, as their home too. And so began the happiest period of my youth.

Shortly before the move to Brierfield we acquired a nationality for the first time. In the formal words of the Home Office, Nationality Division, "a certificate of naturalisation number BZ 2042 was granted on 28 January 1947 to one Jakob Fischbein of 79 Cambridge Road Middlesborough (sic) Yorkshire and that the additional particulars shown on the certificate were as follows: that he was of no nationality (formerly Russian) born at Berlin Germany on 2nd January 1904, that he was by occupation a Company Director and that he was married. The certificate also extended to include his minor son Joachim Fred born 21st June 1931". We had official recognition at last: my father had waited over 40 years for a nationality. We now belonged somewhere. We were no longer refugees, no longer outcasts; we had been taken in and made welcome. We had been able to make our contribution in return. It was a proud moment.

Chapter 32 – Brierfield

Brierfield, in Harrow Road, was a large house, built of brick and stucco, standing in one and a half acres of its own grounds. It was beautiful; the gardens were glorious. It had 200 feet of centrally heated greenhouse, with grapevines running the whole length of the roof. The interior of the greenhouse was taken up by potting tables, exotic plants and tomato plants; it was like a garden centre. The house was sheltered on all sides by tall trees and was not visible from the road. A longish driveway, from the Harrow Road entrance, guarded by two impressive iron gates about 8 feet high, led to the house. A turning circle at the top of the drive left room to park several cars. Immediately inside the gate was a four-car garage, with a flat above. The garage had its own inspection pit of which, as a would-be car mechanic – I serviced my car myself – I was to make much use. At the front of the house was a large lawn with flower beds. Alongside the house was a large lawn which had been, and again became, a tennis court. In front of this there was a garden house, large enough for a party, constructed in the style of a Swiss chalet. There were stone paths from one part of the garden to another. The garden was a dream. With it came two motorised Atco mowers. One was the usual push type; the other, my pride and joy, was articulated, with its own seat.

Behind the chalet there was a stone path with a bower, and behind that at the rear of the garage, there was a a vegetable garden whose produce was more than we could use, and supplied Max and Jeanne and others. Grounds of this size need a full-time gardener. Tom Towel, the school groundsman, had complained about his wages and conditions and I persuaded him that my mother could offer him a better job and he came to work for us. He was a first-rate gardener and made a good team with Mother in the greenhouse and me on the lawns.

The house itself was on three floors. At the front, stone steps led to an elegant front door on either side of which were large windows. The steps were essentially decorative as, although there was a path and gateway leading on to Acklam Road, in practice, visitors rarely approached the house from the front. The front door was only opened for parties in the summer. The usual approach was by the drive from Harrow Road. The entrance, at the top of the drive, was through a small lobby – relatively small because there was nothing small in that house – with washroom, cloakroom and toilet.

On entering the house one was immediately struck by the height of the ceilings and the magnificent wood panelling of the hall and the ground floor rooms. When we bought the house this was dark. Despite my protests, mother had the panelling bleached to a light beech colour. She was right. The result was spectacular. The house suddenly seemed bright and airy. All the ground floor had mahogany parquet, and inlaid floors. My parents' furniture now came into its own and could be seen to its best advantage. The house and furniture appeared made for each other.

The feeling of light and space was epitomised by my good friend from school, George Read, who sitting down on a two-seater settee, said to another of my friends: "I'll take this acre – you sit on that one."

There were three large rooms in the front part of the ground floor. All the rooms had magnificent fireplaces, though as the house was centrally heated these were merely decorative. One of the rooms was a fully equipped billiard room. To have my own billiard room was beyond my wildest dreams. It was too good to last. My mother turned the billiard room into a music room, and replaced the billiard table with a baby grand piano – a rosewood Bechstein, a most beautiful thing in itself. But I did not lose the billiard table. She had it removed to a room on the top floor, with everything that went with it and for good measure had the table re-covered. In order to preserve the atmosphere of a billiard room she had the room papered to look like panelling. The move worked perfectly well apart from in one particular spot where the angle of the roof tended to impede one's cueing. With all the practising I could now do, I became a fairly proficient snooker player; though my best break was only 51, I regularly scored breaks of 30 plus.

The other downstairs rooms were a dining room and a drawing room. This was where the television was installed as soon as it became available, and Dad would settle down on a Saturday afternoon, telephone at his side, with an open line to his book-maker, following the racing.

Off the main hall was the kitchen complex, almost an estab-lishment on its own. There was a large morning room, where life was lived and we ate, except on Friday nights or special occasions. Off this were, respectively, a scullery and a kitchen. Having both of these made keeping kosher simple. One was used for milk and the other for meat. In the kitchen, needless to say, there was an Aga cooker which also fed the very efficient hot water and central heating system. We had a conventional gas cooker as well as the Aga. Off the kitchen was a larder whose size was in keeping with the rest of the house. A corridor led from the back of the kitchen to a walled yard, in which were a fully equipped laundry and a drying room.

An elegant staircase led to the first floor which had four bed-rooms. The largest, which was my parents' room, was on the corner of the house. It had its own dressing room and walk-in wardrobe. There were two toilets and a bathroom, all sizeable. I occupied two of the bedrooms, one as my study and the other, which was actually the main guest room, when available. Another staircase led to the top floor on which there were a bathroom, and another four smaller bedrooms, but still large enough for one to be converted into a billiard room. The largest room was given to Tessie, our housekeeper. One of the spare rooms later became my mother's sewing room.

In my room I had a large fireplace, around which bookshelves were built. The mantelpiece had most attractive wood carvings. My furniture included a desk, a large bookcase about six feet long and five feet high, which my parents had specially made for me, a couch that converted into a bed, and armchairs all in appropriate matching beechwood and materials. The colour theme was orange-red. I had my own radio which my parents had given me for my fifteenth birthday (the latest thing at the time) and a record player. My parents surprised me from time to time with such pre-sents, which came as a complete surprise and without any prompt-ing on my part. They were much more thoughtful parents than I often gave them credit for.

Brierfield was the most marvellous place to live in. I have, over the years, seen many fine homes and beautiful houses; though Brierfield was not particularly handsome from the outside, I have never seen anything to match it for grace, charm, warmth, comfort and good taste, and I do not think that I am simply being nostalgic.

The move from the Grey House was effected with the utmost efficiency. Dad and I left the Grey House in the morning, as usual, and returned to Brierfield in the evening at our usual times, sat down and had our evening meals, as if we had lived there all our lives. Everything was already in its place. We were neither concerned with nor affected by the logistics of the move. How my mother arranged this I shall never understand. The only casualty was my train set, which disappeared, and I know that this time she had not given it away.

The large gardens led my mother to think we should have a dog to keep her company as she did her daily tours. I was only too delighted at the idea. This would not have been possible at the Grey House. Our first dog was a fox terrier, a very pretty little animal. Being of good pedigree, he was highly strung and never stopped barking. Sadly, he caught distemper and despite all our efforts he died. The next two dogs were also disasters. They were given to us by a business acquaintance from Sheffield, a Mr Bernstein.

Mr Bernstein was built like a wrestler, short and stout. He was a man of wealthy appearance, full of bonhomie and generosity; another of the strange charismatic characters who kept turning up in my life. "With it" ahead of his time, he wore very expensive clothes and sported gold chains with medallions and miniature ivory tusks. He drove a large Rolls Royce. He was the very epitome of the successful get-rich-quick entrepreneur which the immediate post-war years produced; a rough diamond, and a very pleasant man to deal with. I met him because I used to drive vans filled with "cabbage" to his business in Sheffield, in return for which I came back with large quantities of cash in notes. Apparently no one else could be trusted with these amounts.

"Cabbage" is a term used in the clothing trade for garments made from fabric that was surplus to requirements. The cost of the cloth has already been written off, and paid for, so the cabbage is waste material, and in theory it is non-existent, but there appears to be a big market for it. Whatever you can get for it is "bunce", and appears in no books of account. This has long been a profitable sideline in the garment industry. I had no idea of this at the time. I was just told to deliver the goods and bring back the money. This may be a tribute to my sense of responsibility, but it is also a measure of my naivety that I had no idea of what was going on until the penny tumbled some time later. I dare say that the proceeds of the cabbage did much to see me through college.

Mr Bernstein, learning of the sad loss of the fox terrier, decided to console us and turned up one day with an Alsatian, called Caesar. This, he said, was more in keeping with a house the size of ours, and would be a good guard dog. Which indeed, he was; so much so that he would not let anyone near the house. All our guests were frightened of him; so were we. If we locked him up in the outhouses, he would just bark until we let him out. Twenty-four hours of this and Dad was on the telephone to Mr Bernstein. He came the very next day, to his credit, with another Alsatian, who went by the name of Prince. Where he got these dogs, heaven only knows; perhaps he got them in exchange for the cabbage! This dog had a real attitude problem – he was scared: a cowardly Alsatian. He would hide under the sideboard in the kitchen, or under a chair. He would sneak out, when he thought no one was looking, for his food. It was a problem to take him for a walk. Most dogs have to be held back; this one had to be dragged, almost carried. The end came when in a moment of blind panic he ran upstairs, and jumped out of Mother's (fortunately) open bedroom window, taking the curtains with him. It was curtains for him too. He was mysteriously uninjured, but when we eventually managed to catch him he too was returned to Mr Bernstein with many thanks and a plea for no further dogs.

A week or so later, Tessie, our housekeeper, brought along the most delightful black-and-white puppy, a cross between a Border Collie and a Labrador, four weeks old and the last of a litter of six. We called her Peggy; she was a joy and pleasure to my mother, to me, and indeed, the whole family. She had an extraordinary intelligence, if dogs can be said to have intelligence. She was easily house-trained and learned her way around in no time. She seemed to understand whatever was said to her and would follow me or Mother, or indeed anyone of the household, without a lead. I never put her on a leash unless there was some park regulation or the like requiring it, and when I did she would look at me reproachfully, as if to say "What's up, don't you trust me any more?" She eventually came with me to London where she lived with Aunt Yetti for some years, finding her way round a completely new environment very quickly. She was a wonderful animal, a great friend and companion, and when she died I could not find it in my heart to replace her.

Chapter 33 – The Hudson Sisters

In her efficient arrangements about the house, Mother was greatly helped by Tessie Hudson and her sisters, Winnie and Joan. Some time before Oma died, Tessie (real name Theresa) had come into our household as a housekeeper. Mother was increasingly unwell, and now suffered from a general physical weakness which she continued to refuse to acknowledge, but which left her too weak to cope both with running the house and working in the factory.

How Tessie came to be engaged I do not know. Household matters were none of my business, and I was not curious. All I know is that one day I came home from school and there she was. Tessie was about 31 or 32 when she started working for us. She came from a devout Catholic family who lived in South Bank, a part of Middlesbrough by the River Tees. Of the three sisters only one was married – Joan to George Cunningham. His brother was a priest of the Marian Order, a charming and educated man, and I had the impression that Tessie was in love with him, a love which, having regard to their strict Catholicism, could not be consummated.

Tessie's father was a widower. He was gentle and wise. Her sister, Winnie, devoted herself to his wellbeing. He was an ardent supporter of the Boro', and he introduced me to Wilf Mannion, a native of South Bank, and one of the greatest footballers of that, or any era, who was a personal friend of his. To meet Wilf Mannion, to shake hands with him, and actually to speak with him was to me at the time like meeting Jupiter on Mount Olympus. Wilf Mannion was a modest, shy, likeable person. Mr Hudson – I never called him anything else – would not go out at night if the Boro' lost their match that day. There were periods when he was at home on a Saturday night – as he would put it – "more often than not".

Winnie came to do the heavy work once or twice a week. Though the household had now shrunk to four, including Tessie, there was still plenty to do. It was a big house and we constantly had visitors. Not only did any visiting family member stay with us but we were a hotel for any out-of-town visitor, particularly those who came on business. There were frequent bridge evenings and other parties as the house was ideal for entertaining, especially in the summer, when the garden looked glorious. Dad had his regular poker game, and there were few evenings when the house was quiet. All this entailed much work. Tessie did most of the cooking and baking, and preparation for parties. Mother had never had anyone so reliable and devoted to her before, and consequently her life was made much easier by this wonderful help.

Tessie was small and rather squat in figure but had a pleasant appearance. She was, in the nicest possible way, ambitious for better things and proud of her status as a housekeeper. She would have been deeply insulted to have been called, or treated as, a maid. She usually ate supper with me when I came home and would bring me a cup of chocolate or cocoa to my room while I did my homework. She adored my mother, and was very fond of my father. She was devoted to me, I felt at times almost unhealthily so.

Winnie was some years older than Tessie. She was formidable – very much a no-nonsense type: not a person to be crossed or who could be easily deflected from her purpose. She had none of Tessie's pretensions. Joan, who had a daughter, also Teresa, was similar, though perhaps a little gentler than Winnie. The Hudson and Cunningham families were typical of many in the area. They were splendid folk, of the highest integrity, all firm Labour voters, solidly and loyally working class; aware of their own worth and confident in their own values. They were hard-working, diligent and conscientious, giving a fair day's work and expecting a fair day's pay – they were the salt of the earth. I like to think that there are still people like them in the North. I loved and admired them all.

Over the following years, and especially during the time of Mother's illness, Tessie had full responsibility for the running of the house. She was soon adept at the disciplines of keeping a kosher household, and was exceedingly strict in this respect. She coped well with us, the rest of the family, and though not always with the best of grace, the numerous visitors who came to stay. Her first concern was with my mother, who found comfort in the fact that everything ran like clockwork. In Tessie's capable hands my mother had no need to worry about the home, and the well-being, and well-feeding, of Dad and myself.

Redcar is a pleasant seaside resort about 9 miles from Middlesbrough and a similar distance from Guisborough. It is not as pretty as Saltburn but has a magnificent wide and sandy beach. The town and all the area between Redcar and Middlesbrough is flat. The road runs almost through what were the ICI's Wilton works, whose lights by night looked like a ship at sea. What it looked like by day is best passed over.

Opa liked to have his family round him, in as close proximity as possible. Max and Jeanne lived just across the road at 38 Cambridge Road. Dora and Joe, when first married, had rented a house on the corner of Oxford Road and Thornfield Road not 100 yards from the Grey House, in true family tradition. But Joe did not share the family's inclination to live on top of one another, and as soon as the opportunity arose to buy a suitable house else-where, Dora and Joe moved to Redcar. They were mistaken if they thought that they could escape the family so easily. Every Sunday the whole family would go to Redcar for the day. On fine days, most of their friends would somehow turn up for lunch or tea. I was only too happy to join these family outings.

Joe, for all his quietness and retiring personality was a gener-ous and welcoming host and Dora revelled in company. They had contrasting personalities, but they were idyllically happy together. This is not to say that they did not have disagreements: Dora's outspokenness and her independent and original mind made this inevitable. Joe knew when and how to humour her and cope with her idiosyncrasies, and she with his.

It was decided, probably by Max – as it was just the sort of thing he would think up – that we should go horse riding on Redcar's glorious sands every Sunday morning. The "we" con-sisted of Max, Dad, Joe, Dora and myself. And so on Sunday mornings we would present ourselves at the stables in Coatham, part of Redcar, mount, and ride off. That at least was the theory. First, we had to learn to ride. None of my family had, I think, ever seen a horse, other than one pulling a cart or similar, or, in Dad's case, as something to place a bet on. Dora took to riding as if she had been born in the saddle. True to her sporting self she was properly and smartly dressed in full rig – jodhpurs, hat, riding coat and whip. As for the male contingent, it would be hard to imagine a more motley or less impressive group of riders. We were no horsemen of the Apocalypse, or, indeed, of anything. To see my father on horseback was a sight so hilarious that I laughed so much that I quite literally fell off my horse, which was a sort of justice, I suppose. He had never in his life done anything remotely resembling a sporting activity. His idea of exercise was to shuffle a pack of cards or pick up the telephone to his bookie; he was out of his depth when it came to engaging in activity involving any sort of movement on his part. However, he was a good sport and persisted, until after a few weeks, he ceased to be afraid of the animal once it became clear that the latter had accepted the responsibility of carrying him at no greater pace than a slow trot.

Joe looked even more lugubrious than usual. He, too, was no great sportsman, but unlike my father he was not entirely sedentary; he loved walking and though also city born and bred, he was very contented in the country. We were all townies. I do not think that any other member of the family could have shut themselves away in Redcar, far less Jersey, as they did later. Dora would certainly have preferred to live in urban surroundings, but she had such an outgoing and vibrant personality that she made any surroundings her own. Her world was where she was, and she and Joe by travelling frequently compensated for the somewhat isolated life which they were to have in Jersey. Joe managed to retain his dignity, even on the back of a horse.

Max was all enthusiasm and raring to go until he was actually sitting on the horse, when he suddenly caught fright, and became paralysed with fear, unable to move. But we had an understanding riding teacher and tolerant beasts who realised that none of us would make proficient horsemen, and over a few weeks we all began to make some tolerable progress.

As for myself, I had the advantage of youth. I approached riding rather as I did cycling; I soon got the hang of getting and staying on the horse, and learned to use my knees to hold myself in the saddle and my hands to control the reins. I was quite sporty, and being a speed merchant soon wanted to go rather faster than my skill permitted. I fell off several times, but was told that every good rider has falls. One fall I recall in particular: I was going too fast, and the horse stumbled, throwing me off. I was unhurt but had all the wind knocked out of me. It was a strange experience. I know that I could stand and walk, but no sound could I make. I enjoyed riding, and was gratified to note many years later when I went on a farmhouse holiday in Devon with my wife and young children, that, like cycling, riding is a skill which is never lost and they were duly impressed by my skill in an art they had never suspected. I was thankful for my early lessons.

Another Jewish refugee family, the Wolfs, had also taken up residence in Redcar. The family consisted of Sigmund Wolf, his wife Wilma and their children Phyllis and Egon. Sigmund was a larger-than-life character. He was short and rotund, and exuded bonhomie, at least until he was crossed, when he was quick to anger. He was the nearest thing to a friend Opa had – there was really no one in Middlesbrough with whom he could have made friends – and they had much in common. They were both men of strong character who knew their own mind, and who dominated by sheer force of personality, not only their families, but all around them. It was as well that they got on as a clash of personalities might have had interesting results.

Mr Wolf was very wealthy. In his case, the Yorkshire saying, "where there's muck there's brass", was literally true. His company, which was well-established worldwide, extracted minerals, ores and such other materials as could profitably be recovered from the slag heaps and waste products of the steel and chemical plants, mines and other industries which produced industrial waste. The debris came mainly from the foundries and steel-making plants of Dorman Long & Co. Ltd., probably the largest ironworks in the country, and the largest single employer of labour on Teesside together with the chemical works of ICI. After anything of value (which could be recycled) had been extracted from the waste, what was still left was turned into briquettes, which could be used as fuel in place of coal or coke. It was a form of recycling, before the term became fashionable, and was very lucrative.

Sigmund Wolf's car was an American left-hand drive Ford V8 – very exotic in that part of the world. It had all the gadgetry and luxury common in American cars but which had not yet reached England. It was a great thrill to be allowed to sit next to him on the bench-type front seat.

His wife, Wilma, was a large, jolly lady more at home one would have thought in Paris or Monte Carlo than Middlesbrough. She was tall with a sumptuous figure. She dressed expensively and always looked as if she was about to go to the opera. She was hospitable and generous, decorative, charming and fun but not remarkable for her intelligence.

The Wolfs held open house and at the weekends there was always a large number of guests, for tea and supper and whatever else was going. I was usually taken along. I loved going there as much fuss was made of me and there was always plenty to do. I enjoyed Redcar with its Pacitto ice creams, promenade, funfair and glorious beach. The Wolf family were not observant Jews, and served "forbidden foods", especially such seafood delicacies as oysters, crab and lobster, which I never touched.

One Sunday, just as everyone else was gorging themselves on these delicacies, the bulky figure of Mr Wulwik, the cantor from our synagogue, was seen approaching. No table was ever cleared so quickly and replaced with inoffensive, though doubtless less tasty, comestibles. By the time he reached the door and rang the bell, everyone was sitting around with an innocent look on their faces, like naughty children, trying to hide their laughter. He was welcomed effusively but to everyone's relief he didn't stay too long; as soon as he went all the forbidden foods returned.

As soon as the war had ended, families who had been separated from their relatives searched for survivors or tried desperately to find out what had become of those caught up in the horrors in Europe. My family had been singularly fortunate in that we had largely been spared the loss of close relations. There were only two left on the continental mainland: Oma's sister, Lin, and Dad's brother, Fritz. Oma's sister was caught by the Nazis in Romania very near the end of the war and died in Auschwitz. Her son Adolph, aka Peter Rockman, did manage to get away in time and spent a few weeks with us, and later turned up from time to time. He blamed Oma for not doing more to save his mother. Whether anything would have helped one cannot know. In view of all that Opa did for more distant relatives, and others who were not relatives at all, this does seem strange.

Fritz had left Germany and was known to be in Antwerp when war broke out. In his case also, no effort appears to have been made to bring him to England. It may be that, as he was in Belgium, he was considered to be safe. No one could have thought that the Germans would circumvent the Maginot Line, the French defence system, by invading and coming through Belgium and Holland. The Maginot Line did not extend along the border with the Low Countries so as not to offend them. Whatever the reason for his being there and not in England, Fritz was marooned in Belgium for the duration of the war.

How he, and others like him, survived, those who have been spared the experience of living in hiding for nearly five years will never understand. How did anyone survive the Warsaw Ghetto, the death camps? The experiences of the survivors demonstrate how people can adapt to the most atrocious circumstances and survive by treating those conditions as normal.

Fritz not only survived, but while living underground he married and had two children. As soon as it was possible, my parents tried to contact him and he, from Antwerp, tried to contact my parents. In the aftermath of the chaos left by the war, with millions of displaced persons in every part of Europe, it was not easy, even though he must have had my parents' Grey House address from before the war. I could not remember Fritz; I had hardly known him. Once contact had been made, however, every effort was made to bring him and his family to England as soon as possible, but nothing went quickly at that time.

His wife, Cecilia, had family in Milwaukee who were able to obtain entry visas to the USA. While they were waiting for these, they came to stay with us at Brierfield. Fritz looked like his father. At first glance there appeared to be little family resemblance between him and my father, but one could see it after a while; they had the same voice. Their elder child was a daughter, Yvonne, a particularly beautiful girl, who grew up to be a beautiful young woman. Their younger child was a son, Michael.

Theirs was a story repeated, in one form or another, many times in the countries under Nazi occupation. The Belgians, for the most part, were extremely helpful to the Jews and protected them as best they could, even at great risk to themselves. The history of the German occupation has been well documented, but everyone has their own story to tell. After Yvonne was born, my aunt gave her to a non-Jewish family who took her in for her protection. The family pretended that she was their child, and my aunt was her nurse, like the story of Moses and Miriam.

My uncle spent most of his time in hiding, often in the countryside. Just before the Allies were about to liberate the Low Countries, when the Germans were in full retreat, my uncle was betrayed to the Germans by one of the local Fascists. A German officer came to the house with a few men. My uncle was hiding in a small cavity behind a wall (an obvious hiding place). The German officer sent his men away, saying it was clear that there was no one there. My aunt knew he knew where my uncle was hidden. It may be that this particular officer was a soldier, and not from the Gestapo, and wanted no part in genocide; it may be that he knew defeat was inevitable and did not want to add to the misery his countrymen had already inflicted; it may be that he was saving his own skin. One would like to think the best of this German officer because he saved the lives of at least one family.

As soon as the necessary papers came through from America, my uncle, aunt and cousins went to Milwaukee. They made their home there, and stayed for many years, until they moved to Los Angeles to be near their son, my cousin Michael. Michael studied medicine, then specialised in pathology, took a PhD, and had a glorious career, becoming in time Professor of Pathology at the Cedars-Sinai hospital in Los Angeles and was later headhunted to be Professor of Pathology at the University of California in Los Angeles. He was regarded as one of the top five experts in his particular field in the world.

Uncle Fritz reached the age of 96, and Cecilia, 98!

Leon and Tosca, other relatives (possibly cousins) of Oma, also came to stay with us for a few weeks while they waited for their papers to the USA. I remember that Leon bore the marks of his treatment by the Germans, with great scars on his head and sudden bursts of shouting and loss of control but he calmed a little in the serenity of Brierfield. Tosca was a very attractive woman who had also managed to survive, protected in hiding, I think, but I cannot recall the details and indeed they were not mentioned as they were doubtless too painful to recount.

Chapter 36 – Business Problems

Oma's death in 1947 had serious ramifications in regard to the business. As long as she was alive, there was some balance in the management of the factory. It was not that Oma took any part in that, but while she was Managing Director, albeit a titular post, no one else could claim the position, and all the other directors were on the same level. As she was also Chairman of the Board she had a casting vote in case of deadlock, which helped to prevent the situation arising. This safeguard went with her death. Max, prompted by Jeanne, thought that as the eldest son he should have primacy, and become Managing Director.

Max was a good salesman, but he had no business sense whatsoever; in my experience, few salesmen do. A conference of salesmen is a manufacturer's dream, because a salesman's sales resistance is in direct inverse ratio to his sales skills. The better the salesman, the lower his sales resistance. Max, as stated, ranked among the best. But, though a charismatic figure, he did not have the necessary leadership qualities. If frustrated in persuading others to his point of view he would soon lose his temper and what he could not achieve by persuasion he tried to obtain by other tactics ranging from pleading to bullying and shouting. Away from the business he was the most charming of people and delightful company, but he lacked any sense of self-discipline.

My mother wanted Dad to become Managing Director of the business, not because he was particularly suited to the position, but because he was the oldest in the family. He had done just as much as anyone to ensure its success, and he would not use the position to throw his weight about. Joe Menasche, who would have been ideal, had no wish to become involved in what he could see would be a long-running battle. He was contemplating something quite different. The compromise reached was that Dad and Max would be joint Managing Directors. This proved no solution.

Max was full of ideas which were sometimes excellent in principle but not always. Even in the case of his better ideas, he did not stop to consider their practicability, which was rather a pity because some might have worked out well given proper planning. He fell victim to every new idea, every new fashion in manufacturing, and had to have every new gadget or machine. For example, work requiring little intelligence, which had been done by the youngest girls, the cheapest labour, such as "cotton ending" which merely meant trimming the little threads left when a garment was cut from the sewing machine, had suddenly to be given over to cumbrous, expensive and inefficient experimental machinery. This often proved less economical, and was certainly less efficient, than the manpower it was intended to replace and was soon discarded. Resistance by the workers, not to say my mother and Dora in particular, and Joe Menasche (for perhaps different reasons) to such ideas was not due to a Luddite mentality but to their introduction without proper feasibility studies and proper planning. Max had no idea of the amount of retraining of the workers which would be involved and the time it would take. These were concepts he did not understand, far less consider. New methods require considerable investment and their benefits take some time to be realised.

The business had prospered in the war. Government contracts were gilt-edged: there were few bad debts. The prices of raw materials and wages were controlled and above all, there was nothing to spend money on. The fire, apart from the disruption caused by the need for emergency measures, had resulted in a bigger and better building, new machinery and improved facilities.

The government contracts were replaced by others, equally as good, namely from Marks & Spencer. These should have secured the company's future. Most of M&S's suppliers became very successful and wealthy. To become an M&S supplier was a big feather in one's commercial cap. M&S were obsessive about quality, and they gave excellent back- up services to their suppliers to ensure that they matched their requirements and would assist any manufacturer with advice and often temporary personnel. They sent regular inspectors. It was not unlike the days of government contracts, except that the M&S inspectors were much tougher. Without my mother in command, quality control was slipping. Though Dora, while still there, did her utmost she did not have

Mother's skills and when she left for Jersey my mother was left fighting a lone and losing battle, not only with the demands of the factory but with her health, of which these demands took their toll. But human frailty, vanity and ambition were to bring the whole edifice to the ground.

Things began to go wrong. The arguments grew worse. Max became increasingly megalomaniac. Joe could no longer stand the atmosphere of rows, disputes, and what he regarded as sheer commercial suicide. He decided it was time to get out, while there was still something left to take out. He could foresee disaster unless there was a radical change in attitudes, and he saw that this was unlikely. Dad had no bottle for fighting, he hated disputes and contention; all he wanted was a quiet life.

Dora and Joe had been to Jersey on holiday shortly after the war ended. Because the Channel Islands had been occupied by the Germans during the war, the only part of the British Isles to suffer that indignity, they were given special treatment when the war ended. Jersey was not only beautiful, with much better weather than mainland Britain, but it was also a miniature Switzerland, with plenty of the food and other goods that were still rationed and scarce on the mainland. In 1948, Dora and Joe sold their shares in the company and their house in Redcar and moved to St Brelade's Bay, Jersey. Dora did not really want to go; her heart was still in the business and she did not want to leave my mother, who came increasingly to miss her. The name "Guisborough" was to her what "Calais" had been to Queen Mary – engraved on her heart!

Max, without Joe, Dora and effectively my mother, though she tried hard despite her illness, had no one to restrain him. My father had neither the strength of character needed, nor the will. It may be that he actually had faith in Max's ideas, and supported him. Max's concept and ambition, as he one day explained to me, was to create a pyramidical structure of companies; to provide not simply the means of production, but also the supply of the raw materials for such production, and the distribution of the produced goods to the public. There were corporate structures such as this; Weaver to Wearer, and Montague Burton were well-known companies at the time dealing in clothing. M&S did this indirectly, in that they controlled the supply of the raw materials to their manufacturers and the quality of the manufactured goods, but they did not seek to own them. They were content for all their suppliers, direct and indirect, to make profits, and helped them to do so. They regarded their echelons as a family.

Max's long-term and laudable ambition was for the business to become a public company, quoted on the Stock Exchange. Max's ideas might have worked had the necessary level of management, the right skills and the necessary finance been available. Unfortunately they were not. The requisite skills would have had to be brought in from outside, not merely outside the family but from other parts of the country. This would have meant outsiders coming in and a consequent surrender – at least partial – of control.

There were three principal difficulties in this. First was that the idea of bringing strangers into the family business was inconceivable to my family; they found it hard enough to appoint managers of any department. The second was that even if this barrier could have been overcome, Guisborough was not an area to which it would be easy to attract people of the necessary quality; it was still comparatively remote, and access was difficult. There were no motorways, no internal air travel, and the main railway line was 45 minutes away. The third was that there would have been conflict with anyone who sought, as anyone worthy of his or her salt would have done, to instil some financial discipline.

Max's ambitious projects required finance. If they were to be realised the strictest economy was necessary; this meant ploughing all profits back in to the business and restricting expenditure, both for business and private purposes. Salaries and dividends paid to directors and shareholders should have been severely limited. Good husbandry was needed. Joe was the strict advocate of this. He could see that lack of financial planning would be disastrous and rather than continue to fight this battle, he left the company.

The company was treated like a milch cow for private purposes. Though a company, it was, as regards the family, essentially a partnership. Theoretically, the drawings of each director were limited, but what happened in practice was that in addition to the drawings, every item of personal expenditure was treated as a business expense. Thus, when one claimed expenses or put private purchases through the business the others also did so, to avoid losing out. In short, the cash in the business was treated as being for private expenditure. One reason for doing this is to minimise tax; though this is a dubious practice it is not uncommon in small privately owned companies, but the prerequisite to paying tax is making profits. The effect of this drain on the company's resources was to leave it short of working capital, and the bank borrowings which had to be guaranteed by the directors were constantly being increased without being matched by a proportionate increase in assets.

One beneficial after-effect of Oma's death was a slight thaw in the relationship with Herman. Though he was still not allowed to participate in the management of the business, a niche was found for him as the company's sales representative. A new company, Harold Stephenson Ltd., was formed to act as a sales agency in London. A plush and quite unjustifiably expensive office was opened for Herman in Regent Street. This proved wholly unsuccessful and another wasted expense.

Herman and Max embarked on a number of trips to America and Canada to look at new production methods, and also to find export customers, another of Max's ideas. These junkets were all very expensive and of doubtful value. It was not the ideas which were wrong; it was the failure to realise that there was no one who could implement them. Max thought he could do so himself and that was the fatal flaw in his plans. I say Max, throughout, because he was the driving force, and he simply steamrollered all opposition. The tragedy was that my mother was not well enough to continue fighting him, my father did not have the guts to do so and Joe and Dora had the sense to get as far away as was possible without actually going abroad.

For some reason, the directors decided that it would be beneficial to invest in large quantities of cloth, as a safeguard against rising prices and to ensure continuity of supply. There was something of the wartime siege mentality in this: it was common to stockpile goods to ensure continuity of supply and keep the machines turning. Large quantities of cloth were bought. This was all striped material, in designs and colours then fashionable. Much of it was made up speculatively into shirts. Unfortunately, the fashion suddenly changed as fashions do; plain white and pastel-coloured shirts with coat fronts, that is, all buttons down the front, became popular and stripes could no longer be sold. Double-fronted shirts with stiff collars were out. Had the cloth not been made up into shirts perhaps the losses might have been manageable, as the material might have found another market. Once made up into unsellable garments, it was a complete loss. This cost the company dearly.

Not long after Dora and Joe had gone to Jersey an offer of some £60,000, a large sum then, was received from a third party for the company. I subsequently worked out that had that sum been accepted, and invested, say, in M&S shares at the time, none of the family – including my generation – would have needed to work again. We could have become rich overnight, rather like winning the pools. The offer was rejected, not because it was considered inadequate, but because the business had ceased to be – if it ever was – simply a means of livelihood. It was an end in itself. No offer would have been enough. The family no longer owned the business: it owned them. It proved a hard taskmaster and exacted a high price.

None of the problems in the business had any immediate effect on me nor was I aware of them except for the constant loud and obviously unpleasant arguments, which I could hardly fail to notice. Whenever they started I went to my own room, where I happily spent most of my time. A side effect of the move to Brierfield was that we were less exposed to these arguments, as it was not quite as easy to get to us from, say, Max's house, which was directly opposite the Grey House but now a few hundred yards away; a sufficient distance to be an inhibiting factor and create a cooling-off period. Moreover, though the rest of the family treated Brierfield as their home, as they had the Grey House, they appreciated that it was our house, not theirs, and did not take the same liberties as they would have done in the Grey House.

Chapter 37 – Illness

My mother's condition was now giving rise to serious concern. Her high blood pressure was disabling, she suffered breathing problems, she was unable to stand for any length of time and could no longer work. She went again to the Zurich clinic and had to live by a strict routine and diet, so that she would be fit for an operation without which her life expectancy would be very short. She weighed 14 stone, and was only 5' 2" tall. Like all the women in her family she was top-heavy: she had a big bust and very thin ankles and legs. Given her condition she was always liable to lose her balance and fall, as she had in Zurich on her first visit. Unable to work, but temperamentally unable to do nothing, my mother took up playing the piano which she had done in her youth, and with her share of the family's musical gifts, soon became quite accomplished. It certainly gave her great pleasure, and I enjoyed hearing her play.

The business problems did nothing to help mother's condition. In 1948, at Guy's Hospital, London, she had the prescribed operation. It was a relatively untried form of surgery performed by a Mr Ross, a highly regarded specialist in his field, by whom it had been developed. It was successful as far as it went, but Mother needed a very long period of recuperation.

Mother decided to reactivate one of her earlier interests, dressmaking. She bought a dressmaker's dummy, took a couple of old sewing machines from the factory, converted one of the rooms on the top floor of Brierfield into a workroom, and began making dresses, first for herself and then for other members of the family. To help her she took on a seamstress, an extremely large Italian lady, for whom she converted the first floor of the garage into a flat. My mother did nothing by halves.

As I've said, we had a very large garden with 200 feet of greenhouse in which we grew tomatoes, flowers, grapes and other fruits, and herbs. When she needed exercise, Mother would walk around the garden, and she loved pottering in the greenhouse, potting and repotting plants, growing her herbs, tomatoes and veg-etables. She proved to have green fingers, showing again how extraordinarily adept she was at any task. She also derived much pleasure from our large vegetable garden though she was too weak to do any gardening. It seemed to me that despite her condition, my mother had never been happier. She no longer had to carry the burden of the business; she could spend her time doing what she really enjoyed and was as relaxed as it was possible for her to be.

Chapter 38 – A Visitor

Saltburn-by-the-Sea was at one time a very popular seaside resort. It is an attractive seaside town, beautifully situated on a clifftop overlooking a magnificent long sandy beach. On a fine day there is no pleasanter spot in England. The only problem is the lack of fine days; even when it is sunny, there is usually a cold wind blowing unimpeded across the North Sea from Russia. Overlooking the promenade stood the Zetland Hotel, a fine example of Victorian Gothic hotel architecture, and an excellent establishment of its kind, with its high ceilings, large public rooms and the best beer in the area; the ideal place to quench your anticipated thirst before the evening's entertainment.

At the end of the promenade just opposite the Zetland, a steep winding road leads down to the seafront. Half way down stands, or stood, "Spa", a dance hall with a real live orchestra. The place was simple but it was pleasant and convivial. There were many very pretty girls. It was a respectable place. As my school friends, who were all a year or two (or even three) years older than me, started to go there, I would join them on Saturday nights. I went by train as I was not yet old enough to drive, nor, if truth be told, to go to the Spa. I was only sixteen, and usually stayed over-night after the dance with one or other of my friends – usually Peter Radford – coming home the next day. There were special late buses to the local villages, but not to Middlesbrough, and in any case, I preferred to finish off the night with my mates and the girls we met at the dance rather than making a long, lonely, inebriated way home.

One unusually hot summer Saturday afternoon, about teatime, that is four o'clock, in late July as I recall, not long after my sixteenth birthday and shortly after we had moved to Brierfield, my parents and I were sitting in the garden when there was a ring at the door. We were surprised, as this was not a usual visiting hour, and in any event anyone we knew would simply walk straight in without ringing – doors were never locked in those days. I went to the lobby door and opened it. I could not believe my eyes. Standing there, with an older lady who was obviously her mother, was the most gorgeous girl. She was about 5 feet 3 inches tall, slim, long wavy brown hair, well made-up – lipstick, eye shadow, mascaraed eyelashes, painted fingernails, high heels, silk (I suppose they were nylon but then I did not know the difference) stockings, well and fashionably dressed: in short, the lot. To have goods like this delivered to the door was unbelievable. It was every boy's dream. Girls like that were not seen in my part of the world, except in films or on the front cover of fashion magazines. When I managed to tear my eyes off her, I heard her equally well-turned-out mother ask whether she had found the right house. I am sure that she said more than this but I didn't hear. So far as I was concerned, she had, and the accuracy or otherwise of my response seemed irrelevant at the time, so I assured her that she had, and took her through to the garden.

The lady was a Mrs Margolin, whose family came from Middlesbrough, and she was here on a visit. She and her family had gone to Canada at the outbreak of the war and now lived there. She had met Max and Herman, some few weeks earlier, while they were there on business. She had been standing behind them in a queue at a post office and had heard them mention Middlesbrough as Max was trying to post a parcel home. She made herself known to them and invited them home. Max had given her our address. Why Max should have given her our address and not his own, I do not know, but I was duly grateful. Tea was served and the adults chatted away. I remained dumbstruck. I could not take my eyes off the girl who sat silent. Eventually I plucked up enough courage to ask her whether she would like to come to the dance at the Spa with me that evening. She referred the invitation to her mother.

I remember the conversation vividly: "Yes," said the mother, "she can go with you, but you must promise to look after her. By the way, I think you should know she's only thirteen." Then after a long pause, during which my face must have been a picture, she said, giving me a chance to get off the hook, "Are you still sure you want to take her?"

My mother expressed some wonder that so young a girl should look so sophisticated. Her mother explained that she was typical of young girls in Canada. The mother herself, with her English background, deplored this preciosity, but felt she had to swim with the tide; that was how all the young girls were where they lived.

Only a Bateman cartoon could have done justice to my expression. But I have, I hope, always been a gentleman. I renewed the invitation and eventually we went off to catch the train. Dad took me to one side before we went, and suggested we took a taxi to and from the station, giving me £5.00 (a lot then) to cover the "extra expenses" as he put it. Never before had he commented on my going out with a girl. Once we were alone it became apparent that she was only thirteen. Her appearance may have been that of a girl aged 20, but her conversation was in keeping with her years. Her looks belied her sophistication. I swore her to secrecy as to her age, which met with no reluctance, pointing out that she was below the permitted age limit for the Spa. When we arrived at the Spa I introduced her to my friends, who buzzed round her like bees at a honey pot. She was a great success and had, she said on the way home, "a fantastic time". Her transatlantic accent added to her allure; my friends had seen nothing like her, except in the movies, and her lack of conversation and immaturity were not noticed. My standing at school on the following Monday was at an all-time high.

I then debated with myself whether to tell them her age. After they had all drooled over their recollection of her for some time, I could not resist teasing them further, and did tell them. To a man, they flatly refused to believe me. There were some crestfallen faces when I managed to convince them.

Chapter 39 – Other Friends

I had a number of good friends in Middlesbrough. Two in particular, Michael Blakey and Geoffrey Bindman, who lived very close, would collect me to go to synagogue every Saturday and on the Jewish Festivals. They were both a little younger than me, but apart from parties and going to synagogue I did not see very much of them. Michael's father was a Professor of Mathematics, and his mother a member of the family which owned a chain of dress shops in the North East. In Middlesbrough it later proved a fruitful source of attractive models.

Arnold Brechner, Louis Lazarus and I were for a long time a threesome. Both were a little older than me. Arnold and I had a number of interests in common. He was highly intelligent, and even more obsessive than I was at any interest he developed. When he decided to take up chess, he got all available chess books out from the library and studied all aspects of the game; he replayed the games of the great chess masters. He imparted much of his knowledge to, and tried his ideas out on, me. He joined the local chess club which played on Mondays at the Literary & Philosophical Society's premises, and got me to do so as well. I was the youngest member, but chess is a great leveller of ages, and I more than held my own.

Arnold later took up bridge with the same thoroughness, and as a result I started to play, rather than just watch my parents, which is how I first learned to play. We shared a love of music, especially opera, and here too, he was my mentor, introducing me to many singers and new music. I did not follow his lead in everything. Yom Kippur is the holiest occasion of the Jewish year. Yom Kippur is treated seriously even by those who have no qualms about breaking the Sabbath laws. One Yom Kippur eve as we were walking home from synagogue, Arnold lit and smoked a cigarette; this was sin beyond redemption. However, the heavens did not fall, he was not struck down on the spot, and the world

160

was no different the following day. But that was not an example I wished to follow, and, indeed, there was in that act an air of arrogance, of defiance, which worried me. Young as I was, I detected a lack of judgment and of balance. I felt a loss of trust which harmed our relationship.

Louis was a very pleasant, gentle fellow, always full of fun and ready to please. He was completely different from Arnold. Unfortunately, Louis suffered from ill health and died young some twenty years later.

I could scarcely wait for my seventeenth birthday. I immediately applied for my driving licence, and for my driving test. Bob Hodgkinson, our wartime taxi driver, had promised to teach me to drive. He still had his pre-war Morris, which he kept in tip-top condition and it says much for his good nature that he entrusted it to me. I took to driving like a duck to water. In fact, I was over-confident, and failed my first test for going too fast, but succeeded the second time, in October. By then I had had considerable practice, as I took every opportunity to drive. Driving brought a new dimension to my life, particularly my social life.

Once I learned to drive, Mother decided she should do so too, and she bought a small Austin 10 for our joint use. My father's Vauxhall 14, which had been laid up for most of the war, was replaced by a Rover 16, which was fast, comfortable, reliable, and technically very advanced.

One consequence of being able to drive was that I spent much more time with my parents. Whereas previously I showed little interest in accompanying them on their journeys, unless they were to go to a show or a wedding, now I would go with them, school and other commitments permitting, at the drop of a hat regardless of the purpose of the trip. I was very keen to drive; my father was happy to let me drive even on our long journeys to Leeds and London. The roads then were bad. There were no motorways. Many stretches were three-lane carriageways, an invitation to disaster. But, like Toad, I enjoyed the open road, and the thrill of driving fast.

One unexpected side effect of my being able to drive was that it seemed to me that suddenly I was being taken more seriously by my family. That may have simply been my conception and that there had been a gradual progression, but passing my driving test was a watershed. It marked the transition from boyhood to adulthood. As mentioned, I also began to see more of my parents. I accordingly adjusted my schedule to enable me to drive my parents to and from Guisborough daily. In going to and fro with my parents I spoke and listened to them more. I also began to understand some of their difficulties. It ended the isolation which our separate routines had created and began the process of bridging the gap in our mutual understanding. The drive to London took about seven hours. It had been a long time since I had spent so long, uninterrupted, with my parents.

Through my new mobility the Spa, and the area east of Guisborough where my friends lived, became much more accessible, and so did girls. My popularity increased. This may, however, have been due to Dad's car, which he lent me when he did not need it, usually on a Saturday night. I was very fond of the Rover. After three years, during which it had done some 150,000 miles (an enormous amount for a car then), he replaced it with a Daimler. This was a "posh" car and I didn't like it. It was heavy and sluggish, and had none of the sporty feel of the Rover. It was an old man's car. I did not feel comfortable in it. It was too showy; it was too redolent of opulence and success. It didn't feel right. The Daimler was inappropriate.

The bare and uncomfortable Austin 10 was soon replaced by a pretty, white Hillman Minx, an excellent little car, with the advantage of a bench-type front seat which meant that you did not have to get into the back seat for amorous purposes! It was also a very nippy car. I drove it at speeds which it was never designed to reach. Mr Toad would have been proud of me.

When his pre-war Ford needed replacement, Max, for some whimsical reason, bought a small two-seater Triumph coupe, with a third seat, known as a dickey seat, at the back. This was open to the elements. Though an attractive car, it was a car for the single man wishing to attract girls. Max may have wished to create a new image for himself, but Jeanne had other ideas, and anything more impractical for a family man, and less suited to Jeanne's dimensions, would be hard to imagine. That car did not last long and Max, as a true Schmulewitsch, went from one extreme to another, and acquired an Austin Princess, a large stately car, the type usually seen in funeral processions or transporting dignitaries, more suited to his standing (and to Jeanne's figure). Max could not be trusted to drive this, if only because it required both hands, and a chauffeur was duly engaged.

This was Gene (actually Eugene) Stratton, an ex-policeman, whose duties became more general. He seemed to spend most of his time in the kitchen at Brierfield. I think he was sweet on Tessie, but she wouldn't look at him, even though she was flattered by his attentions. She could have done worse, because he was a tall, good-looking man, with a large outgoing personality, and like many big men, though strong, he was very kind and gentle. He was also obliging and conscientious. He gave me many police hints on driving, and when I came to go to university would usually take me there or collect me at the end of the year, when I had to bring all my things home. It was on one such occasion that I recorded my fastest London to Middlesbrough time of 4 hours 20 minutes in the Daimler. Today, the same journey can be accomplished with ease in three hours, but in those days to achieve a speed like that was "going some!"

The inspection pit in the Brierfield garage gave me the chance to do my own car maintenance. Rather as Opa had often unnecessarily repaired his grandfather clock, I would change the oil, and the plugs, and generally mess about with the car more frequently than necessary. Car parts were large enough even for my clumsy fingers. This was real-life Meccano. I did not always plan ahead and one day I decided to change the oil. I thought that while the oil was draining I would take the opportunity to wash the car, and instead of draining the sump over the pit, I took the car outside into the open to wash it, leaving a bowl under the engine to catch the oil. I had no sooner finished cleaning and polishing the car when – inevitably – it started to rain, so I pushed the car into the garage, forgetful of the basin underneath it. My mother and Tessie looked on in amazement as I came into the house wearing no shoes, socks or trousers. I felt explanations were superfluous.

Chapter 41 – School: The Final Years

Having reached the sixth form ahead of schedule, and having decided that I would take History, French, English and Latin for my Higher School Certificate, in two years time, I discovered to my delight that the HSC could be taken after only one year. Subjects could be taken as two main subjects and two subsidiary, or three (or more) main subjects. I decided that I had to take the HSC in one year rather than two. I have no idea now why. It may have been simply my competitive urge; no doubt Peter Radford was doing so. On reflection now it was rather pointless, but had I not had the incentive to pass some exams at the end of the year, I would undoubtedly simply have bummed around, which might not have been a bad thing. I am, at heart, an idle fellow and unless I have something to aim for, some incentive or impetus, I can wallow quite happily in a sea of sloth. My redemption lies, I think, in my low boredom threshold. My life has been a constant struggle within me between boredom and indolence; the score is about even.

Despite, or possibly because of, the general discouragement against my taking the HSC in one year I insisted on doing so. To avoid a large amount of egg on my face I had to pass, and thankfully I did. I did well in three subjects. I scraped home in Latin, and thereafter abandoned it. I was now just 16, and could set my ambitions on higher things. I had resolved to go to the Bar, and to go to Oxford or Cambridge, mainly because in effect these were the only two universities of which I knew anything. I knew that there were excellent universities elsewhere, including Durham, and London, but so far as I was concerned it was Oxbridge or nothing.

I took the HSC twice more, rather to stop me from being idle than for any specific purpose. I was a little like the driver who races to be first at the traffic lights and then has to wait while everyone else catches up. The traffic lights in my case were national service. Before that, however, I had to make sure of my place at university. When I took the HSC for the fourth time in June 1948, I also took a special Scholarship paper in English. I remember the first question. The first paragraphs from four books were quoted and the examinee was asked to indicate what sort of book they respectively introduced and to comment on them. I had read and recognised them all. "It was the best of times and it was the worst of times" was the first quotation. It was from *A Tale of Two Cities* which I had read several times, by my favourite author, Charles Dickens. I was given what I was told was the highest mark ever in an S level exam: 93 per cent. There was a considerable element of luck, but it made me wonder whether English, and not History, was my best subject.

Since Geoff Farringdon's return my understanding of and affection for English as a subject had greatly increased, and I seemed to have an aptitude for it, as "foreigners" – that is, people whose mother language is not English – allegedly often do. I cannot say, however, that it was a foreign or second language to me, or that I regarded myself then or since as a foreigner, and to have been called such would have been taken as a major insult. But I was taught English and accordingly understood its grammar.

My parents took no part in any of the discussions, far less decisions, regarding what examinations I took, and plans for university. They felt that because they did not know or understand the system, they could make no useful contribution other than a financial one, and that was never an issue. I doubt if they even knew when I had an examination or, if by chance they had heard mention from me of one, which it was or what it was for. Indeed, their ignorance of my examination schedule led to one of the rare tiffs I had with my mother. My parents' parties were noisy. My family were themselves noisy as large families tend to be, but it was not the party activities which were noisy, in fact they were usually fairly placid as cards were played at most parties; it was the leave-taking at the end. Jewish people seem reluctant to go home after a party. They can stand for hours, with their hats and coats on, at the door telling stories and gossiping and doing all the things they did not have time for through the evening, and as this activity takes place in the hallway, the noise travels up the stairs or through the windows, and disturbs one's sleep. This happened one night before one of my more important examinations. Aroused from sleep at about 2 a.m. by a great din of talking and laughing, I went to the top of the stairs in my pyjamas and remonstrated mildly: at least I thought I was being mild. I merely asked them please to be quiet. My mother soundly berated me the next morning. I pointed out in self-defence that I had an exam coming up and needed my sleep. She more or less indicated that that was my problem; this was her house and the people I was alleged to have insulted were her friends. Words followed, and I left home in high dudgeon vowing never to return. I went round from house to house of family and friends seeking comfort, shelter and solace. No one locked their doors then; every house was open. You just walked in and if you saw no one you shouted. It was incredible, as if there had been a conspiracy, not one person was at home. I went to Jeanne and Max, to Arnold Brechner, to Louis Lazarus, to the Blakeys, to everyone I could think of. I had not yet learned to drive so I was limited to areas I could reach on foot. A frustrated refugee, I returned home with my tail between my legs. Peace broke out. I never complained again, but nor was I given any cause to do so.

Before the summer holiday in 1949, the Head, who was himself at Trinity College, Oxford, called me to his study, and told me that he was putting me in for a scholarship to Exeter. I objected and told him that I was only interested in going to Oxford. He assured me that he meant Exeter College, Oxford. Of course, I had never heard of that college. I said that I wanted to go to Balliol, which I knew of because Rabbi Miller's son, Alan, was there and because it was the first college to admit Jewish and col- oured students – hence the famous remark, allegedly from a Trinity man, who on seeing a canoe rowed by black natives in the film *Sanders of the River*, shouted out "Well rowed, Balliol".

However, Oxford was Oxford, whatever unknown college I had been entered for, and one cold early October day I turned up at Exeter College to sit the entrance scholarship examination. I was not entirely sure what this actually meant. I felt completely strange. Oxford colleges are not always inviting places once you leave the gardens and the quads. Term had not yet started, and the candidates were all accommodated in college. The porter told me my room number and the staircase on which it was situated.

Staircases are to an Oxford college what streets are to a town, and about as easy to find without a map, because it must not be assumed that they are numbered in any logical order, or that they are all in the same quad. The authorities assume a certain intelligence in their applicants, and set them a little obstacle test when they arrive. If you can find your room unaided you have a chance of getting a place.

I duly found my room, and was tempted immediately to turn around and go straight back home. It was dismal. It was small and cold, there was no running water, and although a jug and basin were provided, there was no water in the jug. There was no central heating. Instead, there was a small black fireplace with some paper and coal. As the room had not yet been allotted to any undergraduate, it was bare and bore no marks of habitation. Nor did it bear any signs of having been redecorated at any time since the turn of the century or indeed even since its construction some centuries earlier. I began to wonder whether Oxford was such a good idea after all.

I realised what a great advantage the boys who had been to public school had. They were used to such conditions, not only from their schools, but probably from their homes. For them it was merely a change of location, like being moved from one prison to another. The surroundings would be familiar, and they came up in phalanxes with the same boys they had been with since prep school. Grammar school boys like me coming from fairly comfortable – in my case very comfortable – warm and welcoming homes were unused to such conditions. And it was only October: the mind boggled at what December would be like.

After I had had a chance to become better acquainted with my surroundings, and the first shock had worn off, there was a knock at the door. It was followed by a cheery person wearing what appeared to be morning dress, but turned out to be a black jacket and pin-striped trousers, which had seen better days. It was only some time later that I discovered that as a general rule, in Oxford (and no doubt Cambridge too), a person's style of dress was in direct inverse proportion to his position in the hierarchy of a college. I say "his" because, at that time, "hers" was not a possibility.

"Good day to you Sir," he said in a strong Oxfordshire accent. "I see you're making yourself comfy. I'll bring you some hot water to wash, and a cup of tea, in a moment. You'll find the bathroom on the next floor and the toilets are on the floor below."

The place had obviously been designed by architects whose last thought, typically, was the convenience of the user. This was my "scout", the servant allocated by the college to the particular staircase whose duties included making one's bed, lighting one's fire(s), and in cases like mine, holding one's hand. I had never seen one before, nor was I then sure of his function, but he was very welcome. I thought to myself that the Englishman's panacea for all ills, his equivalent to the Jewish mother's chicken soup, would be most welcome. The tea duly arrived with some biscuits and the scout gave me a short briefing on the procedures of the college, times of meals and where to find what I might need.

Oxford entrance examinations were set in groups of colleges, and in one's application form the candidate's order of preference is listed. Candidates are usually accommodated in the first choice college. We all had dinner in the college hall, which like that of most colleges was austere, but with beautiful panelling and por-traits of past Masters and famous alumni. My epicurean taste buds had not yet been developed and I found the food palatable if a little sparse, but food was still rationed, three years after the war had ended.

I have a selective memory block as regards the few days I spent at Exeter College. The examination papers took me com-pletely aback. I had no idea how to approach the questions, which were set in a way I did not recognise, quite different from those with which I had become familiar in the HSC exams. I had not had the benefit of seeing any previous papers, and it was rather like asking someone used only to multiple choice papers, requiring only an "X" or "Yes" or "No" to be inserted in a space, to write a thesis. I was out of my depth and floundering.

The exams ended on the Friday. I had an interview with the college dons, and by the time I returned to the school on the following Monday my headmaster had received the result. I had failed to be offered a place. I was not surprised, but I was devastated. I had never failed in any examination before. It was not simply that I had done so, but the manner of it. I had, to paraphrase Aneurin Bevan, walked unarmed into the examination chamber. I had no doubts as to my ability, but I realised that I could no longer get by by the seat of my pants or by improvisation; knowledge of the salient facts was assumed by the examiners. What they were testing was the examinee's critical capacity and the original thought applied to that knowledge. This required extensive reading over and beyond the recognised textbooks. It also required a knowledge of political movements, of social influences, and above all the latest thinking and writing on the subject. There was no point in relying on 19th century political philosophers in the context of 20th century discourse. I had not been schooled in this respect by my history master as I had been, in contrast, by Geoff Farringdon in English. I simply did not know enough which was inexcusable as I had had plenty of time to acquire the necessary knowledge.

Fortunately, my old school friend Tony Hearn was home from Oxford researching for his thesis at the time and I discussed the matter with him. He was himself a historian, and clearly brilliant enough to have obtained an open scholarship to Trinity College, Oxford, despite having the same disadvantages at school as I had had, and, indeed, outside school many more. He took me in hand; he gave me a reading list, which included names such as Asa Briggs, Lewis Namier, and others of whom, to my shame, I had not heard, nor, to his even greater shame, had my history master, Mr Thomas. The school, primarily in the persons of Geoff Farringdon and the headmaster, rallied round me. Geoff Farringdon simply said that he would take charge of ensuring that I was properly prepared for the next try.

Application was immediately made to enter me for the Balliol Scholarship Examination in December, and "Operation Freddy" was set in motion. I was relieved from all school duties and attended school only as required by Mr Farringdon. I worked at home or in libraries. As a backup, I was also entered for the entrance examination to St John's College Cambridge, which was to be held in January 1950, this time for English as opposed to

History. I read all that Tony Hearn had prescribed; I obtained and worked on previous scholarship examination papers, and did virtually nothing else for the next few weeks. My Saturday night at the Spa was, however, sacrosanct.

I returned to Oxford to sit the Balliol exam in December. Balliol was no more luxurious than Exeter College had been, and my room overlooked Broad Street and Exeter College. But this time I knew what to expect. Strangely, I felt at home as soon as I walked through the Balliol front gate. I was more at ease, better prepared and my heavily shaken confidence was gradually returning. I resumed acquaintance with some of the October candidates who had been similarly unsuccessful. We greeted each other like long-lost friends. The food was better at Exeter; Balliol's reputation for academic excellence was then equalled only by that for the poor quality of its food, except on special occasions.

I took the exams and felt very much more at ease with the papers. On the Thursday afternoon, in the middle of the Latin paper, I was called out for an interview. The panel of Balliol dons – I cannot recall how many there were but there seemed to be about eight – included the Master, Sir David Lindsay Keir, Theo Tylor, the Law tutor, Christopher Hill, a history don and Russell Meiggs, a classicist and Praefectus of Holywell Manor. I was in a slight daze, as I had been exercising my powers of concentration on the Latin translation, and was not quite sure why I had been interrupted in the middle of the paper. When asked to go for the interview I at first demurred on the grounds that I had not finished my paper but I was assured that that did not matter, and that I really could go. I thought to myself, in that case, why bother with the Latin paper at all.

I was put at ease, and was asked a number of questions. One I remember was what could I do for Balliol? I replied that the reputation and standing of the college were such that it would be pretentious for me to suggest that I would be able to affect it one way or another. However, I would endeavour to be a conscientious member of the college, if admitted, and devote to it such talents as I had.

I was also asked whether I needed to rely financially on the grant of a scholarship or exhibition to come up to Oxford. Rather caught off-balance by this question, but sensing that victory was at hand, I spurted out that, financially, I was quite independent of any grant, but in any event I had already been awarded a Middlesbrough major scholarship (the equivalent of a county major scholarship) which would see me through. All I was really after was a place.

I then went to Aunt Yetti's in London and returned home on the Sunday. I went to school on the following Monday to report to Mr Farringdon. I arrived there some time after the morning assembly, when classes had already started. I was standing alone in the sixth form common room when he came in.

"Have you seen the Head?" he asked. "He was looking for you."

"No," I replied, wondering what I had done wrong.

At that moment the headmaster appeared and put his head round the door. "Come into my study," he said.

I followed him somewhat nervously.

"This may be of interest to you," he said, handing me a letter. It was from Balliol.

I did not need to read beyond the first few words: "I am pleased..." I could not restrain a whoop of delight which the whole school must have heard. I then read the letter again in full. It was a short letter to say that they were offering me a place, and that my tutor-to-be, Theo Tylor, would be writing to me. They required me to come up after I had completed my national service. I reread the letter a few times, just to make sure that it referred to me and that there was no mistake. The Head congratulated me very warmly; Geoff Farringdon, who had been lurking outside the door knowing about the letter – in fact, everybody seemed to know about it but me, as the Head had mentioned it at assembly from which I was absent – shook my hand and hugged me with pleasure, a quite unusual display of emotion. It had been a team effort, largely orchestrated by him, and it was as much his achievement as mine to have turned me from a no-hoper to a successful candidate in under two months. Then I ran all the way to Dad's office with the news.

This time I had not been anticipated. My father was not an emotional man – at least not demonstratively so – but the look on his face and the tears shed by my mother when I saw her later in the day, expressed not only pride and pleasure but a vindication of their policy in regard to my upbringing, which involved considerable sacrifice on their part, though this had not always been obvious to me. And, though I had obtained, in most years, a school prize or received some sort of mention my parents had never once, in all my school days, attended a school sports or prize-giving day.

To put the matter in perspective, however, Neville Cohen, my cousin by marriage, was awarded an open scholarship to St John's College, Oxford to read Classics at the age of 16. He was at the City of London School which may have helped him, although Tony Hearn got his open scholarship, and Peter Radford obtained a place at Keble College, Oxford to read Divinity, without, apparently, any of the difficulties I had, and coming from the same school as me. Where I did lead the way was in my single-mindedness and determination, from an early age, to get to Oxbridge. I think this may have encouraged others to do the same, at a time when it was still considered difficult to get into Oxbridge without a public-school education, and sending his boys to Oxbridge was not within our headmaster's contemplation.

In due course, I received a letter from Theo Tylor, the Law tutor, containing a list of books he wished me to read before going up to college and confirming that to avoid a break between leaving Oxford and starting a career in Law, I should complete my army service before going up. He was quite right.

I had received my call-up papers shortly after I reached 18, in June 1949, but had obtained a postponement to enable me to take my various entrance examinations, and would have been granted a further postponement to go to university had that been requested. Now that I had my place I was anxious to get into the army and out again as quickly as possible, and there was no one who appeared keener to join His Majesty's Forces than me. I attended the recruiting office, of which I was to see much more before long, daily. I went for my medical which was uneventful, though I was in no mood for the jocularity shown by the medics. My call-up papers arrived in February requiring me to present myself at the Army Selection Centre, Aldershot on 11 March 1950.

It should be noted that not all my energies were devoted to scholastic effort. I never worked on Saturdays, or Sundays if I could help it. The Sabbath day was sacrosanct but, unlike my father, I extended it as long as I could, not for the sake of religious observance, but to give me a full clear day without work. I have kept up that practice throughout my life. On Saturday nights I continued to go to the Spa. I had many girlfriends but none was in any way regular. In fact, my hormones were in overdrive; I felt like Cherubino, the sex-mad page in *The Marriage of Figaro*. I loved dancing and despite being overweight, about which I was slightly self-conscious, but not so that I felt in any way inhibited, I was light on my feet and danced well.

A very different sexual climate existed then. Victorian *mores* still prevailed. In this respect the culture was not different from that at home, where sex was not spoken of, though there was no suggestion that it was considered sinful. My part of the world had both a large Catholic population, and a strong Wesleyan influence among Protestants. Both regarded sex outside marriage as sinful. It was also Yorkshire, where girls did not "flirt or flaunt". Sex, in the sense of full intercourse, was not readily available (at least for free), and certainly not from the sort of girls we knew, unless there had been commitment to marriage, and often not even then. Many of these girls were the sisters of friends and there was an under-standing that they were untouchable. It was not easy to get a girl into bed, and there were certain girls with whom you did not even try. My approach was to keep on until the girls said "No", which at some stage, varying from one girl to another, unfortunately they usually did. The Monday morning round-up of the weekend's activities was full of tales of frustration, often at the last gasp.

There were good practical reasons for girls' reluctance to go the whole hog. The Pill was still unknown; condoms, or French letters as we called them, were not easily available. They were not displayed openly on chemists' counters; they were generally sold only at gents' hairdressers. When we were young few of us had the temerity to ask for these in a shop full of people, and there was no guarantee that the barber would sell them to you if you looked too young. Later, as we got older, the barber, after he had finished his task and was about to take his 1/6d from you, would discreetly through the back of his hand or from the side of his mouth ask, "Would there be anything else, Sir?" But it was some years before I was old enough to be "Sir". The risk of an unwanted pregnancy was great and the social services did not look favourably on the unmarried mother, nor did society at large. Abortion was back door, done by some unauthorised person, and was expensive and dangerous. The cake was not worth the candle.

Bras had not yet been burned; women's sexuality and their demands were still stifled by male domination; Germaine Greer had not yet published her seminal book *The Female Eunuch*. Women's liberation, if it had been thought of seriously at all, was dismissed as unimportant. We were living in the age in which parts even of *Gulliver's Travels* were considered pornographic. Classics were bowdlerised. Even some ten years later, Crown Counsel in the failed prosecution of Calder, the publishers of *Lady Chatterley*, did not think it ridiculous (though the rest of the world did) to ask the jury whether they would "allow their wives and servants" to read it. As against that, this sort of morality did place an obligation on the male to act responsibly, and it had, so far as I was concerned, with my Jewish background, an inhibiting effect. I cannot say that it castrated me, but I was more careful, and possibly more caring, than I imagine I would have been had I been that age today.

The girls' school equivalent to my school was the Saltburn High School for Girls. It was the school to which my friends' sisters went. Its girls went to the Spa as we did and it supplied most of my class with their girlfriends. I first saw Norma at the Spa. She was stunning – tall, about 5' 7" – she looked like Vera-Ellen the film star, with her colouring (a sort of blonde auburn), and had a figure like Rita Hayworth. I asked my pals who she was. "Forget her," I was told, "she's too big for her boots, and doesn't look at anybody." I gathered that I had a number of frustrated friends.

One night at the Spa I went over to her, introduced myself and asked her to dance. She replied, "So you're Freddy Fishburn! I've heard a lot about you." I expressed surprise that she had heard of me and was delighted that she agreed to dance. She danced well, as I flattered myself I did. There was an immediate mutual attraction.

Norma was the great passion of my youth. She was as intelligent as she was attractive; she had a ready wit, a great sense of fun, and she was passionate. She had a gift for clothes. She could look wonderful wearing a sack. She had a wonderful body, which fulfilled its promise of pneumatic bliss. But above all, she loved me. She was the first girl with whom I had known this mutual love. For all my apparent self-confidence and no lack of girlfriends, I was self-conscious about my weight. It did not hinder me, particularly in any activity I chose to indulge in, but most of my friends, and I suppose as regards girls, competitors, were slim or muscular and good-looking. I looked at them with some envy. Norma did wonders for my self-confidence; she was good for the ego.

Norma was not Jewish. Quite what my parents thought of the matter I never found out. My relationship with Norma was never mentioned, though my parents must have known all about it, if only from Tessie, who appeared to have given Norma her seal of approval. I now realise that this was symptomatic of the increasingly different worlds in which my parents and I lived.

I rarely brought Norma home, and then only briefly, on the way to somewhere else; to go to a party, or to meet friends. Both Norma and I knew that our relationship could only be short. It is hard to realise now that we were only sixteen at the time and at eighteen we would have to go our separate ways, Norma to university and I to the army.

We went out together, until Norma went off to university. My parting from Norma was sorrowful. I cannot speak for her but I tried to put on the best face I could. She left a great void in my life. However inevitable it was, and however much we had conditioned ourselves to that day, when it came it was not without tears.

I did not see her again until some twenty years or more later. She telephoned me out of the blue at my office to say she was coming to London and could we have lunch. The day she chose, out of 365 in the year, was my wedding anniversary and my wife was less than pleased but I felt it would have been churlish to refuse. And in any event, I wanted to see her again. Norma had changed very little and maturity sat well on her, but seeing her again I realised that I had been lucky to have had such a wonderful time with her but that was a youthful fling and it ended at just the right time.

There had been other girls before Norma, but my relationships with them had been brief. One, however, was and remains an enigma. The family doctor, Joe Israel, had three daughters. Eleanor was the eldest. She was six months older than me. She was a real tomboy. She could climb trees, run faster, swim better, and do almost anything physical better than most boys, and very much better than I could. Her boyishness contrasted with the somewhat effeminate upbringing I had had and she enjoyed teasing me. Her favourite sport seemed to be to climb up a tree and throw things at me.

Eleanor grew up to be beautiful. She was a free spirit, totally uninhibited, and exuded sexuality. I cannot pretend that I found her anything other than extraordinarily attractive, and she certainly appeared to be attracted to me. However, rather as Groucho Marx would not join any club which would accept him as a member, I was suspicious of girls who made advances to me – that is if I was ever aware of the fact, as I was particularly insensitive in this respect.

It was Tessie who pointed out that Eleanor was "sweet" on me. However, remembering how she had humiliated me in my youth, I was always a bit scared of her. She had a strong, outgoing personality. I had had enough of strong, outgoing personalities within my own family, and regarded such personalities with some caution. Eleanor, like everyone else of my age, was invited to all my parties and it was at one of these that I found myself alone with her. She took the initiative, which was very exciting, but I was too young and inexperienced to fully appreciate her; her ardour frightened me. As girls mature earlier than boys, she was, I suppose, sexually some years ahead of me, even though she was only six months older. I felt instinctively that this was a situation I would not be able to handle. There was about her a generosity of spirit, a joie de vivre, and a lust for adventure, a restlessness, which I found overwhelming. I still regret the missed opportunity, but perhaps it was just as well.

She disappeared from the district about the time I went to university and I had no further contact with Eleanor. I did hear many years later, through the grapevine, that at some stage she had become an air hostess, married an airline pilot, divorced and after a somewhat disjointed and unhappy life, had died quite young of cancer. How true this was I do not know, but it seemed to be in keeping with what I knew of her.

Chapter 44 – Holidays

Though the Swiss holiday is the only one I can recall having had with my parents, there were many holidays with other members of the family, mainly by courtesy of Auntie Jeanne. After Geoffrey, Jeanne had three more children, Rochelle, Stuart and Michael, who was not born until 1953. For several summers Jeanne took a house in Scarborough. The owner was a dyed-in-the-wool communist. He had a lovingly maintained pre-war Jowett, a strange motor car, which had many features ahead of its time about which he would enthuse at great length. He was a strange man, long and thin, and needed little prompting to enter into long diatribes against capitalists and capitalism. He would not accept my argument that by owning property and accepting rent he was himself a capitalist and if he were true to his convictions he would let us have his house for nothing. Not only did this argument fail but he put the rent up every year.

Scarborough was one of the finest holiday resorts in the country. Its setting on a clifftop, overlooking two long and beautiful sandy beaches, was spectacular. The road to Scarborough from Middlesbrough ran through the dramatic scenery of fishing villages such as Staithes and Runswick Bay, the fishing port of Whitby, and part of the North Yorkshire Moors, an area of outstanding beauty. Apart from the sea, which at the height of summer is just about warm enough for a hardened northerner to swim in, Scarborough had many fine public facilities. Every summer a show, usually Edward German's "Merrie England" was staged in Peasholm Park, Scarborough's main park. The stage itself was situated on an island in the lake in the park, and the seats were on the shore opposite. The setting was very attractive, and the conjunction of land and water gave much scope for the producer's inventiveness. The performances were in the evening. In the long northern summer days, night fell late but the weather was frequently uncertain, and the evenings, however hot the day had been, were usually cool. Jeanne ensured that there was a plentiful supply of blankets, hot drinks, sandwiches and cakes. The term "sandwiches" in the context of my aunt is not to be confused with the small, white, delicate, barely visible pieces of cotton wool containing specks of cucumber served for tea at pretentious cafes or in hotel lounges; Auntie Jeanne's sandwiches were American-sized, huge.

She did nothing, at least in the food line, by halves. She was afraid that unless fed regularly every hour or so, we would starve. "A growing boy must eat," she would say. She did not specify in which direction. Having reached my upper limit, quite young, there was nowhere to expand but outwards. I think Jeanne enjoyed having me there with her; her own children were still small, and I was someone to talk to, and to eat with. We got on very well, and we spoke the same language. She was generous and kind, outspoken, without any snobbishness, and bore no grudges after a disagreement.

The proximity of Scarborough both to Middlesbrough and Leeds ensured that there were family visitors every weekend. How they were all accommodated I do not know, but all our houses, even those taken for holiday lets, seemed to have expandable walls. Scarborough was one of my favourite places.

When Jeanne tired of Scarborough she moved the family holidays to Sandbanks, a promontory forming part of Poole, in Dorset, which has the second largest natural harbour in the world. Though the scenery around Poole is not as dramatic as that in Yorkshire, there are many beautiful parts, particularly the Isle of Purbeck, Corfe Castle and the harbour with Brownsea Island in the middle. Its main advantage over Scarborough was the weather. Scarborough was cool except for a few hot days in the summer. In Sandbanks the weather was usually warm, and swimming in the sea did not leave you blue and shivering with cold. In future years we would take our own children there year after year. But the change of venue did not alter the nature of the fare provided by Jeanne, and the holidays I had with her and her family are among the happiest memories of my youth. Wherever Jeanne was there was an open house and no few people to take advantage of it. Neville Cohen often came at the same time as I did and we went off together doing whatever it was that boys do, but never without an adequate supply of sandwiches and other foods. These were the sort of days that Laurie Lee wrote about, days when you hoped that time would stop and you would not grow older.

Dora and Joe settled in Jersey. They had a modern house with a beautiful garden which was Dora's pride and joy and a spectacular view over St Brelade's Bay. That also became a favourite place for holidays. Indeed that became far more than a holiday resort for me, it was a second home. I went there every summer for many years both before and after I was married. The first time I went, in 1947, there were still great shortages on the mainland; rationing in one form or another lasted until 1954 but Jersey was, like Switzerland, a cornucopia. Steaks, butter, cream, sweets, chocolates, and luxury goods which had not been seen since before the war were all readily available in Jersey. Joe had his favourite eating places, usually run by eccentric ex-sailors, some of whom were a parody of themselves, but engaging characters nonetheless. As I did not eat shellfish much of the local produce was of no interest to me but I gorged myself on the steaks.

Joe never learned to drive and if Dora was not available to ferry him about he would take a taxi. Once I had passed my driving test I was only too happy to drive him around, and in return they would let me have their car, when Dora didn't need it, and I would explore the island and its different beauties, which was a happy compromise. Jersey roads made even the worst English roads seem like motorways by comparison.

Joe was a keen reader and far more widely read than any other member of the family, except perhaps myself. He had a large library which doubled as the spare bedroom and is where I slept on my visits. He was not inhibited in his collection and I found many books there which were not readily available in England being considered obscene and hence not available for purchase. Among these was Frank Harris's *Lives and Loves*. This, like *Lady Chatterley's Lover* was banned in England under the Obscene Publications Acts as being likely to "deprave and corrupt" its readers, when a nanny state thought it had the right to decide what its citizens should not read.

I enjoyed the feeling of wickedness at reading something which was forbidden, though I was impressed neither by the literary style nor the veracity of the author's accounts of his sexual exploits. It all seemed rather pointless to me. There was nothing there to compare with the passion of *Blood and Sand*, or even the suggestiveness of *Forever Amber*, an eminently forgettable book, which was all the rage at one time. Joe's library was unexpectedly eclectic and introduced me to a number of foreign writers such as Thomas Mann and Stefan Zweig.

After Paris and the two Swiss holidays, it was very much a matter of holidays at home. The years immediately after the war were still times of great shortages. Food rationing continued until 1954, but at times it seemed as if there was actually less food available then than there had been during the war. Clothes rationing ended in February 1949. Foreign travel backpacking or hitchhiking were not then known and would barely have been feasible in a continent still full of displaced persons, and countries trying to repair the ravages of war. Europe was far from safe, and until May 1949 the Russians were blockading Berlin. I later envied my children's and grandchildren's generations who could spend their holidays travelling not just around Europe, but the whole world.

Most of my holidays, at Easter and Christmas as well as during the summer, were spent in the factory, carrying out various menial tasks, for which I was paid. Usually, I would put shirts into boxes to be loaded on to lorries for delivery, and then I would also do the loading. The factory had its own fleet of vans – fleet is perhaps an exaggeration: there were probably three or four vans of different sizes. Once I had learned to drive I upgraded myself to driver and drove all over the country delivering our goods. These vehicles were not easy to handle and took a considerable amount of strength, particularly high-sided vehicles in strong winds. They did not have the comfortable gearboxes of cars; you had to double-declutch, that is, bring the gear to neutral and then engage the target gear. Doing that going up a steep hill needed a strong hand and a steady nerve. I developed considerable understanding and sympathy for lorry drivers, and learned to appreciate just how skilled they are.

Working in the business also gave me an insight into exactly what was going on and what all the rows were about. I learned a lot from talking to the employees, who would talk to me as they would not to my elders. As is often the case, they knew more about the mechanics of operating the business efficiently, and the problems on the ground, than did the management. Ever since those days I have been suspicious of administrators, and have distrusted management who do not take into account the views of those on the shop floor. There was little evidence of any Luddite mentality; there was, however, a reluctance to accept change for its own sake, and a lack of confidence that it would be for the better or that the ground had been properly prepared. I found the experience of actually working in a factory both exhausting and exhilarating but I knew it was not something I wanted to spend a lifetime doing. It was fine as a holiday job, and there was satisfaction in actually earning a bob or two, and not having to depend on one's father, however generous.

The Middlesbrough Empire was typical of the provincial music hall which was killed off by television. It is salutary to remember that an artiste today, a comedian for example, has a larger audience from one appearance on television than he would have had from all his live appearances in the theatre. We were fortunate that the Empire was on the national circuit of all variety artistes. The most popular acts were the comedians, the funny men, many of whom were Jewish, such as Issy Bonn and Maxie Bacon. When they were in town they would be invited to the synagogue for the Saturday morning service. If they came, without a doubt they would be given some *"Mitzvah"* (liturgical honour), and we would meet them and chat after the service. Their connection with Orthodox Judaism was at times somewhat tenuous, however. I remember that Issy Bonn after being so honoured and asked what he wished to give by way of a donation – which was not expected to be paid there and then as money is forbidden to be carried on the Sabbath – put his hand in his pocket and brought out his wallet to the horror of the pious and the amusement of the rest of us.

The only serious theatre in Middlesbrough was the Little Theatre, a very good amateur group. For opera and professional theatre one had to go 40 miles north to Newcastle, or down to Leeds, 70 miles south-west, or London, 240 miles away. We often went to the Town Hall at Leeds, a fine, large building, a memorial to the prosperous 19th century entrepreneurs of the wool and cotton industries whose profits paid for it, where the big operatic stars of the day – and, it has to be said, often the day before – would appear on their several farewell tours. We went to "farewell" concerts given by Benjamino Gigli and Tito Schipa, and I felt very privileged to have been able to hear in person two of the greatest tenors of the 20th, and probably any other, century. Their style of singing may no longer be fashionable, but in my opinion few singers since have been able to equal the beauty of their voices and their technical skill.

My mother.

A rare occasion, my family en masse. L-r: Herman, a friend, Karl, Yetti, Ray, Jeanne, Dora, Max, my mother, Dad.

Phoenix risen from the ashes (courtesy of Guisborough Museum).

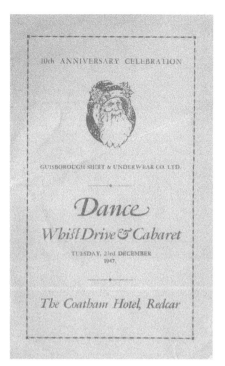

Left: Souvenir programme: "We won the war". Right: Happy Tenth Birthday – any excuse for a party!

My bar mitzvah – with my parents.

Left: On Grey House steps: at my bar mitzvah. Right: My dog, Peggy, disapproves of my uniform.

Left: A rare occasion – with my parents on holiday. Right: The cyclist.

My 21st birthday party.

Tod (Vernon) Handley and I at Balliol.

BA (Oxon).

5 Menckestrasse, Leipzig: the apartment block where I was born.

24 Landsbergerstrasse, Leipzig: my parents' home.

Wedded bliss – and they lived happily ever after.

We often went to London, usually only for a few days. These visits generally coincided with some business meetings or family occasion. By this time my aunts were producing cousins at frequent intervals necessitating visits to mark the occasions. Ray had two more daughters, Diane and Sandra, and Yetti had Harold and Sarah. By the time they had all finished I had ten cousins, on my mother's side.

On these visits to London we always took in a show. My parents, particularly my father, loved these. I was fortunate enough to see Danny Kaye at the Palladium on his first visit to London. I doubt whether British audiences had seen anything like him before, and we certainly have not seen his like since. He was sheer magic. I can find no other suitable word. He came on stage, all alone, walked to the front in total silence, sat down with his feet dangling over the orchestra pit and started, very quietly, to chat to the audience. He held the huge, packed theatre in the palm of his hand. Then slowly he went into his song and dance routines, joked, and kept us all enthralled for the rest of the evening. There was no other act. There were no rude or offensive jokes, no lewdness, no sex, nothing but wit, good humour, fun and enormous talent. The nearest thing to a risqué remark was a lifting of the eyebrows at the name of the county of Middlesex. I am very glad to be able to say, "I saw Danny Kaye in the flesh."

I came to London a few times on my own when I would stay either with Yetti or with Neville and his family. Yetti did her best to entertain me and arranged various outings. One day she thought we should visit the Crystal Palace. We duly took the no. 2 bus whose route went all the way from Golders Green, where my aunt lived, to Crystal Palace. It was a long journey – about two hours – through the heart of the West End, Victoria, Brixton and through parts of south London, whose squalor made Middlesbrough seem inviting. So far as I am concerned, London south of the river is a different country. It is unknown and uncharted territory and I am lost as soon as I cross the River Thames. We eventually arrived at the terminus and my aunt asked for directions to the Crystal Palace. She was met with loud laughter. The Crystal Palace had burned down years before, in 1936.

We turned round and came home in the same bus. At least I had seen some different parts of London, some of which still bore heavy scars of war.

On another occasion, I must have been about 12, when the war was not yet over but the bombing had stopped and the danger seemed over, Yetti took me as a special treat to see my first opera, the Carl Rosa Opera Company's performance of *Madame Butterfly* at Sadler's Wells Theatre. I cannot remember much of that performance but I came out weeping: I was so moved and upset at the dastardly behaviour of Lieutenant Pinkerton, abandoning Butterfly, that it was many years before I could see the opera again. It must have been a good performance!

We went to Madame Tussauds, and to the zoo, and did all the touristy things. Yetti was not that much older than I was and she approached all our outings with almost childish enthusiasm. Apart from the Madame Butterfly episode, she may have been right by Schmulewitsch standards, where everything was done at full volume and fever pitch, but I am my father's son and only averagely effusive. She enjoyed our outings as much as I did; even if they did not always prove conspicuously successful, they were never less than entertaining. Apart from her other many fine qualities, she was a person of considerable gusto, fun and enthusiasm, which made her an entertaining companion. She was easy to tease; one day as we passed a stationary Post Office van I told her that the mudguards were made of rubber.

"Go on," she said, "tell me another one!"

"You don't believe me?"

"No, you must think I'm stupid."

Whereupon I went up to the van and pushed the mudguard to show her.

She was a good sport; we had much fun together.

Chapter 46 – The Army: 1

Though, in fact, it did not entirely work out that way, I regard the start of my national service as the day I went out into the world and became a man, as it were. The age of majority had not yet been reduced to eighteen, but so far as I was concerned what was left of the umbilical cord was now cut. All other considerations apart, I was earning for myself for the first time and not reliant on nepotism or my father's generosity.

I took the train, my fare paid for by an expectant country, to Aldershot where I, with hundreds of other unwilling recruits, was met by army lorries. I was not quite sure how to get on one of these as beckoned to do so by a soldier with one stripe on his arm, as there were no steps and the lorries stood several feet high. Somehow, with some pushing and pulling we all managed it, together with our bags and cases. This was my first taste of army life. We were taken to the main depot where we were kitted out, given our army numbers and little plastic tags to be worn round our necks to remind us who we were and to enable identification to be made in case of death or injury. And then inducted into His Majesty's Forces; I became no. 22348636, Private Fishburn F. J.

The kit included formal battledress, consisting of a tunic and trousers, and fatigues which seem in the modern army to have replaced battledress. Army specifications to their manufacturers, as I well knew from the factory, were very specific, but the personnel handing out the kit were not as particular in their selections. Inevitably, therefore, it was only by coincidence that anyone was issued with a uniform that fitted. Recourse was necessary to what was optimistically called by the army, "the tailor", to ensure that the uniform bore some approximate relationship to the figure it was intended to adorn. We had to press our uniform trousers which were thick and unwieldy and not easily amenable to army requirements, until a crease sharp enough to look as if you could cut yourself on it had been achieved. The tunic had box pleats, and to obtain any sort of definition of these a considerable amount of effort with cardboard inserts, a very hot iron, and wet – damp was not enough – cloths was needed. But it occupied time which the army feared might be spent on less worthwhile pursuits. Once you had mastered the art of pressing, I admit that the finished product did look smart, and you felt the achievement of honest sweat.

I was not impressed by the army issue shirts, however. These were not the product of the Guisborough Shirt & Underwear Company Limited. I was used to better quality than this and sent home for reinforcements. By return six beautifully ironed khaki shirts arrived. The only problem was that these were officers' shirts, made of best quality poplin rather than the serge cloth of which those of other ranks were made. I wore the officers' shirts for going out, when civvies (civilian clothes) were not allowed, and later, becoming more daring, even in camp. I got some quizzical looks but, I do not think anyone ever actually identified what was unusual about my uniform. Certainly no one ever mentioned it, except my CO (commanding officer) once, who seeing me, complimented me on my shirt! I do not think that in fact I was committing any military offence. I was, after all, wearing official army shirts.

My experiences were, I imagine, typical; the depiction of the life of a recruit in such films as *Carry on Sergeant* and *Virgin Soldiers* is fairly accurate, jokes and all. We spent two weeks in the selection centre, starting our basic training and going through various selection processes to ascertain where one's talents could best be employed to the army's advantage. I had no objection to the principle of this, but the army, being what it is, paid no attention whatsoever to the results of the tests. I had hoped that the fact that I spoke German might have secured some posting in Germany, but that was too much to expect.

On the second or third day in the army, we were all paraded and marched to a cinema. The army does not hand out programmes of proposed activities to its recruits. Rumour was all we had to go on until we arrived anywhere. We were told what to do and where to go on a need-to-know basis. "Oh," I thought to myself, "this is a pleasant surprise," though after the experience of the temperance meeting while I was at school in the Lake District, I was naturally wary. The army was very concerned for the health of its soldiers. The films we were shown were certainly eye-openers. They dealt very specifically and in graphic detail with the effect of venereal disease, with special emphasis on syphilis and gonorrhoea. I personally thought that I would restrict myself, given the opportunity and need of choice, to the latter. To anyone not yet acquainted with the facts of life, these films would have been sufficient to deter them from any sexual activity forever.

After exhaustive testing of my ability to put pegs into holes, to differentiate patterns, to identify shapes and to be able to read, write, and count, it was decided that my abilities would be best exercised as a clerk in the Royal Army Ordnance Corps. The RAOC (now the Royal Logistic Corps) is responsible for the army's inventory. Originally responsible only for the supply of guns and ammunition, the RAOC became responsible for supplying any piece of equipment the army might need, from paper clips to tanks. When I joined the army it was the largest corps with an apparently insatiable demand for clerks.

The pre-selection tests were given by army sergeants, known as sergeant testers, who looked no older than me: I assumed that they were national servicemen who had been in the army only a little longer than ourselves. One of them looked relaxed and friendly; not all did, even national service sergeants can seem fearsome. It is wonderful how quickly even the slightest whiff of power and authority can turn a person's head. I commented to the friendly NCO – his name was Louis Schaffer – whom I was to meet again many years later, married to one of my daughter's teachers, so small is the world:

"That looks like a nice job. How do you get it?"

"You have to apply for it."

"How?" I asked.

"You go to your CO and apply!" was the answer. "They have to put your application forward so you have nothing to lose."

There was – perhaps there still is – a rule that any application for a particular post or training made to your commanding officer had to be forwarded by him to the appropriate army authority, provided that you had the necessary qualifications. As I could read and write and was not entirely innumerate, I reckoned that I had the necessary qualifications for almost anything in the army, except highly specialised fields like medicine and physical training. So I went along to my CO and made the appropriate application. That was not as easy as it sounds as commanding officers, indeed any officers, are godlike in their remoteness, but I did not know that at the time. The CO was a somewhat disenchanted-looking major, who was pleasant enough, and undertook to process my application but warned me that these things "take time".

As part of the selection process we also had what passed as an interview. When asked where I wanted to be in the army, I was about to say "Out" but thought better of it and mumbled something about using my knowledge of foreign languages; perhaps the Intelligence Corps might be able to use me. I soon learned that modesty is not a useful quality in the army.

Our barracks for these first two weeks in the army were wooden huts, set out in H-blocks. They were comparatively spacious and by army standards reasonably pleasant. The army was going easy on us until we had been sorted out; as we were merely passing through a clearing house, our first initiation into basic training was fairly benign. No one could really be bothered, and the main object was to move us on ASAP.

We were shown how to make our beds, fold our blankets, put on our uniforms – not as obvious as it sounds because the belts and their buckles, the webbing and the fold of the trousers into anklets above the boots, caused problems until you became familiar with their intricacies. The mysteries of the application of Blanco to webbing, and boot polish and spit (literally), to secure a mirror-like toecap to your boots, were imparted to us, though the art was only acquired by long periods of practice. This passion for cleanliness is known as bullshit, and its sole purpose was to keep you busy on the principle that idle hands make mischief.

After the selectors had used their blindfold pin methods we were dispatched to our various training camps. Mine was Badajos Barracks, Aldershot, so I did not have far to go. This was one of a series of blocks named after Wellington's Peninsular battles. Salamanca was the next block. These blocks, we were told, had been used as prison blocks and had been condemned as unfit for human use even before the war but had been retained for reasons of economy. Every untenable official decision is justified on the grounds of economy. The economy is usually illusory.

The blocks were made of grey brick, on four floors; the billets led off concrete and iron verandahs which were reached by an iron staircase at each end. Anyone used to current health and safety regulations would have been appalled, and any self-respecting fire officer would have had them closed down immediately. There were 14 of us to a room: 12 rookies, a lance corporal and a corporal, who were responsible for our training. The beds were set out in rigorously straight lines.

There were communal latrines and "ablutions" – the army term for baths and showers – of primitive design, but they worked and the water was hot. When we arrived, we were met by a shower of abuse and spit from the floor above, whose occupants were veterans of 14 days standing, being the intake immediately before ours. We would in our turn greet the next intake in similar fashion.

As Passover was about to start, and as the one aspect of Jewish religious observance I was then very particular about was the prohibition against eating anything leavened – in effect anything which has not been specially sanctioned by the rabbinate – during the eight days of Passover, I applied for leave on compassionate grounds. I was told that I could not have leave within the first month of service. My application had been dealt with initially by a subaltern. I demanded to see the CO which could not be denied me. He said the same. I pointed out that it was the army's fault, not mine, that I was in that position, because for three months I had been hammering at the army's door to let me in, and if he could not give me leave, I would have to take the matter up with the padre. Why this should have frightened him I do not know, but he relented and I got my leave which I spent with Yetti in London. We, that is Yetti and Karl and family as well as me, went to Herman and Ray's home for the seder nights, which are the first two evenings of Passover when the festive table becomes an altar, and the story of the exodus from Egypt is read from the Haggadah, a book of specially written and selected prayers and songs. Time did not allow for me to get home, but

Herman and Ray entertained lavishly. Herman, in the family tradition, was musical and sang well. His voice was not as strong or clear as Max's but he was a devout man; he understood and felt the prayers as he sang them so beautifully. It was a welcome return, albeit short, to civilisation.

Looking back, I can only wonder at my own temerity in my dealings with officialdom, as represented by the army. Any member of my family with their continental background and respect for authority, especially when it wears a uniform, would have been horrified had they seen me. They would have had visions of my being thrown into jail, being starved or beaten, for even daring to approach a superior officer. It says much for the education I received that this attitude, this awe of authority, never occurred to me. I would not have been terrified of a policeman coming to the house, as my family had been. It also has to be said that I might not have fared as well in a guard's regiment, or the infantry, where there were more professional soldiers and where discipline is perhaps taken more seriously. But even there I would have had nothing to fear as long as I kept within the rules. One other aspect of the matter is that a civilian army, which is what we were, is difficult to deal with. In a period of service limited to 18 months there is not a lot you can do with reluctant and often downright recalcitrant recruits, whose main interest in the army is to become ex-servicemen as soon as possible, if there is no war or crisis of some sort, natural or manufactured, to keep them busy after they have finished their basic training.

In the army you acquire a completely new vocabulary, which lasts during your service and is largely abandoned on demobilisation. The first thing is that every other word must be a swear word connected with the sexual act, usually the gerund if an adjective, or featuring some part of the female anatomy, if a noun. In conjunction they form the basis of a typical description of anyone of higher rank, or with whom you may be displeased, or even, used in the right tone of reverence, a compliment. It is not a large vocabulary, well short of the 800 words in basic English, but correctly used and inflexed it seems to cover most situations. Imaginative variations of both nouns and adjectives may be used. Verbs seem superfluous; if used at all they are usually in the imperative, eg., "Go screw yourself". Verbs, when used are in the future, promissory, tense – "I'll…" – except when referring to women, when they are all in the past tense. I did not know what a "nig-nog" was, though the word has a certain onomatopoeic quality, but soon discovered that I was one.

Then there are the usual phrases, calls to arms, you might say:

"Stand by your bed".

"Get your hair cut, lad".

"Get fell in".

"By the left, quick march", and other marching orders.

None of these is in the slightest comprehensible: you just learn to recognise the various grunts or other sounds which represent them. Shakespeare had it right when he referred to the soldier "full of strange oaths". But as to "bearded like the pard", things have changed since the 16th century; clean-shaven was the order of the day.

The first thing the army does to destroy individualism and reduce all to standard army issue, is to cut your hair. Long hair, blown upwards, quiffed and heavily Brylcreemed or kept in shiny place by some other similar unguent, was the pride of many a raw recruit, reduced to tears at the sight of his locks falling about his feet. There was something sadistic about this. Army life is inevitably brutalising but it seemed to my young eyes that much of what was perpetrated on young, unhappy, and reluctant recruits was more than was necessary to instil good military discipline. I distrust anyone with power; he is bound to abuse it.

My co-recruits were, as one might expect, a varied crew, and I found them fascinating. There was one other Jewish boy in the squad, Julius Deinstein. He was from the East End. A big, bruiser-type, he looked strong and acted accordingly. He had unruly, jet-black hair, and the appearance of a round-faced Sylvester Stallone. There was a defensive aggressiveness about him. He was the sort who got his retaliation in first. Swift to anger, at the smallest slight, he had an outsize chip on his shoulder and saw an anti-semitic remark in what seemed to me the most innocent comment. He certainly was no respecter of authority and had many brushes with our corporal, a man called Fisher, who was equally bloody-minded. But Julius, once he settled down, became more friendly with the rest of the squad and was very loyal to us all. He was a good man to have on your side, and whatever disagreement he might have with any other of his colleagues, he would always spring to their defence against any "outsider". I liked Julius; you knew where you were with him.

My closest friend was Bernard Howson from Leeds, an easy-going, thoroughly likeable lad. He was more like the boys I went to school with than were any of the others. He was a secretary, an unusual occupation for a man. He could type 120 words a minute, and do shorthand. The army, in typical fashion, sent him on the same clerk's course as the rest of us.

Then there was Jock from Kilbirnie, in Ayrshire. I assume he had another name, I think it was Ferguson, but I doubt if I ever actually knew it. He may have answered to his surname at the pay parade roll call, but everyone knew him as "Jock". He was about 5' 7" tall, very wiry and strong for his size; he was red-faced, and generally of nondescript appearance. In the chip-on-the shoulder league he was way ahead of Julius. Julius had an attitude in that he was oversensitive about any (usually imagined) slight to his Jewishness. Jock had an attitude about everything, but he really came into his own when he was drunk, which was most nights. During the day Jock was prickly but comparatively amiable; after a pint or two of beer, he would take on all comers. He would go looking for trouble, and had to be handled carefully. Usually, he finished up for the night with the Redcaps, the Military Police, who handled him anything but carefully. I liked Jock and got on well with him. Like Julius, he too would come to the aid of his mates, so in terms of combat we were well protected.

Corporal Fisher was also a big man. He had seen too many army films, and imagined himself as some sort of martinet, but he did not have the personality or the air of authority to carry it off. As a result, he had to resort to trying to bully us. He hit on the wrong squad: Julius and Jock were, in their different ways, no respecters of persons and had no fear of punishment. They were quite capable of taking Corporal Fisher to a quiet corner and sorting him out, and he knew it. I pointed out to him, gently, that cooperation might provide better results, and an accommodation was reached. Once he had been straightened out he turned out to be quite pleasant. It was merely that power had gone to his head. He was in due course promoted to sergeant, and I told him that he had us to thank.

As for myself, I learned that in the land of the blind the one-eyed man is king. The fact that I was literate and had, as my colleagues saw it, the gift of the gab, gave me a moral authority which was altogether unjustified. When my colleagues learned that I was going up to Oxford to read Law, I was immediately appointed as spokesman for the squad, and looked to for advice on all manner of things, advice which I was not competent to give. But of course this was something which I could not admit. I have never allowed lack of knowledge to inhibit me in giving advice. I was, in my ignorance, undeterred by authority and always ready to represent my constituents when called upon to do so. When necessary, I made sure that I was accompanied by my "minders", Julius and Jock, and my experiences in advocacy at that time convinced me that I did indeed have a vocation for the Law.

More touchingly, I was often asked to read letters which some of my colleagues had received from their family or girlfriends. The illiteracy of some was such that I wondered why they had been taken into the army; they could not read the letters which their senders must have had difficulty in writing. I also began to learn a little about the problems of those who had not been blessed with social advantages, skills or intelligence, and those to whom life had simply dealt a bad hand. Unbelievably to me, some at the age of 18 already had wives and children; in those days they would usually actually be married. To them, being in the army was almost a financial blessing but the troubles at home, cruel landlords, unthinking families, and doubts about their girls' fidelity did lead some to disappear absent without leave, and find themselves brought back by the military police and in greater trouble than before. Fortunately, being in England and not too far from their homes, with understanding officers (and they usually were), this sort of defection was kept to a minimum in my squad. In fact, my assistance was often sought from other squads in our barracks, so my reputation must have spread.

Living together in one room, drilling, marching, running and doing everything together, even for only a few weeks, creates a surprising comradeship between disparate types. This is the stuff of so many war films, and it is true. Though in many respects I considered my period of army service as a deplorable waste of time, I feel that this aspect of it, the chance to meet so many different people with such varied backgrounds, the comradeship which is created, and the pleasure of achievement at the end of the training, provided a most valuable experience which I would otherwise have missed, and I am grateful for it.

The period of our square-bashing coincided with the run-up to the King's birthday parade which was to be held on 14 June, and we were among those selected for special training to take part in it. Unfortunately, this involved extra exercises at 6 a.m. daily. We had, among other exercises to prepare us for the great day, to swing our rifles around our heads and use them rather like Indian clubs. Apparently this strengthens the muscles so that one can stand at attention for long periods, with the right arm holding the rifle at an angle of 45 degrees to the shoulder. We also had to stand a great deal, and my flat feet collapsed under the strain. I was in great pain, and was sent to the Cambridge Military Hospital in Aldershot. I had to stay there for several days for tests, X-rays and the like. My condition was diagnosed as permanent, and I was excused boots. I no longer had to go on parades, except for pay. I was disqualified from becoming an officer, which worried me not at all as I had no intention of seeking a commission. It did not stop me from becoming a non-commissioned officer (NCO).

In the army nearly everyone smoked. Most of my squad fell asleep with a cigarette between their lips and next morning, before opening their eyes, they would light another, which they managed to keep dangling from their lips during morning ablutions, breakfast and until they had to go on parade. Training is what happens between smoking breaks, which occur about every ten minutes, except when on full parade. Squaddies are friendly chaps, and I got so tired of saying "no" to the frequent offers of a fag that I thought it easier to say "yes", and I became a smoker. I rarely smoked before 11 a.m. but once lit up I more or less chain-smoked until I went to bed. I started with Wills Woodbines which were smaller than most other makes of cigarettes, but stronger. Their size made them ideal for a short intermission for a smoke, and they were the cheapest cigarettes.

Odd things happen in the army. One morning, our staff sergeant, a very exalted NCO, came into our room just as we were about to go on parade. He called for six volunteers. Almost the first thing one learns in the army is to remain silent when volunteers are called for. He wanted the six tallest in the squad. I just qualified. He told us that we would be under his sole command for a few days. He needed us for an army funeral; an old soldier had just died and had expressed a wish for a military funeral. As the Ordnance Corps supplied everything which the army needed, other than food, it was called upon again. We trained for a few hours every day practising carrying a coffin on our shoulders without using our hands to steady it, how to get the coffin up and down, how to slow march – all good vocational training for an undertaker, but it was better than the alternative exercises on offer. I did not think it necessary to mention the fact that I was not of the deceased's religious denomination. I knew what the answer would be.

The funeral was surprisingly stately and strangely moving. The coffin was put on a gun carriage, which we drew (fortunately not very far), and it was not very heavy. The Union Jack was draped over the coffin, and the full obsequies were observed. A rifle salute was followed by the Last Post, which to hear at any time is emotional. After the ceremony, as the pubs were not yet open and it was too early for drinks, the staff sergeant treated us all to tea and buns at the NAAFI (a canteen run by navy, army and air force institutes), apparently at his own expense; an unexpected and unusual but welcome gesture.

One day Jock suddenly became quite ill with a very high fever. We were moved out of the barracks and quarantined in some disused building which seemed as if it might at some time have been used as stables. We cleared it out, and managed to make our temporary accommodation quite comfortable. Our food was delivered to the gate and left there. We were treated like lepers. We were relieved from training, and had nothing to do, apart from reading and amusing ourselves by playing football. We all got fed up with this and went to the NAAFI or into town. So much for the quarantine! It was a pleasant interlude. It appeared that Jock may have had some food poisoning. I suspect it was more likely to have been alcohol poisoning.

Eventually, we finished our period of basic training. I had qualified as a Clerk Class 1, which meant that I could read and write and type 20 words a minute. After the leave we were entitled to at the end of our training, I was posted to the RAOC depot at Bicester, one of the largest in the country at the time, where I had my worst time in the army. The place was a disgrace by any standards. The accommodation, in old Nissen huts, was bad enough, with the same old inefficient, smelly and I suspect health-damaging, cast-iron stoves we had had in Aldershot. There, the floors had, through our efforts, been highly polished, here, they were made of stone.

I was sent to work alone in a small office, clerk for the use of, in a huge warehouse containing millions – literally – of vehicle parts, most of them obsolete. They were catalogued in true army fashion in language of its own: "seats, toilets, officers, for the use of", type of thing. And of course, every single part, every type of screw had its own number and location. It was quite ingenious, really. Theoretically, anything could be found within a matter of minutes, always supposing that it was where it should be. I never had the chance to find out if the system worked. The excitement of waiting to be called upon to enter the vast Dexion forest, possibly never to reappear, to find an essential screw, was unnerving. To ensure that I was ready for that trial when, and if, I was called upon, I spent my time relaxing by reading. When challenged by authority, in the form of an officious second lieutenant, the lowest rank in the army in practice if not in theory, I explained that I was holding myself back; unless I relaxed by reading, the fever pitch of excitement if asked to do anything useful would be too much to bear. I indicated that I was willing to undertake any useful commission but I was already wasting enough time by being there and, apart from reading, could anything more useful than twiddling my thumbs be thought of. My ability to express myself grammatically, and I hoped with some humour, seemed to let me get away with what might be regarded by some as insolence and others as insubordination which, of course, it was.

But it was the food that made the place unbearable. It was uneatable. One does not expect good food in the army but until then it had been wholesome and plentiful. The kitchens had been clean and the washing facilities adequate. Here in Bicester, the stench of rancid food could be smelled a mile off. Most of us ate in the NAAFI, and needless to say Tessie, as she had done since I joined the army, ensured a continuing supply of food parcels from home. However, on one misguided occasion I did eat in the cookhouse, and became severely ill with food poisoning. Not wishing to risk army medical treatment, to embark on which requires a level of fitness I was unable to achieve in my condition, I went home for a weekend leave, saw my own doctor and on his certificate stayed there till I was better. I calculated that out of the 84 days I was officially at Bicester, I was there only 37 days.

The journey from Bicester to home was long and unpleasant. The travel vouchers issued by the army required you to take the shortest route. The quickest route would have been via London, but the shortest meant changing trains at Bletchley which is a station on two levels. It is only a small station and had no particular comforts, and changing trains there involved a long and cold wait. But it took less effort than reporting sick would have done. Unless you were so ill that you had to be removed on a stretcher, to report sick you had to hand in all your bedding and non-portable equipment to the quartermaster's stores in case you were sent to hospital; and having done that you had to report on sick parade in best battledress, all spick and span and highly polished, with your kitbag loaded with your own belongings, clothes and kit. There was an element of self-protection about this. If you didn't do this you were not likely to find them there on your return. And if you were really ill and the M.O., medical officer, who was likely to be a doctor just qualified and doing his national service and to whom you were just a guinea pig to practise on, didn't finish you off there and then, the army hospital would. It really wasn't worth the effort. It was easier just to die quietly in your bed.

While I was on sick leave at home, the posting to the sergeant tester's course which I had so long ago applied for came through. I had several times asked for information about the progress of my application, but typically of the army, no one knew or cared. Nevertheless, army wheels do, surprisingly, grind, however slowly. I had to be in Barton Stacey near Andover for the course within some five days, and by the time I had been notified at home three of these had gone. I was not going to lose this opportunity, so ignoring my condition I packed my bags, returned to Bicester to collect what equipment and uniform I had there, went through the necessary formalities, collected my tickets, and then departed for Barton Stacey. I was glad to leave Bicester. I learned later that there had been a general outbreak of food poisoning, that the whole of the kitchens and mess had been condemned; the cooks had been charged with various offences and the place cleaned up. I did not find out how true this was, but if it wasn't, it should have been.

From Bicester to Barton Stacey was a move from the catastrophic to the sublime. Barton Stacey was a WOSB (War Office Selection Board) and we were treated like gentlemen from the moment we arrived. We were immediately promoted to the rank of corporal, high rank indeed to a recruit. Some soldiers do not achieve that rank in many years of service. Some indeed have no ambition to do so. At Bicester there was one soldier, a private, whose long-service stripes, which are the same as those of a sergeant but sewn upside down on the lower part of the sleeve of the tunic, filled most of the available space. He had joined the army when he was 17, as a boy soldier, some 25 years earlier. He seemed to have no fixed duties, and came and went as he pleased. I asked him about his apparent lack of ambition. He explained it quite simply: he enjoyed army life; he had free accommodation, food and holidays. He was respected on account of his long service. His duties were minimal, and he earned enough for himself. When he retired he had enough saved up to buy himself a little house in his home town and his army pension would more than cover his needs. What need had he of responsibility?

Chapter 47 – The Army: 2

Our training at Barton Stacey consisted of a series of lectures and seminars on the assessment of aptitudes and intelligence. They were of high quality and fascinating. The fact that the army ignored its own mechanisms did not invalidate them. The methods used for testing abilities and the need to ensure that round pegs were not put into square holes were explained. We all had to do the various tests ourselves which we all passed. My companions at Barton Stacey were all, like myself, expecting to take up university courses on completion of their national service, and it was a very different army from the one I had been serving in up to then.

On the day before the course was due to finish, the CO referred to one other form of testing which had not yet been mentioned. Training soldiers was costly: there were some recruits who were untrainable and these had to be identified before they were taken into the forces, even for national service. There was therefore a pre-selection test which was held at army recruiting offices. These were in civilian centres and it was sometimes difficult to staff some of them. He asked whether anyone would be interested in taking up such a post. It would involve an extra week's training but promotion would not be affected. He read out a list of places they were seeking to fill. Among these was Middlesbrough. I said nothing at first. I knew no one else would volunteer for that. I let the matter ride for a short time. I asked exactly what would be involved. I then indicated that if it helped the army, I would volunteer for the Middlesbrough posting. I modestly dismissed the effusion of gratitude shown by the major. Even more pleased than the major was Alec Crosland, a delightful lad from Leeds from whom I took over, who was relieved to be relieved; he thought he would never be replaced.

And so, having left home for good, I was back there with the rank of sergeant (fully paid), that being the place a grateful nation thought I could best serve it. Though I remained in the RAOC and continued to wear its badges, I was no longer of it. I had been seconded to the War Office to whose offices in Berkeley Square I reported directly. My commanding officer was a roving major who went round the country visiting such as me. I was officially attached to a RASC (Royal Army Service Corps) unit where I had to go for my pay at Sedgefield, near the village of Fishburn. The unit there had no idea that I existed, and my appearance at my first pay parade caused considerable confusion and I had some difficulty in getting paid.

Having to travel to Sedgefield, albeit only once a week, was an inconvenience not only to me but to the unit, causing an unnecessary administrative burden. I should have been quartered there, as Alec Crosland had been. This would have involved travelling to Middlesbrough daily. I had an understanding CO who negotiated permission for me to live out, for which I received an appropriate lodging allowance. After a while, I had a word with my CO and it was arranged that my pay would be sent direct to me. Following this, for the rest of my national service, my physical connection with the army was tangential.

There are many advantages to being a sergeant. I think it is the best rank in the army. No rank carries more immediate power. Generals may rule over armies, and majors over companies, but a sergeant had immediate access to and hence direct power over his men. He is also more immediately subject to their dislike. Officers are out of their reach, too remote for the ordinary soldier usually to have any relationship with or feelings directly towards them. The sergeant is the key in the chain of command.

Apart from the heady power of their position, sergeants and more senior NCOs have their own mess, of which the sergeant cook, the Raymond Blanc of his unit, is a member. Sergeants always eat well. If they have cause to complain, their remedy is close at hand, or rather the object of their protests is. The officers' mess may be well provided with silver and cut glass, and wines and spirits, but the best food is reserved for the sergeants' mess.

My office was in the Army Recruiting Centre in Corporation Road, in what the Americans would call "downtown", insofar as Middlesbrough could be said to have such a thing. Here were employed three regular soldiers, and a member of the ATS, the

women's section of the army, who was a not unattractive brassy
blonde in her middle twenties, into whose pants the two men
tried, unsuccessfully so far as I am aware, to enter all the time I
was there, and which seemed to form the main subject of their
conversation. My work was, happily, interesting but not taxing. It
consisted of administering the appropriate pre-selection tests to all
new recruits. Few of these were volunteers, but occasionally I did
get some who were.

The tests were all standard and I checked them against a
matrix. There were 80 non-verbal questions with multiple-choice
answers. Most were expected to get not less than 60 correct. I
would interview anyone who had scored less than 40 to make sure
that they were genuinely of low intelligence, as some were wise to
the nature and purpose of the test and tried to fail it. These were
not difficult to identify because they did not know which were the
hard questions and which the easy ones. To an intelligent person
they were all easy and if they tried deliberately to fail the test they
would probably have answered all the hard questions correctly.
The standard was not meant to be high and after eliminating
chance guesses one could soon see who was not genuine. These
recruits soon gave themselves away when I interviewed them.

Some volunteers for the regular army, having failed to reach
the required standard, were sent back for testing for national
service. Many of those who failed were sad cases, and I asked
myself what possible careers or future they could have, even
within their own very limited ambitions, if their mental capabili-
ties were inadequate even for national service. Their sheer gorm-
lessness made interviewing them difficult and depressing. I
wondered at their family circumstances. It was not necessarily a
matter of poverty: though many came from deprived backgrounds,
not all did. The most difficult and at the same time most interesting were the travellers, didicoys or gypsies. Travellers, as we think
of them today, people seeking a different lifestyle, hardly existed
then. The travellers were either circus people, market traders, or
tinkers and their like. I used to wonder how they had managed to
be called up for national service. Most had no fixed address; it was
unlikely that they had registered for service when required to do

so. Most of them were illiterate. This did not mean that they were necessarily unintelligent, but to train them to become useful soldiers in the comparative short period of national service was, in most cases, not something that the army considered a proper use of its resources.

Strangely, most men turned up for their national service preliminaries dressed in what seemed like their best clothes; even allowing for the fact that everyone, at least on Teesside, dressed more formally 50 years ago than they do now, I often remarked on this. It may have been innate respect for the uniform but more probably many only had one suit.

I settled in well in my new billet, receiving living out and subsistence allowances for so doing. But it was an odd sort of existence, much as I enjoyed it; living at home and going to work in army uniform. I had an excellent batwoman in Tessie; my battledress was always impeccably pressed, my shoes brilliantly polished and my shirts factory-ironed. I do not know what my parents thought of it all. They had always suspected that they had come to a crazy country and here was living proof right under their own roof.

Chapter 48 – Israel

When my parents visited Israel for the first time in 1950, it had just celebrated its second birthday. The first Israelis they met, after welcoming my parents, in the usual inquisitive Jewish way, enquired whether they had any children. My mother said that she had one son.

"Why isn't he with you?" she was asked. "Where is he?"

"In the army," my mother replied.

"Oh, that's wonderful. Where is he?"

"In England," Mother replied.

"In England? What's he doing there?"

"He's in the army."

"The English army!" came the response which I can only imagine must have been in a voice rather like Dame Edith Evans' "A handbag!"

"What's he doing there, he should be here in the Israeli army."

My parents' explanation that I was merely obeying the law of the land cut little ice with their Israeli friends.

Their visit to Israel was the fulfilment of a lifetime's dream for my parents. All my family were keen Zionists. The Jewish youth movements of which my uncles and aunts had been members and the camps they had gone to while still in Germany, were all very much orientated to Zionism and they encouraged settlement in Palestine. Had the British Mandate authorities permitted it, immigration would have been much greater. A family such as mine would probably have settled there rather than England, but the English government of the time, with that lack of logic which characterises so much of government policy, seemed rather more willing – even though reluctantly and in inadequate numbers – to allow immigration to the UK than to Palestine, no doubt because the Home Office was staffed by Arabists. Perhaps they had a hidden agenda too, because the contribution to the life of this country from those immigrants in all fields has been enormous.

My father was heavily involved in raising money for Zionist and other Jewish charities. In my home, Zionism was synonymous with Jewish identity; religious observance was much less important. Our permanence in England was by no means firmly established or guaranteed. The events immediately following the end of the war shook our confidence. We thought we had found a safe haven. A Tory government with more than a smattering of notorious anti-semitic supporters, among them the local MP for Cleveland, Commander Bower, had somewhat reluctantly allowed entry to many (though still too few) refugees into the United Kingdom. Winston Churchill, the Tory premier, had supported a Jewish state in Palestine. Most Jews of my parents' generation were naturally left wing; not Communists, though many Jews in Germany – Rosa Luxemburg to name but one – had been active in the Communist party, but Social Democrat in outlook, and Labour in terms of British politics.

My family's Zionism was allied to socialist principles: the idea of the kibbutz, equal opportunities, justice for all, no discrimination, that is to say the principles set out in Ben-Gurion's Declaration in May 1948, on the founding of the State of Israel. The result of the 1945 elections, which swept the Labour Party to power with a large majority, had been greeted with joy and expectation.

Ernest Bevin betrayed our hopes. His policies were a denial of everything that we had expected of a Labour government and of what we had expected of an England which had led the fight against Nazism. It was for us a denial of what the war had been fought for. Not to allow refugees, survivors from the Nazi death camps, displaced persons with nowhere else to go, into Palestine because of Arab intransigence was bad enough. To send them back to the very places (in countries from which they had been fortunate to escape with their lives), to the concentration camps from which those same troops (or perhaps their comrades) who were now forcing them back there, had liberated them, was inhuman and unconscionable. Whatever the economic and political reasons may have been, to us it appeared clear that Bevin could only have been motivated by anti-semitism.

There have been many examples of Albion's perfidy and cruelty, which reflect no glory on the history of this country, from the burning at the stake of Joan of Arc to the massacre at Amritsar, from the treatment of the Irish to the imprisonment of the Boers in concentration camps. But in all those, with the exercise of a vivid imagination, some military or political purpose, however unworthy, can be identified. It is hard to see what military or political purpose can have been served by this crass conduct, by sending people back to their concentration camps. I did not understand why the country did not rise in protest, why no votes of no confidence were passed in Parliament, why protesters did not lay siege to the Foreign Office. To me this was further evidence of anti-semitism, open, not simply latent, in high places. It explained and justified Jewish paranoia. My disillusionment was great; my ideas – perhaps I should say ideals – of what this country stood for, my confidence in my position in it, were shattered. Bevin is regarded by some as an outstanding Foreign Secretary. From my (Jewish) point of view he was an unmitigated disaster. I have not changed my mind over the years.

The idea of betrayal went deep and brought about a major re-evaluation of where I stood. If, I thought to myself, a party whose policy had been wholly supportive of the establishment of a Jewish state, which had been highly critical of the previous government's policies, which purported to stand for the same principles of justice and equality as those of the Zionist movement, could be held in thrall by one of its ministers and allow such matters to happen, what guarantee was there that Jews would be safe here? If it could return Jews to the concentration camps from which they had thought themselves liberated, what guarantee was there that there might not be anti-Jewish legislation and the encouragement of pogroms here at some future time when it suited the politicians? Attacks on Jews had happened here before, as recently as 1913. If Jews could be returned on sinking boats from Palestine to Germany, why not from London or Guisborough? The anti-semitism latent in the English establishment is clearly demonstrated in the books of John Buchan (otherwise known as Lord Tweedsmuir –eminent in the Diplomatic Service), G. K Chesterton and Hilaire Belloc to name but a few and beautifully portrayed in Ishiguro's *Remains of the Day*. The German Jews had also thought that they were safe.

My loyalties were torn apart. I loved this country, and was grateful for the home, shelter and education it had given me. I loved where I lived and where I went to school; I loved my friends; but I was Jewish, and when the chips were down no one would look after me except myself; no one would provide a refuge for Jews except their own country, Israel.

Yet I was not totally disillusioned, for two reasons. The first was that I recalled that the pre-war Fascists, Mosley's Blackshirts, had despite police protection if not positive support, been stopped in Cable Street in London's working-class East End at a time which seemed propitious for their success. And secondly, because I felt from my own relationship with my friends that they no more approved of these policies than I did. I felt that there were certain things the public would not stomach. Of course, we were very young and tended to see things in black and white, but we read the papers and we were intelligent. There may have been issues beyond our knowledge, and our comprehension, but humanitarian principles were involved and they should not have been sacrificed on the altar of one man's vanity and prejudice.

Neither my family nor I subscribed to the fascist philosophy or the terrorist policies of the Stern Gang and the Irgun. There was a reluctance to believe what was alleged against them. Much was regarded as anti-Zionist propaganda, but it soon became clear that the reports were accurate, if not understated. The incidents of the bombing of the King David Hotel and the hanging of the British sergeants caused great grief and embarrassment to the Jewish community as a whole, and I expected a rough ride at school. Far from it: when I was asked what I thought about it I replied that wars cannot be fought with one's hands tied behind one's back. When I was asked: what would you have done? I quoted the saying by Rabbi Hillel, one of the greatest of Jewish sages, in the *Ethics of the Fathers*: "If I am not for myself, who will be for me?" And, "If I am only for myself what am I?" and "If not now when?" That, it seems to me, is the core of practical Jewish and particularly socialist Zionist philosophy.

I felt that my friends understood my argument and our relationship was not affected. In fact, the courage and determination of the Haganah and the Zionist settlers were greatly admired, and their success in the 1948 War of Independence seen as a modern miracle. Looking back, and having lived through and read much about those times, I now feel that the tactics of the Irgun were justified, in the same way, though to a different degree, that Hiroshima was justified: they expedited the inevitable; had the fighting been allowed to continue, it would have cost many more lives. Those were stirring times, and it was gratifying that one could now be openly proud of being a Jew instead of shamefacedly and fearfully trying to hide the fact, as my parents and grandparents felt they had to do.

The establishment of the State of Israel gave Jews a self-confidence that they had not known for centuries. It also gave them a position on the world stage, and that small country today has politically, militarily, economically and strategically an importance totally disproportionate to its size.

It was many years before I went there myself. I found the experience fascinating. It is a place where I feel at home. I may disagree vehemently with its government, its constitution, its policies, the secular/religious divide which is its greatest danger. There may be many reasons for not settling there myself, but I like to know it's there, and while it is, I, in common with others, feel safer.

Chapter 49 – Patronyms

In September 1950 my surname was officially changed to Fishburn. I had been called up for my army service under that name. In this respect, not having a birth certificate was actually an advantage, as there was nothing to indicate that that was not the name I had been born with. The law of this country is quite informal on this point. You can call yourself whatever you wish, as long as you do not assume an unauthorised title. You might encounter delays in getting a passport or other official document. For some time my parents and I officially used different names. I do not know why my father waited so long to change his name or why he bothered to do so when he did. It may have been that he needed a passport but the real reason I suspect was quite different.

Auntie Jeanne had for some time been grumbling at the name "Schmulewitsch" and wanted Max to change it. This caused considerable controversy in the family. None of the Schmulewitsch daughters would brook any thought of change. It had been their maiden name and what was good enough for their father was good enough for his sons.

The most vociferous "anti" was Dora. Herman said that he would not change his name, but in this he was a little disingenuous because he usually went by the name of Mr Herman anyway. Jeanne argued, understandably, that it was easy for the sisters to complain, as their married names caused no difficulties – Fishburn (or even Fischbein), Menasche and Katz were not difficult mouthfuls like Schmulewitsch.

Opa had been called "Mr Papa", Oma "Mrs S", my mother "Mrs Fishburn", Dora "Miss Dora", Yetti "Schnucky" or "Yetti" and Max was "Mr Max". Jeanne was concerned for her children. Schmulewitsch might not be out of place in London's East End or Stoke Newington, but it was a very cumbersome and foreign name in Middlesbrough. I thought she had a point. I should not have welcomed being called "Schmulewitsch". But the name had done my family no harm and it was, to say the least, distinctive.

Many European Jews, refugees from Nazism, were very self-conscious about their foreign origins and sought to hide them. During the war when Polish, Czech and American soldiers, many of whom had names of European origin which they wore with pride, were welcome visitors, their names appeared to cause no problems. English people were still conceived to be inherently xenophobic and even anti-semitic. No doubt many were, but no more so than elsewhere and many Poles, for example, who served in their own air force or army units and then opted to remain here, perhaps having married and started families, retained their Polish names which were usually much more difficult to pronounce than Schmulewitsch, and impossible to spell.

Ethnicity and pride in one's ancestry were not then fashionable. Many golf clubs and other institutions excluded Jews. It was never "official policy", but somehow Jews never became members. It was very difficult for a Jew to find employment in London at the large City firms of solicitors and accountants or the clearing banks. I do not know if it was any easier at large provincial firms, but the matter probably rarely arose. Golf clubs all over the country discriminated against Jews, not only in denying them membership, but in not even allowing them to play as guests. Considerable progress has been made in the last 50 years in legislation and education, and it is, perhaps, difficult for those who have not been affected by discrimination to understand its damaging effects.

However, it seemed to me that Jeanne's attitude was born of snobbery. She wished to send Geoffrey to Clifton College, and felt that his patronym might prove a disadvantage. She wanted a change of name which totally hid the family's origins, and the name she chose was Selwyn. I was amused by the whole argument. Her maiden name was Glick, not exactly an Anglo-Saxon name, which did not inhibit the many members of her family who reached eminence in their chosen professions. There was a hidden agenda in her intentions which, I think, were to separate her family from the rest of the family. The upshot of the matter was that Uncle Max's family changed their surname to Selwyn. I do not know what great effect it had on or difference it made to their lives. I did think that it was a matter entirely for them and that interference by other members of the family was unwarranted, but the members of my family never accepted such restrictions or allowed such liberal views to influence their attitudes. But the fact is that in time, they ceased to think of themselves as Schmulewitsches, they were now Selwyns, and separated themselves from the rest of the family.

Chapter 50 – Home And Army

The rest of my army service was uneventful. My school friends had all gone off in various directions, doing their own national service in less beneficial surroundings than mine or having gone on to university. I saw little of them except occasionally at the Spa when they were on holiday, but I became much more friendly with George Read, who was now living in Middlesbrough. We had known each other at school but because of the difference in our ages, had not then been close friends. He was three years older than me, and a class ahead of me. We met up, as it were, in the sixth form. We had also been in the school Scout group together. George had left school and started his army service in 1947 and went up to Durham University in October 1949.

At Durham, George met Nancy, on whom he showered limitless praises, all of them justified from my own impressions of her, but the greatest compliment, the ultimate accolade, was that she drank beer, which he considered an excellent thing in a woman. I went to Durham several times to see them, when suitable and invariably delightful company would be provided from their large number of friends. Those were very liquid, and would no doubt have been memorable, weekends had their recollection not been drowned in alcohol and clouded by tobacco.

George had been, for most of his time in the army, in Gibraltar, though from his accounts he appears to have spent most of his time in the bordellos of Tangier. His education in sexual matters seemed – and no doubt was – practical and comprehensive. He appears to have been an eager pupil, and passed on to me as much as he could of what he had learned. I was an avid listener. Though I had few opportunities at that time to turn theory into practice (an aspect in which I envied him), my education at George's feet stood me in good stead later in life. He is the only one of my school friends with whom I have kept in touch over the years. We spent a lot of time together when we were both at home, and continued our outings to the Spa, especially at Christmas and New Year.

George was my guru not only on matters sexual but in matters liquid. We would spend some time at the Zetland Hotel bar in Saltburn before going down to the Spa. One Christmas we had a few drinks before dancing, but met some (male) friends at the dance and decided to revert to the Zetland. As Norma was at university I had no steady girlfriend just then so no reason not to drink. A series of beers with rum chasers soon left us legless. When the bar closed we had to go home. After some difficulty we found the car. I was in no fit state to drive, nor was George to navigate. Though drink-drive laws were not as strict as now, they did exist. We discussed – for lack of a better word – what to do. It was too far to walk (some ten miles), too cold to sleep on the seafront; how would we explain our absence? There was nothing for it but to drive back. After a few efforts at walking up and down to try to sober up, we got into the car. We had further discussions as to what route to take. There were two possibilities: one was the fast route to Redcar and then along the straight wide road all the way back to the Borough. This would be full of traffic, other drunks and policemen. We decided to take the longer, windier, back roads, and to stop whenever we saw another car approaching. We drove very slowly for a few miles: all was well, and we were feeling rather pleased with ourselves. Then we saw a light approaching and stopped. We waited. The light came no nearer. I sent George to investigate. He came back ten minutes later to report it was only a street lamp. We continued our journey, albeit with frequent stops for comfort breaks, and got home some two hours later, safe and still free. I told George I was driving no further; he was welcome to our couch or whatever other accommodation was available. I cannot say with hand on heart that I thereafter always drove entirely sober, but I was never as drunk again.

I began to make new friends. I looked west rather than east, to Stockton. Though the Stockton and Middlesbrough Jewish families were all very friendly and formed part of the same social milieu, I barely knew my contemporaries as they were at public schools. They were now home, waiting to go to university or for their army call-up. Most chose to go to university first.

I had always been friendly with Brian Levy, who lived only a few houses away in Cambridge Road but saw little of him during our schooldays as he was away at Marlborough College and only came home for the holidays. His father was Victor Levy, the local pharmacist. Victor was short, round and bald. He was a quiet and gentle man, charming and urbane. Brian's mother, Esther, was tall, very attractive and much younger than Victor. She had an outgoing personality and quick wit. I liked her enormously. They were one of the several disparate married couples in the small Jewish community. They were mismatched in every way. I had the impression that theirs was not a happy marriage, and rumour had it that they each found solace elsewhere, but they never divorced; people – especially Jewish people – didn't.

Brian had his father's personality and his mother's looks. He was one of the nicest people I have known. He was always obliging, ever ready to join in our various activities, and never acerbic, bad-tempered or rude; I never heard him speak ill of anyone. He was without guile. We became very close friends. After university, Brian qualified as a solicitor, where I am sure his kindness and sympathetic manner put many a troubled client's mind at ease. Brian and I maintained our friendship even after I left the North East and settled in London. Some time after I was married, I was idly turning the pages of the *Evening Standard* on my way home from work on the Underground, when my eye was caught, for no particular reason, by a small paragraph at the bottom of a column on an inner page. This reported that the person killed in a motor car accident on the Great North Road had been identified as Brian Levy.

The shock must have shown on my face. As I arrived home my wife immediately asked what was wrong. I showed her the paragraph. "Surely it can't be your Brian Levy," she said. "What would he be doing down here?"

I prayed she was right, but a telephone call to his cousin Adrienne, confirmed my fears. No other car was involved, there was no apparent fault with his car, an Austin-Healey, nor any outward mark on his body. There was no apparent cause for the accident. Brian was not yet 30.

The small number of Jewish families in Stockton, though nominally subscribing to the Middlesbrough Hebrew Congregation did not really seem part of it. Stockton had no synagogue of its own. They appeared to be even more assimilated and detached from any observance of Judaism as a religion than the Middlesbrough Jews. My father tended to be somewhat critical – but only to himself – of those who appeared to have abandoned all religious practices and "kept nothing". It may have been easier to do this in Stockton than Middlesbrough where the social pressures in this respect – at least as expressed by my father – were greater.

Harry and Lena Cohen were one of the Stockton families. Harry was Esther Levy's brother, Brian's uncle. He was a very dapper figure; he was a man of few words and tended to keep his own counsel. Lena made up for him. She was a large, voluble, motherly person whose life, as did that of most of her generation, revolved around her family. She reminded me a little of my Aunt Jeanne; she was big-hearted and generous. They had one son Martin, and a daughter Adrienne, of whose existence I was at that time still unaware. They gave the impression of substantial wealth without any open display of extravagance, apart from their very large house, but this was no bigger and much less attractive than Brierfield. Harry Cohen was not a showy person. He was, in North Country terms, a "careful" man. He was not an easy man to get to know.

Martin was very different from his father and they had many spats. Looking at matters objectively, I am sure that his father was invariably in the right because Martin was one of the naughtiest boys I have known. Parties at Martin's house when his parents were away, or even just out for the evening were wild affairs. His favourite hiding place for his cans of beer was the piano. However well his father thought he had locked up the drinks cupboards, Martin found a way to open them. There was nothing nasty or vicious about him; he was kind and generous and would put himself out to an extraordinary degree to help a friend, but he was wild and, at that time, undisciplined. He and I became great friends, and he, Brian and I spent much time together.

Martin was a natural born leader, by example rather than by precept. He was medium height – about 5' 9" – very athletic and exceedingly handsome. He had something of an Errol Flynn look about him. He had charisma and was very macho. He also had great sex appeal; he liked girls and they would welcome him with open arms and more. I have known many men with charisma, but none to compare with him. Brian and I used to watch in wonder and envy. Where we had to work hard to score, Martin needed only to bend his little finger. His smile would win any heart, male or female. Even his father, at his crossest with Martin, could not resist that smile. His mother, needless to say, idolised and indulged him.

Martin was a County standard tennis and squash player. His style was his own and not one to be, or indeed capable of being, emulated. He was very fast about the court, in either discipline, had the quickest reflexes of anyone I have known, and an absolute determination not to be beaten. He was not bookish or intellectual, and had some difficulty with examinations. This was due not to any lack of intelligence or ability, but to his impatience, his hyperactivity which made him reluctant to sit still for any length of time. Though many of his friends may have envied his easy success in whatever he set out to achieve, they did so with admiration and affection. Martin, extrovert though he was, did not show off or throw his weight around with his friends. Our friendship long survived my departure from Teesside; indeed, we remained on very friendly terms till the day he died.

The group of friends which developed was very mixed. What we had in common was a sense of fun, wild spirits and the wish to indulge in the fling of youth before duty and serious life took over. One of this group was Bill, whose father had high military rank, a general, I believe. Bill was a real tearaway; he put Martin in the shade. Bill would do the most outrageous things; he was the upper-class equivalent of my old army mate, Jock from Kilbirnie. Though we all drove very fast, he was the worst; he was dangerous. He was small, fair-haired and neat. His room would have won the Gold Medal or Sword of Honour at any military inspection. Everything was in its place; symmetry ruled. There was no speck of dust; nothing disturbed the immaculate formality of that room. I found it astonishing and in a sense frightening because it was the last thing I would have expected from him. There was something psychopathic in all this measured (quite literally) order. Bill seemed to have no sense of propriety nor responsibility. He would not harm anyone deliberately but he seemed to have no idea of danger or thought what his actions might entail. He was a kind person but something of a loose canon. Yet his obsessive tidiness seems at odds with his behaviour otherwise. It may be that he simply liked taking risks. For all that, he was good fun. Bill one day persuaded me against my better judgment to go for a ride with him on the back seat of his motorbike. I was so terrified that I have never been on another. I do not know what happened to him.

Another Stockton family were the Mannings, Dr, Mrs and Michael. Dr Manning was a tall upright gentleman whose stern expression belied his friendliness. He was a local GP and gave the impression of being very competent. What Mrs Manning was doing in a place like Stockton is hard to know. She was a very smartly-dressed, attractive, urbane lady, whom one would have expected to meet in the social milieu of Chelsea rather than Stockton, which would not appear to provide a satisfactory social setting for her. She was wasted there.

Michael was a tall youth, somewhat camp, affected and pompous in his manner. He lived in the past. He was a rather engaging dinosaur even then. Gertrude Lawrence, Jack Hulbert and Jack Buchanan were his artistic heroes rather than the then current cinematic and theatrical favourites. He adored his mother and dressed in colourful waistcoats and velveteen jackets. His manner was more suited to a man of sixty than one of twenty, but no doubt he grew into it in time. He formed no part of Martin's tearaway mob, and we rather unkindly thought of him as a figure of fun. But this was unfair; Michael was a kind and good-natured sort, full of bonhomie and a genuine love of his fellow creatures. He affected an effeteness and aestheticism which did not fit in well with the area or society in which he lived. He was playing a part, but he enjoyed doing so, and was able to laugh at himself. I believe that at some stage in his youth he had been seriously ill and this had left him physically weakened. Michael "collected" all sorts of people, many of them Jewish officers stationed in nearby Catterick Camp, who were only too anxious for some civilised company at the weekend. And whatever his failings may have appeared to be to us, he was certainly that. I think that of all the crowd with whom I mixed I was the only one who appreciated and was friendly with Michael. I realised that culturally he was not our contemporary. He had social graces, albeit old-fashioned and somewhat pretentious at times. He was an excellent host and provided good and entertaining company. Michael was not a person I could – or wished – to get close to, but I liked him and always enjoyed his company which was an oasis of peace and quiet compared with the rumbustiousness of my other regulars.

I always enjoyed female company and after several months without I felt in need of it. Though memories remained, and my yearning for Norma was great, a chapter had been closed and life had to move on. There were reports that one of the local ladies' dress shops, part of a chain of shops owned by my friend Michael Blakey's mother's family, had just taken on a particularly attractive new model. My mother was a customer of the shop and as Mrs Blakey managed it, I had to be circumspect. I wanted to see for myself, if the reports were true. I had to find some excuse to go to the shop. My mother could not understand why I was so enthusiastic about returning some garment, a mission that normally I would have died rather than undertake; if she suspected my motives she said nothing and thus I was able to approach the real object of my mission and ask her out. My invitation was accepted without demur, without any of the usual pretended prevarications traditionally then adopted by young ladies for good form's sake, which immediately raised her in my estimation.

Jane was quite beautiful. She had a lovely, warm face with a beautiful complexion and wore very little make-up. As might be expected of a model she was quite tall and slim, but still well-rounded in the right places. Models then did not have the androgynous, cadaverous looks which Twiggy first made fashionable and which modern models have taken to the stage where even Twiggy looks overweight in comparison. Jane had long slim legs, she was always beautifully dressed, and was a flatteringly attractive companion. Conversations with her did not require any great exercise of the intellect. She had one interest, which we at least had in common. She was loving, affectionate and generous, but much as I liked her I was unable to reciprocate the feelings she showed for me. All went well for some time, until one evening as I was saying goodnight to her in my car, we were caught by her father, no doubt jealous for his daughter's reputation. I beat a hasty retreat, discretion, in my case, being the better part of valour and our relationship ended soon after. Jane turned up again some 20 years later, when she came to my office in London to ask me to undertake some legal work for her. She had lost the bloom of youth, but the years had dealt kindly with her, and she was as smart and attractive as when I had known her.

My army service was drawing to its close, and though it had been comfortable and for its last year uneventful, I was looking forward to going up to Oxford. I had not taken any leave. There seemed little point. I was already at home which is where I would normally have gone on leave. As I was on active service I was unable to leave the country without specific permission, and where would I have gone had I been able to? Europe was still in a mess recovering from the war and benefiting from the Marshall Plan. Backpacking, then still virtually unknown, did not appeal to me, nor did any sort of social work such as now undertaken by the VSO which did not then exist. I thought it better to carry my leave entitlements forward to ensure that I could get to Oxford in time, and indeed I started term while still on leave.

As I was seconded to the War Office I had to go to its Berkeley Square Headquarters in London for my demobilisation. One of the conditions of early release was that I was required to join the Supplementary Reserve for five years. After the necessary documentation had been completed I went straight up to Oxford. I kept my uniform and equipment as this would be needed were I required for immediate call-up, and for the annual camp.

I was officially demobbed on 16 October 1951, which was after term had started. At my first annual camp I was persuaded to volunteer for the Army Emergency Reserve, which meant that I was on the Reserve for a minimum period of five years. My rank was guaranteed and I was entitled to an extra £90 bonus, a considerable sum at that time in addition to the full regular sergeant's pay. The transition from Supplementary Reserve to AER was effected on 18 July 1952. I was discharged from this in August 1957.

Chapter 51 – Balliol

The start of the academic year at university is always chaotic. The main gate to the college is crowded and the porter's lodge besieged. Trunks, crates, cases, golf clubs, bicycles, tennis rackets, typewriters, and all the various paraphernalia brought by freshmen expecting a minimum stay of three years, as well as those returning from the long vacation at the start of their second and third years, were all over the place. Freshmen were besieging the lodge looking at the lists showing their allocated rooms trying to find where these were, asking the porter for directions and general information, others were shouting recognition to those they knew; there was a general hullabaloo. The whole scene was supervised by the imperturbable and splendid Cyril North, the head porter who, assisted by his staff, godlike, was creating order out of chaos.

My own luggage was not inconsiderable. As I had gone straight from being demobbed at Berkeley Square, Gene Stratton, the family chauffeur, brought my clobber down separately and met me at Oxford. I had a large trunk, several suitcases, a case of 33 rpm records (bulky and heavy), my life-saving Dansette record player and a large number of books, including those law books which had been on my required reading list which I now had hurriedly to read. I also had my football boots, my chess set, my little radio, my tennis racket and my bicycle, which I had abandoned when I started to drive but now resuscitated. Not forgotten were some tins of food (kosher, of course), in case I got hungry, courtesy of Tessie, who took over where my grandmother had left off, together with the appropriate two sets of eating implements and dishes (meat and milk). My clothes included dinner jacket and black tie, as well as a couple of formal suits. I was all set for the next three years.

My excitement was intense. My great ambition was being realised. I knew that the next three years would be the last time I could enjoy complete irresponsibility and independence. I was answerable to no one but myself. I could work as much or as little as I chose. The appropriate consequences would follow, but they would be of my own making.

I was allocated a room in Holywell Manor, which was not part of the main college building but an annex some seven minutes walk away, or two minutes by bicycle. I acquired a short gown (not being a scholar) and mortar board from the college porter for a small sum. The trade in these and the bicycles, which were traditionally left to him on leaving college, were a perk of his job. I was disappointed at first at not being given a room in college. The general rule was that you had a room in college for two years and spent the third in lodgings. My disappointment turned to joy on seeing Holywell Manor. This was a fairly small (by college standards) building of grey Oxford stone. Its appearance from the outside was inauspicious, as it presented a blank wall with a doorway and some small windows to the road. The narrow entrance led to a small courtyard overlooked by a small porter's room. From the yard some steps led to a hall, which in turn led to the various rooms on the ground floor and to the first and second floors, where most of the students' rooms were. The entrance and access generally were not impressive but the rest of the building was.

The rooms were modern – by the standards of the Oxford of 1951 – spacious and comfortable. Suites consisting of two bedrooms, each with its own wash basin, a lounge/study, bathroom, and toilet, were shared by two freshmen. Single rooms were usually for second- or third-year undergraduates. There was hot and cold running water and central heating, far from the conditions of the rooms I occupied when I sat my Entrance Scholarship. This was unexpected luxury. Every room looked out on the gardens. The house, some 200 years old, had been acquired by Balliol in about 1931 and after considerable reconstruction reopened in 1932. It was in a traditional Oxford renaissance style and U-shaped. The gardens occupied the space between the wings and the areas all round them. The central area of the garden was partly sunk and paved, an ideal setting for plays, dances and parties. The place was idyllic, and I could think of no more convivial surroundings in which to work, or not, as the fancy took. Holywell Manor was to be my Oxford home for the next three years.

Russell Meiggs, a classics don, was the Praefectus in charge of the Manor, assisted by his charming and very attractive wife Paula, also an academic. Both had a great sense of humour and exercised their authority with a very light hand. They had two young daughters, charming girls, and they created a family atmosphere. Russell typified what the outside world expected a don to be and look like. He had long flowing hair, or to be more accurate, hair which looked as if it would have been flying along behind him like a mane, had it not been cut off halfway along its length. It was rather like a modern racing bicycle helmet made of hair. I do not know how he managed it, but for all the years, both at university and after, that I knew him, his hair never changed, except that in later years it grew slightly greyer.

Mr and Mrs Ward, a homely couple, who embodied all the finest traditional qualities of college servants, looked after the daily operation of the Manor, which included the provision of an excellent breakfast, much better than was served in college. They were always ready to oblige with any personal request outside their normal duties. I do not think I was given any special treatment, but so far as I was concerned, no request was ever refused; they spoiled me as completely as if I had been their child.

The Manor had its own Junior Common Room, that is a committee of its inhabitants, to which was delegated the policymaking function, including such matters as what newspapers to have, what pictures to hang, and what festivities to provide. The President of the JCR, who also represented the Manor ex officio at the college JCR was David Bucknill, a charming and unassuming man.

My co-tenant was Mike Hodgson, from Wyggeston Grammar School in Leicester. He was slightly taller than me, about 6' 1", with disproportionately small feet which seemed to affect his stability. Though we got on well we were not on the same wavelength and did not have the same interests. He was pleasant enough but our relationship was never really warm.

The Freshmen's Dinner takes place on the first night of the Hilary (autumn) term, the start of the academic year. Thus it was that I found myself walking to college with a number of others from Holywell Manor, and ended up sitting at Hall next to or opposite a number of people who were one way or another to have an impact on my life and with whom I formed long – indeed lifelong – friendships. Their names were Clive Tayler, Vernon, then better known as Tod, Handley, and Glen Petrie.

We had to eat dinner in Hall at least five nights a week. It was not compulsory but you were charged for the meal whether you had it or not, and having regard to the usual impecuniosity of undergraduates, you did not throw money away lightly. This was intended to, and did, create a collegiate spirit. Dinner in Hall, was in a way, the keystone of college life, and was almost ritualistic. It was usually preceded by a drink, generally a pint or two of beer, in the Buttery, the college bar, conveniently placed directly under the Hall, and followed by coffee in the JCR afterwards. Dinner was at 7 p.m. and the steep steps leading to the College Hall would be full of men (no women then) waiting for the doors to open. The seating accommodation, which has not changed for decades, is uncomfortable but fit, I suppose, for students. Except on very formal occasions there were no set places, it was first come, and, if lucky, first served. Hall did enable you to meet contemporaries from other years, other disciplines and interests. This was one of the few opportunities to do so. At the top of the Hall on a plat-form was the High Table where the Master (if he attended) and the dons sat with their visitors. The quality of the food left much to be desired, though the college chefs could perform well on special occasions. Remarkably, when I started at Balliol there was still food rationing and I had to hand in my ration book.

Balliol is not a particularly beautiful college. It has a pleasant garden, and is homely. The Hall, though beautifully panelled is not exceptional by Oxford standards. The social centre of college was the JCR in the main quad. It was then an exclusively male preserve. The JCR, after dinner, was usually full as people queued for their coffee, talking incessantly, trying to read the papers or planning the rest of the evening's, or the week's, activities. George Steiner was one of the orators often to be heard, among many. He has not changed much. All the gossip and scandals were heard in the JCR; many probably originated there.

One evening as I was standing in the coffee queue I heard Len Barden, one of the leading English chess players, and still the chess correspondent of the *Financial Times*, discussing chess matters with John Sykes, who later became the crossword editor of the *Times*, and himself no mean player. I mentioned that I had played a little chess for, among others, Middlesbrough Chess Club in the North Yorkshire and South Durham League, and Yorkshire County in postal games, and that I had had some success at club and these levels. Len suggested we might have a game, then and there. Chess was commonly played in the JCR and there were plenty of sets available. We found the nearest thing to a quiet corner, and started the game. We were soon surrounded, and I felt very nervous and sorry that I had opened my big mouth. However, I began to recover my confidence and to my surprise as well as that of most of the onlookers, I managed to hold Leonard to a draw. On the strength of that I was chosen to play at fourth board for the college, which I felt was not bad, as the first three boards were Leonard, Israel Persitz, the Israel National Junior Champion and John Sykes. I played chess regularly for the college after that with a fair measure of success. Our highlight was when the Balliol A team (the first three boards) met the Balliol B team, the next three boards, of which I was the first, in the Chess Cuppers (the university chess competition). We drew all three games.

I joined the Oxford Union, mainly for its excellent billiard and snooker tables and bar, rather than for its debates, but these were often interesting. To someone like myself, the formalities of the debates, the officers – president, librarian, secretary – the purported emulation of parliamentary procedures – were fascinating. Balliol has traditionally been influential in the Union and there was a natural gravitational pull to it, but I had no desire to stand for office or even to speak. I admired the confidence and polish of some of the speakers. Patrick Mayhew, later QC and cabinet minister, was one of the Balliol presidents of the Union in my years. He was a year or two ahead of me. He was also reading Law, so I saw something of him outside his public persona, which was impressive then and remained so.

Theodore Tylor – many years later to be knighted – the Law tutor and Balliol College bursar, was one of the most remarkable personalities not only in Balliol but in legal academia generally. He was effectively blind, with perhaps five per cent vision. He had attended the Worcester College for the Blind of which, in due course, he was to become the president. He had a frighteningly comprehensive knowledge of all branches of law. Whereas other colleges sent their pupils to tutors in various subjects or to other colleges, he taught us everything himself. He was a big man in every way. Well over 6 feet tall and corpulent, he was a distinguished figure as he strode through the college with his white stick which he seemed never to use for its intended purpose. He was single-minded about his subject and demanding of the highest standards. He was also an excellent chess player, and seemed able to recall all the games he had played. When I arrived for a tutorial he would say: "Ah, Fishburn (no first names with him), you will be interested by a game I had last Saturday. I was black and my opponent opened with a Queen's Gambit which I declined and the game developed..." He would then go through the whole game at breakneck speed, explaining finally the intricacy of the ending, in which he had captured the White Queen with a fork, or some similar coup, ending up: "What do you think of that, eh?" I had lost him at move three. I could hardly have followed it all written down.

I have known bridge players who are able to recall every hand played during the course of an evening but they were not blind. Surprisingly, he also played bridge very well. Exactly how, I never discovered, though I did play some bridge games with him and his sister. He seemed to hold his cards very close to his eyes and could just about see them, and as the various cards were played to each trick they were called out to him and he memorised them.

His mother and his sister Peggy kept house for him. They were a very close family who devoted their lives to his well-being. Every term, Theo would invite all his law students for tea, the fare at which never varied, and halfway through he would change places with his sister. These were formalised rituals, which we tended to mock, but anyone not invited would have been mortally offended, and it was very generous of Theo and his sister to give these tea parties. Theo was very formal. Even in 1951 it was common to address one's tutor by his (or exceptionally her) first name, and be so addressed in return, but no one would have had the temerity to address Theo Tylor by his, and we were all called by our surnames, even at the tea parties. I even now feel some diffidence in speaking of him as "Theo".

The essence of Oxford teaching is the tutorial system and as a method of teaching I can think of nothing better. The person-to-person dialogue allows for a proper exchange of ideas and the direct criticism has an immediate impact. Two would share a tutorial, and Theo tended to move us around so that we were likely to have a different partner each term. No doubt he saw some advantage in this but I did not, as not all sharing a tutorial were of equal ability. Presumably, in theory this should not happen, but in practice it did.

Oxford then was a place of strange contrasts. The first thing one noticed was the absence of women; Oxford was very male-oriented and that is the greatest contrast with Oxford today. Old practices which may have had some logic or reason in past times, when the university was largely a place for clerics, were retained long after their purpose had been exhausted. Among other such rules, inconsistent with the idea that students were adult citizens, women had to be out of college by 10 p.m. College gates were closed at midnight and students had to spend a given number of nights each term in Oxford, otherwise they would not have "done their terms" and would not have qualified to take their finals at the end of their third year. I had to obtain an exeat, a leave of absence, to go up to London to eat my dinners at the Middle Temple, another anachronism, which had to be done if I wished, as I then did, to go to the Bar on leaving Oxford.

It is true that many of these rules were difficult to monitor. Many undergraduates were in lodgings for two years out of three. Every college had its unofficial climbing-in route for after hours. Holywell Manor was so easy even I could manage it, thanks to the tomb or catafalque of A. G. Skeat, the Anglo-Saxon scholar and ecclesiastical historian. But occasionally a student, who had had just that little bit too much to drink, would fall and hurt himself, sometimes seriously, so this was not altogether harmless. For the most part these rules were honoured in the breach rather than the observance, but they were an affront to many of my contemporaries who had spent several years in the forces, some having seen active service, and to the many mature Rhodes scholars from the United States and elsewhere. One of our residents at the Manor was Andy Remson, an American, who had reached the rank of colonel in the US Army. Undergraduates needed special permission from the college to have cars in Oxford. Andy had a huge American car which he had difficulty manoeuvring around Oxford. Exceptionally, you might receive permission to have a car in your last year – I did – but you had to attach a small green light to the front for identification.

To enforce university discipline there were two proctors, elected by the various colleges in turn, and their bulldogs. The proctor was a sort of university policeman and the bulldogs, who were college scouts, or servants, his assistants. They were identifiable by their bowler hats. (They reminded me of the Military Police and their distinctive red caps.) They had the power to fine or rusticate, or even send down, that is expel, a student for what they considered to be a wrongdoing, which might simply be the failure to wear a gown at night. J. C. Masterman, in his book *To Teach the Senators Wisdom*, quotes the story that complaints were made to one proctor because an undergraduate had been observed bathing naked late one summer evening. Unsure how to deal with this transgression, because that was not itself prohibited, the proctors fined the student five shillings (a large sum at the time) for not wearing his cap and gown after dark. The proctor was doubtless a necessary invention when there were frequent clashes between Town and Gown, that is between the students and the townsfolk, to ensure that authority for matters of discipline was retained by the university. Town and Gown have physically grown so far apart that such clashes rarely occur.

In contrast to these anachronistic rules, which sought to impose a paternalistic authority, was the reality that once in Oxford you were on your own. There was no parental help, no back-up service or support. You had to find out everything for yourself, often in the face of what was either uncaring ignorance or what appeared to be deliberate obstructionism. In this respect, being at the Manor was a great advantage as we were a close community, and you could usually get help or advice from Russell or Mrs Meiggs, or the Wards. The lodge porters at college were as helpful as they could be but they were usually busy or did not have the required information. No one ever seemed to know where anything was or could be obtained, even simple things, like shopping. You had to find everything out for yourself. When it came to trying to find the reading matter prescribed by your tutor for research, my experience was that in general the librarians were particularly unhelpful.

They gave the impression that they did not trust you with their precious books. As I disliked reading in libraries, and had the money to do so, I would buy the books when I could but there were many which were available only in libraries such as the Radcliffe Camera or the Bodleian. I actually enjoyed researching. All Souls College had an excellent Law Library and I exempt the librarian there from any criticism. One could only have access to that on the personal recommendation of a Fellow, or one's tutor, and, no doubt, Theo Tylor's fiat commanded respect.

Those who came up to Oxford in my years there and those in the preceding years after the end of the war, were fortunate in that most of the male undergraduates were comparatively mature. Nearly all had done their national service. Some had been in the forces for several years, some had served in battle and some had, like Andy Remson, achieved high, commissioned ranks. Though they were well able to join in the frivolities of undergraduate life, and often instigated them, and were there to enjoy the experience of Oxford, they had a serious purpose and usually knew where they were going. They had much catching up to do and no time to waste.

Chapter 54 – Three Men And Me

I was happy to live in my own world, or would have been had I been allowed to, but my friends had little respect for my privacy in that respect. I had, as mentioned, three particular friends.

The most remarkable of these was Vernon Handley, otherwise known as Tod. He was a grammar school boy, from Enfield. He was slightly older than myself, about the same height, of slim build. He was a man of many parts, and good at all of them. He played football and tennis well. He was also a keen ornithologist; I remember that he once made a study of the whitethroat, and became sufficiently expert to write a paper on it. He had a quick wit and keen sense of humour which could, however, sometimes be biting, as tolerance was not among his qualities. He was ego-centric and single-minded, qualities which may have been neces-sary for his success in his career against all odds, but which did not endear him to all. Diplomacy and tact were not words in his vocabulary. He made as many enemies as friends. There was an element of defiance in his attitude. Given a choice of how to go about things or what course to follow he always chose the harder route. He had something of a chip on his shoulder perhaps because his background had been modest. His finances were always tight, which was not surprising when his local authority scholarship was worth only £250 p.a. as against mine which was worth £440. Yet he was able to motivate people of all sorts, even those not necessarily sympathetic to him, by sheer force of person-ality, and inspire great loyalty and devotion: there was no shortage of Tod "groupies", of whom, I suppose, for a long time, I was one.

Tod read English, and, typically, decided to specialise in Norse and Old English. His tutor in these was a female don, who did not succeed in escaping his charms, not that she wanted to. But Tod's overwhelming passion was music; his all-consuming ambition was to become an orchestral conductor, not easy to achieve for one who could play no musical instrument and had had no formal musical education. He put much more effort into his music than into his prescribed subjects. Tod, self-taught, would spend hours poring over orchestra scores, mainly of modern English music, humming the various parts *sotto voce*, but still loud enough to be heard. His musical memory was prodigious.

Through Tod, I found a new world of music. His interests lay in Bax rather than Bach, Bliss rather than Beethoven, and Moeran rather than Mahler. He introduced me to the music of Gerald Finzi, Edward Rubbra, and other English composers of whom, to my shame, I had not heard though I cannot say that I always came to share Tod's enthusiasms. Much of his career was devoted to furthering the cause of British music, and its current popularity is in no small measure due to him. My own musical education inevitably flourished, almost by a process of osmosis.

Oxford has always had an active undergraduate musical life, much of which was centred on the Holywell Music Rooms, just around the corner from Holywell Manor. Tod joined the Musical Society and soon made his mark. Never shy, he wrote to his idol, Sir Adrian Boult, then the leading English conductor, and to my surprise, but not to Tod's, he received an invitation from the great man. Tod went to see him and Sir Adrian was so impressed that he took Tod under his wing. As conductors must have a musical instrument, Tod took up the double bass after leaving Oxford and went on to music college for a formal musical education.

Tod, who reverted to being called Vernon Handley for professional purposes, achieved his ambitions, and made a very successful career, even being invited to conduct the Last Night of the Proms. Some of his recordings of the music of Elgar, Vaughan Williams, Malcolm Arnold, Walton and others are regarded as authoritative interpretations of these works. But all this was far into the future. I always felt that Tod, for whatever reason, did not receive the recognition and status that might have been expected in the light of his abilities and his popularity with the musicians who played for him.

Life with Tod was not easy, as I was neither the first nor the last to find out, and required the exercise of considerable tolerance. He undoubtedly used people, and discarded them when they were of no further use, particularly his women. He was one of those men whom women found irresistible. He never lacked for female companionship, even at a time when women were scarce in Oxford. Tod's own account of his latest form of brush-off went as follows: "Oh, Tod, why haven't I heard from you? I thought you wanted to see more of me!" Tod: "Why, is there any more?"

With Tod around there was never a dull moment. He had enormous energy and imagination. I learned much from him, and admired his better qualities. I enjoyed his company and life would have been much poorer without him, but there were aspects of his personality to which I became increasingly unsympathetic. To Tod, friendship meant unquestioning admiration, which is not how I saw it. I could be just as outspoken as Tod, though I tried to be so with an element of diplomacy. He was never visibly put out or at a loss for words. If someone upset him, he would usually be a person with a "pointed head who must be very unhappy". Tod was not a deep analyst of people. But throughout our time at Oxford, though we lived in great proximity and shared rooms, and were nearly always together, we never had a cross word. Strangely, in light of the time we spent together and how close we were at university, his influence on me was evanescent. We kept in touch after college to the extent that I tried to attend all Tod's concerts in London and went backstage to see him and to dinner afterwards if possible, but these occasions became increasingly rare. We did not correspond or speak on the telephone as I did with Clive and Glen. Every time I met Tod he seemed to have another wife; I don't know how often he was married.

Tod, among his other abilities, had considerable talent as an impresario. Towards the end of our first term, David Bucknill, the Manor JCR president, asked for help to organise the traditional Christmas Dance at the Manor. Tod and I, in effect, took over the whole matter. Tod looked after the organisation of the event – the decorations, the band, the buffet – and I took charge of the finances. These annual dances had been running at a loss, putting a burden on the JCR funds rather than contributing to them. My first move was to substantially increase the price of tickets.

David was horrified. "No one will come," he said. "Did you have any tickets left over last year?" I asked. "No," he said. "We won't this year either," I assured him. Russell Meiggs was equally worried, but rather on the grounds that perhaps we were not projecting the right image. I inquired exactly what image did he want us to project, and assured him that he could safely leave the matter to us.

Marketing such events is strange. There is a snobbery about attending expensive functions. Everyone wants to be seen there, in case it is thought that they cannot afford to go. It seemed to me that we should tap into this market and put the Holywell Manor dance on the social map. On the other hand, a balance has to be struck, so that you do not discourage those who really could not afford the price. We kept back a few tickets for deserving causes, like our friends. The dance was a tremendous success. This was in very large part due to Tod's organisational talents. He cajoled, bullied and marshalled all the available resources to design the decor and make and put up the decorations. His enthusiasm and drive ensured that there was no lack of helpers. It was quite a tour de force on his part. Mine was the easy part; selling the tickets and counting the profit. We could have sold twice the number of tickets, and the JCR coffers were back in the black. There was an immediate waiting list for our next function. Even this did not quite satisfy David and Russell. They still had misgivings about making a profit. It really wasn't the "done thing". This was my first experience of Oxford's lack of any sense of commerciality.

Tod and I ran the Balliol dances the three years we were there. His talent for organisation and for driving others was the key to their success. I found him easy to work with, and learned much from our theatrical – because that is what it was – cooperation. We each brought to the venture complementary skills and neither of us interfered in matters outside our respective agreed responsibilities.

Glen Petrie was another great friend, and still is. His father was a general practitioner in Ulverston, on the edge of the Lake District. Glen had been at Bradfield College, a public school noted for its Greek Theatre. He took me there once to a performance in Greek of a play by Aristophanes. Though I could not understand a word, not having learned Greek, I understood everything. It was an experience I have not forgotten.

Despite having served in the army in the Far East, and reaching the rank of sergeant, Glen was remarkably unworldly. It was almost as if his life had been spent in a cocoon, a world of his own. Glen was, in a strange way, an innocent at large. He was probably the most civilised and cultured of the four of us. He appeared to have read everything and remembered it all. He had a great love and knowledge of music, but, above all, he was a cinema buff, and introduced me to a world of which, apart from my brief and unconsummated love affair with Arletty (*Les Enfants du Paradis*), I knew nothing. It was Glen Petrie who had the greatest influence on me, and who started the process of civilising an unpolished Northerner.

Glen did not get on well with his American roommate, Fred Frey, who had a somewhat regimented idea of life, no sense of humour, and even less charm. Though he disliked Mike Hodgson, my roommate, Glen more or less set up camp in my room and effectively, cuckoo-like, evicted Mike from his nest. I enjoyed Glen's company; he was witty and urbane. Several times a week he would drag me off to see the latest foreign film or classic at the local cinema. Thus it was that I came to see (often several times) the great Orson Welles films, *Citizen Kane, The Magnificent Ambersons,* and incomprehensible and arty French films, although some such as *Orphee* were even quite good. We watched sexy or tear-jerking Italian films, dour German classics, and mind-blowing Russian masterpieces, *The Battleship Potemkin* and *Ivan the Terrible* to name just two.

Glen read History, or to be more accurate, was meant to do so. He had spent his life before Oxford, it would appear, only in the company of men, apart from his mother. The attractions of Oxford and the sight of girls – few as they were – and one in particular, completely distracted Glen from even the minuscule amount of work required to pass Mods. The Oxford exam system is not easily explained. My parents were not able to understand it. Most academic institutions have exams at the end of each year; Oxford has Moderations, defined as "the first public examination in some faculties for the BA degree at Oxford University", after the first two terms. If you fail this you can resit at the end of the third term. A little application and effort are sufficient to overcome this initial hurdle. The compensation, however, is that there are no more public examinations until finals. You can enjoy four terms of comparative idleness – you had to work for the last three – except at Balliol, which takes its academic reputation seriously and insists on setting internal exams each term.

Like all undergraduates, I suppose, we had long philosophical discussions; we drank up the culture now freely accessible, we learned to dine well, to tell one wine from another, and some of us occasionally put our nose in a textbook. Glen was probably the most academically able of us all, yet he failed his Mods and suddenly he was gone. All this I discovered later. There seems to be a conspiracy of silence at college about anyone who leaves. There was no farewell, no leave-taking, no news. He came to my 21st birthday party in June 1952 and yet when we started term the following year there was no Glen, no news, no notice, no letter. Glen was expunged.

I missed him. We had become very good friends in that short time, even visiting each other's homes. His influence on me was wholly beneficial. I can only wish that I had had an equally beneficial influence on him. It seems that Glen was so intoxicated by the absolute freedom he enjoyed for the first time in his life, that he forgot to exercise the self-discipline necessary to ensure that he did enough work to overcome the small hurdle of Mods. I was very cross with him at the time for what I considered a waste of talent, but even more so for the loss – I did not know then that it was only to be temporary – of a valued friend.

I saw nothing of Glen for a long time, except once out of a train window at Didcot, on my way back to Oxford, so I knew he was still alive. Long after I was married, I was driving up one of the local streets very near my home, when I saw, walking on the pavement on the other side of the road, a figure remarkably like Glen, accompanied by what proved to be his wife and family. I stopped my car in some disbelief, ran across the road and called his name; my identification was accurate. The true mark of friendship, I think, is that you can immediately pick up where you left off after a gap of many years. Since he had left Oxford, Glen had been a schoolmaster, gone back to university at Exeter, met and married Pat, an outstanding personality, had several sons, and settled not a quarter of a mile from where I was living with my family. I made sure that I kept him under surveillance thereafter. I owe him much, especially in regard to this book.

Clive Tayler, was the third and by no means the least of my close friends. He was the youngest of us, not yet having done his military service. Clive was, like Tod and me, a grammar school boy. He was tall, slim, fair-haired, diffident and engagingly modest, not a quality common at Oxford, and less self-confident than was appropriate in the light of his abilities. His father was an agent for hop-growers, and his mother a schoolteacher. Clive was also reading Law, and this brought us close. I like to think that I taught Clive something about life and people from the vantage point of two years' seniority and a brilliant army career – his father seemed to think that I had had that – and he taught me some law. He was highly intelligent, and mastered his subject with great speed. He also worked very hard, by my standards, not his. Clive had decided he wanted a first-class degree and worked conscientiously to get one. He studied for at least 4 to 5 hours a day every day. He could always explain to me some abstruse point of law which I failed to understand, but his caution and accuracy kept in check my wilder flights of fancy. We complemented each other.

Clive and I both intended to go to the Bar, but he still had to complete his national service. Clive was one of the most patient and forbearing people I have known. I have never seen him angry, or ill-tempered. He saw some good in everyone, and I have never heard him speak ill, or even critically, of anyone. His tolerance, in the face of my frequent lack of it, had a calming influence. Though I did not appreciate it then, he had the qualities to make the good judge he became later in his career. Clive may have been younger, less experienced and perhaps somewhat less confident at first than the rest of us, but he had mature qualities which belied his years and which it might have benefited some of us to have adopted. At times I became a little exasperated with him when he showed what I considered an excess of tolerance to some I could cheerfully have strangled, but Clive did not allow a close friendship to influence his own views, whether about people or otherwise. In this respect, as in curbing my wilder legal flights of fancy, he exercised a moderating influence on me which was wholly beneficial. Above all, Clive was a friend you could always rely on.

Holywell Manor was fortunately situated just across the road from the Balliol playing fields, tennis courts and squash courts. Clive and I played tennis or squash according to the time of year and the weather virtually every day throughout the time we were at Oxford together. We usually played before breakfast when the courts were empty, but sometimes more than once a day. Most of the games were very close, but whether it was my extra years or my extra weight, I do not know, on balance I won more often than Clive. He and I kept in touch, and met regularly. Sadly, he died unexpected in February 2017 while I was writing this book.

Chapter 55 – Settling In

The first term at Oxford is inevitably a confusing time. Oxford was a culture different from any other, except perhaps Cambridge, and it took a little time to adjust. Everything was new and, to me, exciting. I was in one of my periodical states of wild enthusiasm. Oxford terms are short – only eight weeks. Allowing for the time it takes to find your feet, the first term seems considerably shorter. The novelty of strange surroundings, the making of new friends, finding your way around, and the process of starting a new subject from a position of complete ignorance, combine to leave memories of the first term a mass of confused impressions from which only a few images stand out. Being in the Thames Valley and in the shadow of the Chiltern Hills, Oxford is subject to autumn mists and there were days of matchless beauty. I was constantly reminded that this was the "Season of mists and mellow fruitfulness" which Oxford in autumn defines. The autumn colours, the few still warm days, and the weakening sun shining on the Oxford stone created a beauty which I had not seen before, and which is unique. Though I had never been much given to walking, except where it was the only means of getting from one place to another, I would often wander alone around the streets near Holywell Manor, which was particularly happily situated for such excursions, to Magdalen College and along the river, or in the parks or just through the various colleges, enjoying their quiet beauty. I was never lonely in my own company, and these little meanderings were often my only solitude. It was not that I did not enjoy company, but I needed a little breathing space now and again.

One of the idiosyncrasies of Oxford was the dress code. The basics comprised a scarf, ties bearing the college colours or crest and the badges of any society you had joined, bicycle clips, and an umbrella. I stuck at this. l was astonished to see young men carrying umbrellas, both furled and open. No man in my northern part of the world would be seen dead carrying an umbrella. That was the ultimate symbol of decadence. Umbrellas were nearly as bad as galoshes. Only women and toffs carried umbrellas. (Michael Manning, my friend from Stockton had an umbrella.) Our only concession to the weather was to wear a heavier coat. But umbrellas were very definitely out. It took me some time to overcome this hang-up, but that was not until well after I had come to London.

I suppose that most undergraduates aspire to be different, to foster an individual characteristic, if only to retain some private identity, by their dress or manners. In my case it was probably my northernness. This must have stayed with me, because some decades later, after I had lived in London for many years, my youngest daughter, who is not usually at a loss for words, baffled and frustrated by what she considered my obtuseness or more kindly, obstinacy, having considered what might be an appropriate insult without being offensive, said "Oh, Dad you're so, so – long pause – Northern." But for someone seeking an identity it was as good a place as any to start.

The other traditional Oxford teaching method, apart from the tutorial, is the lecture. Attendance at lectures is not compulsory. Tutors would recommend certain lectures. A good lecturer – few and far between – will maintain his audience throughout the series of lectures.

There are, in effect, only three good reasons for going to lectures, unless you happen to be one of those rare people who actually derives some benefit from them. These are, first, that the lecturer is charismatic, and is worth listening to for his or her own sake; secondly, that he or she is dealing with a subject which is constantly developing and has something new to say about it, and last, that the information is not available elsewhere.

Rupert Cross, who lectured on Criminal Law was in the first category. He was a tall, handsome man, completely blind, another alumnus of the Worcester Royal College for the Blind, whose lectures were spell-binding tours de force. Criminal Law, as opposed to Roman Law, is constantly changing and there is always something new to say. Rupert Cross's lectures were among the few which I found it worthwhile to attend, and from which I actually learned something. My first term's studies therefore consisted of preparing and writing the weekly essay, the weekly tutorial, and attending Rupert Cross's lectures.

Professor Hart, to whose lectures on Equity I was directed some terms later, was the complete contrast to Rupert Cross. Professor Hart's academic brilliance is beyond dispute. He was acknowledged to be an unchallenged authority on his subject and a fine and original thinker. The only trouble was that he thought aloud. His lectures took place in the Schools, the university building on the High Street. There was a full house, standing room only, for his opening lecture. His second lecture played to a half full house, and the attendance reduced proportionally thereafter, so that by the middle of term there were fewer than a dozen people. He was quite unable to make any contact with his audience, if that was indeed his intention. He could hardly be heard, he looked out of the window when talking, like a singer with his back to the audience, he went off his subject at tangents.

The first term was far too hectic for me to settle into a routine. As for girls, I had had no time to think about them or miss them. Neville Cohen had come up one year earlier to St John's, which is conveniently next door to Balliol but I only saw a little of him during the first term. He was already well established and had his own coterie of friends. I was still a rookie. At Oxford you make a large number of acquaintances and move in several circles at once, which do not necessarily overlap. Lawyers will mix with other lawyers; you join a special interest club, and move within that circle; you play football or chess or row, and you make friends with those interests in common. These are not limited to your own year. I joined the Jewish Society, which is in effect socially obligatory. Though I was not a particularly active member I made a number of friends there. Oxford is not very different from society at large in this respect; the main difference is that like everything else in Oxford, the effect is far more concentrated, and there never seemed time to do anything in-depth, at least, not if you spread yourself as widely as I did.

Chapter 56 – Storm Clouds

The Christmas vacation was suddenly on us, and Stratton came with the car to fetch me, spoiled brat that I was. My parents and Tessie were clearly anxious to hear all about my life at Oxford. My parents had rarely shown any direct interest in what I did or in my academic life, but Oxford was another matter. I was questioned in a way that I had not previously known from my parents. I had been used to, and would have expected, severe questioning on every aspect of my doings from Dora and Yetti, who were both insatiably inquisitive. I was as mystified by this altered attitude as I was gratified.

I saw much of my local friends, but had no regular girlfriends at the time. We – Brian Levy, Martin and I – ventured further afield, as I had heard that there were some dances at Whitley Bay, near Sunderland, where one might meet Jewish girls. Sunderland and Newcastle had sizeable Jewish communities. I met one very pretty dark-haired girl, on whose account I repeated the journey a few times, but I decided that she was not really worth a detour, far less a journey, in Michelin terms.

Martin Cohen's parents were at our house one evening, when Lena Cohen asked whether I would like to meet her daughter. I did not know she had one; Martin had kept very quiet on the subject. No doubt he had forgotten to mention the fact. I said I should be delighted, not knowing what to expect, but there was no harm in being polite.

Adrienne was a breath of fresh air. She was very young, sweet sixteen. She was fair-haired, fair-skinned, and pretty; she had the looks of a typical English rose. Like Martin, she was high-spirited and full of fun. She was much more disciplined and actually more mature than Martin. She had the family athleticism and sporting skills, and though I rather fancied myself as no mean tennis player, I rarely beat her. She hit the ball like a man and was exceedingly fast around the court. We saw a lot of each other that vacation and on subsequent vacations, and I always felt better for having been with her. She had a cheerfulness and natural sympathy and understanding, which belied her years. She diverted me from the increasingly bizarre, but harmless, antics of Martin and the rest of the Stockton gang, and, indeed, had a civilising influence on us all. She had the added advantage that I need have no inhibitions about bringing her home.

But at the factory, all was not well: storm clouds were looming. My parents, and indeed my family as a whole, had always tried to shield me from the unpleasant things in life. I had a very protected and sheltered existence. They did not seem to have noticed that I had grown up while they were not looking. I became aware that there were serious difficulties at Guisborough from the heated and often personally abusive discussions conducted at high volume with Max. I was quite used to these from early youth, but now they were far worse than any I had known before. My family all had the saving grace that, however bitter the vituperation, however insulting the exchanges, however harsh the language, and though they might start to row again the next day, where they had left off, once tempers had cooled, there was no rancour or hard feelings. They immediately forgot what had been said, indeed, even often the cause of the dispute. Whereas a neutral observer might have expected them not to talk to each other ever again, their relationships were not adversely affected by their rows. Before my hypertension was diagnosed I had a similar disposition. I could completely lose my temper, but five minutes afterwards I was not aware that there had been any unpleasantness, or that I may have said things which, had I remembered them, I might have regretted. But these arguments seemed different. There was a distinct palpable after-effect, a feeling of unease, frustration and deep concern, as, indeed, proved to be justified. For the first time, these discussions spilled over at home into arguments between my parents and affected the easy tenor of our home life.

At that time, M&S had a large number of manufacturers producing the same line of goods, shirts, for example. In order to achieve standardisation they imposed stringent requirements. All their suppliers had to obtain their raw materials from designated sources and goods had to be manufactured, labelled, and packaged in the same way. To a large extent, M&S treated their manufacturers as glorified outworkers, but they gave their suppliers every possible advice and assistance in satisfying their requirements and maintaining quality. M&S goods were sold on the basis of quality, they were never too cheap but their suppliers were always paid a fair price. To be a M&S supplier was greatly desired, and many companies made their fortunes that way, but there was a price to be paid, namely excellence.

M&S regularly sent inspectors to their suppliers, unannounced, to check quality and these inspectors reported back to Head Office. If the reports were unfavourable, M&S would send along their production experts to see what was going wrong and to try to correct the faults. Sometimes problems arose from sudden style changes, or some similar policy decision by M&S. The immediate problem at Guisborough was that M&S were not satisfied with the quality of the shirts being made for them. The factory was treated no less favourably than any other supplier, and considerable practical help was offered.

At Guisborough the cause was more deep-rooted. There were two basic problems. The first was bad management. Max, the Managing Director, was convinced of his own infallibility and refused to take advice from anyone. By his temper, his shouting and his sheer willpower he overrode all other opinions. My father lacked the strength of personality to stand up to him and my mother could no longer stand the strain of trying to run the production side of the factory with the constant shouting matches. She knew what was wrong and what needed to be done, but Max knew better. When it came to bringing in new personnel he had a talent for constantly appointing the wrong people. He was easily taken in by anyone who had an impressive CV and interviewed well. Like many salesmen he could not read between the lines, or see behind the person. My mother knew her girls and the staff she had to deal with. She knew that what was needed was someone with an understanding of the business who could bring out the best from the workforce. Unfortunately, she was probably the only one who had the necessary qualities, and perhaps her expectations were unrealistic. Max accused her of being obstructive out of jealousy, of being unwilling to relinquish control over what she regarded as her baby. That she did regard the factory as "her baby" is true, and the girls in it were "her girls" but she was far too much of a pragmatist to stand in the way of a suitable replacement, because she knew she could not carry on.

The other very serious problem, again not new, was that too much had been taken out of the business. There had been no differentiation between the needs of the business and the personal needs of its directors. Everything was paid "out of the business". Instead of the directors living within their salaries, they sustained their personal lifestyles from the company's income, not a novel phenomenon in family companies. The company had been milked dry of the financial resources it needed and when funds were required for retrenchment and reorganisation it was too late, the cupboard was bare. No one had contemplated the possibility that they might lose their biggest customer, something which can happen to even the best managed and most efficient organisation.

For the first time, my mother began to confide in me and tell me something of what was going on at the factory. Her main complaint was that no one would listen to her. She was constantly being sidelined and she blamed my father for not taking her side. "If only I had been a man," she would say. "Because I am a woman no one listens to me." This complaint was not entirely new; the problem first became serious after Oma died and Dora and Joe, Mother's mainstays, moved to Jersey. My mother was left exposed, and her health could not withstand the repeated battles she had to fight.

There had been no indication at home that there was anything wrong. Even then our standard of living was unaffected and no one appeared to exercise any financial restraint. There was always a feeling of financial security which was not justified by later events. My parents never discussed money matters with me. They did not seek to impose on me any budgetary restrictions or any financial discipline. They did not try to warn me that there were problems ahead and that perhaps I should be rethinking my intentions of going to the Bar, which was an expensive exercise. This would not have occurred to them.

As for myself, I spent my vacations working in the factory, driving the vans, packing and doing what I could to help. I was also trying to find out exactly what was going on, because my family, my mother included, had another major fault: in regard to the factory they became divorced from reality. They could not accept that the business was in a state of terminal decline. They were unable to identify, far less accept, the real problem. They would not understand that no amount of good money being poured in after bad would help. The problem was much deeper than cash flow. This was, in due course, to have literally fatal consequences.

But none of this impinged upon my social life. I spent time with my friends, with Adrienne, dancing, drinking and generally having a good time. I did only a minimal amount of academic work in the vacation. Christmas and New Year were celebrated in the usual liquid manner, and soon, to my relief, it was time to go back to college. I had been looking forward to returning throughout the vacation; much as I loved my home and family, and friends, male and female, that is where I wanted to be. It may have been a form of escapism, but this was my last chance for that.

Chapter 57 – Halcyon Days

When I arrived back at college for my second term, the Hilary term, all feelings of novelty and strangeness had gone. I was back in my new home, and very relieved to be so. Consolidation was the order of the day. The immediate objective was to pass the first public examination, "Mods", at the end of the term, and I was able to get into a routine which I more or less followed for the rest of my time at Oxford. I would rise early, at about 7 a.m., and play an hour's squash at the college courts. Exhausted after this exercise, I would shower and shave and then have breakfast in the Manor's equivalent of Hall. We sat at a long table at one end of the room and the breakfast we had was immeasurably superior to that available in college. We had a full English breakfast, bacon, eggs, mushrooms, tomatoes, toast, butter, marmalade and jams, and as much coffee as was wanted. I was less delicate in my observance of the dietary laws than I had been at home and later again became. Though I have always risen early, a habit formed in my school years and developed in the army, I was never a "morning person". I spoke little and read the newspapers. No one objected. You did as you liked. If anyone smoked, no one objected. I never smoked before 11 a.m, another habit from army days.

After breakfast, if time allowed and I did not have to go to a lecture or tutorial, I would rest for an hour or so. Then I would start work, going to the law libraries, looking up the cases recommended by Theo Tylor, reading the articles in the *Modern Law Review* or *Quarterly Law Review* or similar other journals he prescribed.

Lunch might be taken in Hall, or more usually at one of the local hostelries or restaurants. You could get a full three-course meal with coffee for 1s.6d. (12.5p in decimal terms). The afternoon from about 2 to 5 p.m was devoted to sport, football in winter and spring, tennis or cricket in the summer. If weather prohibited outdoor activities, I would usually play squash. Most of my racket games were played with Clive. I played soccer for the college (2nd XI), and also cricket. The college's standards were not so high as to exclude my abilities, but the great thing was that sport was available at any level. Colleges had second, third, and sometimes even fourth teams, and you found your own level. I did not try rowing, but the same applied there; there were crews at several levels, and all enjoyed themselves. I was fortunate to be there for three successive rowing successes which were appropriately and traditionally celebrated by ceremonial dinners in Hall at the college's expense. Balliol's success on the river, which I applauded but had no part in except as an increasingly happy participant in the celebrations, caused some of the dons to question whether the college was not losing sight of its main *raison d'etre*, namely academic excellence.

University working hours, that is when lectures took place, were 9 a.m. to 1 p.m. and 5 p.m. to 7 p.m. which I considered somewhat odd. I rarely had lectures in the afternoon, though there were some highly specialised lectures in the second year given by M. Fifoot (of Cheshire and Fifoot fame) on the Interpretation of Statutes with particular reference to Legislative Orders, by which much of the law which governs what we can and cannot do, is effected. He chose to demonstrate the subject by reference to some highly esoteric Order called the "Kegs, Barrels and Casks Order" (or similar). He gave these lectures – they would probably be called seminars today – to a small audience of about twelve sitting around the library table in his college, Hertford College. I can remember little of the arcane points of law involved because throughout the whole of the series of lectures we were convulsed by laughter. He showed the difficulties of interpretation, and hence the counterproductiveness of legislation framed in incomprehensible jargon. His points were well and wittily made and the principles remain ingrained in my mind.

Dinner was usually taken in Hall and was followed by the day's social activities, planned or ad hoc. I was usually back in college by about midnight when I would start my serious work, the preparation and writing of my essay. Considerable amounts of coffee were consumed and cigarettes smoked during this exercise accompanied by records on my record player. I had a series of these, though my favourite accompaniment for some reason was

Stravinsky's "Petrouchka". Other favourites were Strauss's "Till Eulenspiegel" and "Don Juan", and the Beethoven piano concertos and odd-numbered symphonies. I liked full-blooded romantic music. Much as I loved opera, I did not find listening to it conducive to work, though I sometimes played some Gilbert & Sullivan for light relief. The midnight candle usually blew itself out at about 2.30 or 3 a.m. I was, in terms of work, an owl not a lark. I found the early hours the best for working; there was no noise, and no distraction; no one to entice me to a meal or a cinema or other entertainment. I found it difficult to resist such temptations – indeed, why should I? – and worked when they could not arise. However, I do not wish to give the impression that these work sessions were diurnal, or even weekly. They usually only occurred when need arose, such as the day before a tutorial, when the essay had to be read, or immediately before an exam. I made it a strict rule never, even at moments of crisis, to work on the Sabbath day, which I interpreted in the widest sense to include both the Jewish and the Christian.

The hurdle of Mods was duly overcome; Roman Law and Criminal Law were abandoned. Common Law subjects of Contract and Tort, The Law of Real Property, Equity and Jurisprudence took their place, and Constitutional Law, and Private International Law were added in due course.

The last term of the year, the summer term, was eight weeks of pure lotus eating, a period of hedonistic pleasure and relaxation disturbed only by the weekly tutorial. The Manor gardens were ideal for idling; cricket at the parks was only a few minutes walk away, the river and its punts and pubs were idyllic; life was, for a short time at least, as perfect as anyone has a right to expect. The term, which I recollect as having occurred in a blaze of sunshine – if it rained I did not notice – ended on an appropriately high note, with the Holywell Manor Dance and a series of Commemoration Balls ("Commems", known in Cambridge as May Balls).

The Commems are all-night balls, given by several colleges on a sort of unofficial rota at the end of the academic year. The tickets were expensive but, having regard to what was on offer, good value for money and the price included a running champagne buffet. Huge marquees housed the dance floors and provided protection against inclement weather and cold early morning mists. The most eminent dance bands or groups of the day were engaged to play, and a variety of music was provided. A ticket to one ball somehow seemed to include entrance to any others which coincided with it, as it was common to do the rounds. Everyone wore their best finery: the men wore tails or evening dress; the ladies' gowns were a brilliant display of colour, glamour and wealth. There was no shortage of female company, as those who had them would import "their sisters, and their cousins and their aunts". Rare was the girl who would refuse an invitation. Indeed, these were the only occasions of the year when men's company as escorts was at a premium. Debs fought to be invited; their names and faces would inevitably appear in the fashionable society magazines. The girls always looked beautiful and charming at the start of the party, however disillusioning their exposure to the morning light might later prove. The Commems demonstrated two things: the capacity of the British for sheer unadulterated enjoyment, and the fact that the capacity to imbibe enormous quantities of alcohol was not the prerogative of the working classes.

Chapter 58 – Twenty-One

The Commemoration Ball was followed shortly by one of my own. My parents threw an extraordinary party to celebrate my coming-of-age, which was then still at 21. It was undoubtedly the social event of the decade in Middlesbrough; a black tie affair. It was the biggest party given by my family since they came to Middlesbrough and outdid even the weddings of my aunts in splendour. The grounds of Brierfield were ideal for such an occasion. There was ample space for a very large marquee, even though I resented the harm done to my tennis lawn, and for once the weather justified its midsummer date. Being on the longest day of the year, which is very long indeed in North Yorkshire, gave the impression that there was no night. The food was catered by a Manchester caterer, apart from the additional dishes prepared by my mother and her "staff", and was abundant and delicious.

While we did not have Edmundo Ros, Joe Loss or Geraldo we did have Charlie Amer and his Orchestra from the Coatham Hotel, Redcar, who gave a very good account of themselves. The party went on all night and most of the next day. To avoid complaints all the neighbours were invited. Indeed, everyone was invited; the whole family, school friends, Clive, Tod and Glen, all the Jewish families from Middlesbrough and Stockton, young and old, Neville and all his family from London, various members of Jeanne's family from Leeds; in fact, it seemed that everyone whom my parents and I knew, and even some we didn't, were invited, and all came, except Dora and Joe who found that they had to be in New York. But my parents saw it as an opportunity to make up for the barrenness of my bar mitzvah, which had been in wartime and the year in which two grandparents had died which made it anything but a happy occasion, and they were determined to make it impressive.

It was the first "grown-up" party that my cousin Judith, had been to. She was only 15, but she was tall, and slim. She had long flowing black hair and the beautiful legs and full bust of the

Schmulewitsch women. She looked 21. She was a sensation, outstanding even among the many attractive girls there. The young – indeed even some of the older – men flocked round her. Her father did not let her out of his sight and chased away any prospective wooer. I think he was a little too old-fashioned and rather spoiled her fun but she still enjoyed herself immensely.

This wildly extravagant party was held at a time when matters at the factory were at a critical stage; effectively, the point of no return had been reached. On any logical basis my parents had no business to indulge in such extravagance at that time. Dora and Joe were, by their absence, demonstrating their disapproval of what they regarded as an act of financial irresponsibility on the part of my parents. In a way they were right; had the money been put aside for my own future use, I might have benefited more and the story of my life might have been different, but then life is full of "what ifs", and I do not resent or criticise how my parents chose to spend their money. I think they were fully justified, certainly in the light of subsequent events.

That my parents' decision was none of Dora's business would not have occurred to her. No one in my family ever took the view that what concerned any other member of the family was not his or her business and this characteristic appears time and again, almost like a leitmotif, in the history of the family. Dora had her father's stubbornness, and once she had made up her mind about something, no amount of reason or logic would change it. My parents and I were hurt by her and Joe's absence and, so far as it was within her character to do so, Dora subsequently regretted her decision. But by then it was too late.

One of my mother's justifications for this party was that it was to compensate me for the fact that my bar mitzvah was disturbed and not the celebration she would have liked. It was the last "simcha" she could make for me. Even if she lived long enough to see me married, which she had often expressed misgivings about, it would be the bride's parents' responsibility to make the wedding. Both my parents, but for different reasons, tended to live for the moment and let tomorrow look after itself: my father because he was by nature an optimist; my mother because she expected to die young. Her life had been prolonged once; she had no confidence that this would be repeated. This expectation of an early death runs like a refrain through all her actions, certainly, I feel, so far as they concerned me. It was not obvious at the time, and no one would voice, or even dare to think, such fears and they never occurred to me. My mother's forebodings were, unhappily, to prove correct.

I am very glad they did provide a memorable 21st birthday party. I, and I believe others who were there, still have memories of it. The house and its grounds provided appropriate amenities and cover for every sort of activity. The dancers danced, the card players played, the lovers loved and the gluttons ate, the whole night through. Some managed to do all these. Legend has it that one quartet of bridge players were found still playing 24 hours later. I cannot vouch for the accuracy of the story, but from my knowledge of the parties involved, I am quite willing to believe it. It took the tennis court the rest of the summer to recover. How long it took those present I do not know.

Shortly afterwards I had to go to my annual army camp. This was now Her Majesty's Army. Elizabeth's accession to the throne just preceded my 21st birthday. I reported to the depot at Feltham, which was by usual army standards of the time a comparatively civilised place, and my sergeant's stripes doubtless helped. As there was no intelligence testing to do, the army decided that I should become an ammunition examiner, and having acquired the necessary knowledge, impart it to others. I was thus one lesson ahead of my pupils. I had to master the intricacies of the marking of ammunition. All ammunition is marked and one needs to know the codes. For volunteering to join the Army Emergency Reserve I received an additional sum of £90 for the two weeks in camp, which, on this occasion, was not under canvas. Ninety pounds was a lot of money in 1952.

Chapter 59 – The Phoenix

The remainder of my vacation was not much fun. Every effort was being made to rescue the sinking ship of Guisborough, and good money was being poured after bad. Any suggestion that they should let go, and save what resources they still had to start again, were rejected out of hand by Max, and I cannot pretend that my parents', or so far as I know Herman's, attitude was any different.

The factory had been an obsession. As I said earlier, the factory owned the family, not the reverse, and now it was to consume them. For the first time, they sought my opinion. This may have been desperation as they were clearly not receiving the advice they wished to hear. Perhaps they thought that my short acquaintanceship with the law was sufficient to qualify me to express an opinion on some of the letters and documents which they were being asked to sign. If they were looking to me for some sort of comfort or encouragement, I was unable to give it.

I was horrified by what I read. In order to obtain finance they were being asked to put their joint and several other necks on the block by way of personal guarantees and mortgages of their homes. Financiers, contrary to Max's views, are not charitable institutions. Indeed I was surprised that anyone was willing to lend them any money on whatever terms. Some who were well disposed to my family refused to encourage them in their headlong career to disaster, which is all that any finance would have meant. Had there been some vague hope of turning the business round, had there been an array of orders for goods waiting to be fulfilled, had there been a potential investor in or buyer of the business, some justification for taking such steps might have been found, but there was none of these. Marks & Spencer had withdrawn their custom.

Max's great charm (though he was not in my father's league in this respect) had made him popular and given him access to the Finance houses who had been patient, indeed, long-suffering but despite the personal goodwill that he and my father enjoyed, reality had to be faced. The company was bust. The liabilities were such that several profitable years and the greatest possible economy, both corporate and personal, would have been necessary to discharge them. The idea of putting the company into liquidation, the acceptance of commercial failure – not a crime or sin and not unknown to many successful millionaires – was anathema; the family could not face the shame, the affront to their pride. It took some forceful language to bring this home to them. I learned at an early age one of the basic principles of business, namely that one's first loss is the best loss. Cut your losses and don't throw good money after bad. Salvage is for the experts.

Fortunately, at this point, Aunty Jeanne, who had had no direct involvement in the business, intervened. Jeanne was at her best in a crisis; she was indomitable. She was not considered by the rest of the family as particularly frugal but she simply decided that they would have to start again from scratch. My mother who welcomed help from any quarter, supported the motion, and the two ladies started a new company of which they were the directors and shareholders.

They would not let the men have any say in the running of the new business. Thus, early in 1953, the Rockville Manufacturing Co. Ltd. was formed, named after my cousin Rochelle, Max and Jeanne's second child, who had been named after Jeanne's mother. Premises were taken in Stockton-on-Tees, just off one of the widest, oldest and most attractive high streets in the country. The men, Max and Dad, were taken on as employees, Dad to do the books, and Max to do what he was best at – selling. Herman was not involved, and he went his own way in London.

Naturally, they made shirts and adopted a trade name which Max had first proposed at Guisborough, "Kadema," which means "forward" in Hebrew. Some of the girls who were prepared to make the journey from the Guisborough area were taken on and new girls were trained. Machinery was acquired, largely through the good offices of the Bellow Machine Co. (Jeanne's family) and they were back in business, albeit a very small one even compared with the first days of Guisborough. Jeanne, who had worked in an office before her marriage, revived her old skills, and looked after the administrative side of things; my mother ran the factory. How financially successful they were I do not know, but morally and psychologically they felt much better; they had turned despair into hope.

While this was happening, I was back at Oxford having put Guisborough out of my mind. There was nothing I could do to help, and I was not going to allow a small matter such as insolvency to worry me. As I have pointed out, nothing in my parents' conduct or financial way of life appeared affected by the demise of the business and I had no reason to suppose that this would impinge on me. My allowance continued as before; I still received my food parcels, and still sent my shirts home to be washed.

For our second year Tod and I shared what I can best describe as a suite of rooms in the Manor. They were the best rooms in the place, in the centre block directly overlooking the gardens. We planned and executed the second Manor Christmas Dance, which was even more successful that the previous one. We gave splendid dinner parties which were largely prepared by ourselves, with the help of supplies from home to meet our particular requirements. For the rest we engaged one of the chefs from the Balliol kitchen, and our favourite scout, who served as bartender and waiter, and gave us a few useful tips such as placing slices of cucumber in a room to keep the atmosphere fresh.

Many of our friends had left Oxford; some for good reasons in the appropriate fullness of their time, some for bad ones. Glen Petrie's absence was neither commented on in official circles nor explained. I was as close as any undergraduate could get to the Manor Praefectus, Russell Meiggs, but he never mentioned Glen's absence, far less volunteered an explanation, and avoided all questioning on the matter. This was typically Oxford, which seemed to adopt a Bishop Berkeleyan philosophy: objects and, presumably, people exist only if you can see them. I have some friends who adopt that philosophy in regard to their wives or girlfriends, but Oxford has perfected it.

As for the rest of that term, indeed the rest of that second year, a fortunately selective memory protects me from the agony of recalling some of the excesses, committed I hope, at least, in a moment of insobriety, the recollection of which made me cringe even the following day. Life at Oxford was studded with such events. Various items try to surface, such as trying to date, by leaving messages at their rooms, the young ladies who had arrived as freshers and the fame of whose beauty had quickly spread, the potential Zuleika Dobsons of their day. There were not many of these. Then there were the nurses, mainly from the Radcliffe, usually willing and sometimes even attractive. One of these must have been the original for Rigor Mortis in Richard Gordon's *Doctor in the House*. She was flat-chested and skinny, not my type at all in fact. She never moved. A blow-up doll would have been more animated. Whether she was just closing her eyes and thinking of England, I do not know, but I doubt whether she was capable of that much thought. What she got out of it, I cannot imagine. Other similar follies can be left to Lethe, and remain undisturbed.

Holywell Manor was a close community and the distinctions between the years and subjects and pre-Oxford history (e.g. which school you went to), which to a large extent determined your friends, were unimportant. Tod's ubiquity and reputation, and perhaps mine too, brought a constant stream of visitors to our room. One afternoon, while Tod was doing his usual tumpety-tumpety-ing from some complex symphonic score, and I was idling at something or another, there was a knock at the door. I called to our unknown visitor to enter. Another knock; I repeated the invitation, and went to the door to open it. An old wizened grey-haired man stood there. In a croaking voice he asked whether a Mr Handley lived there. I confirmed that he did and asked him in; I was completely puzzled. Who the devil was he? He began some rambling account which went on for a couple of minutes until Tod suddenly collapsed in helpless laughter. Only then did I realise that our "visitor" was Jack Good, who later became the successful producer of *6.5 Special*, a TV show for teenagers which ran for a considerable time. Jack was a very fine actor. He had joined and in due course became president of OUDS (the Oxford University Dramatic Society). To have taken in me, innocent and gullible as I was, was easy, but to have fooled Tod for so long at such close quarters was a fine display not only of acting, but of

257

make-up. Jack came up a year after we did. His talent soon ensured he made his mark on Oxford society. Like so many showmen, he was not a modest person, and conversation with him tended to be a monologue by him, but he was a great entertainer and excellent company. He was a regular at our dinner parties. I later saw him in several films and kept running across him in London. Some years later when we met at a Gaudy – a reunion of college men (and now women) he told me he had retired at an early age to San Diego, California, where he abandoned the theatrical world and developed his talent as an artist. We have met at subsequent college functions and he was always interesting and amusing. Sadly, he died in October 2017 while I was writing this.

Another regular visitor, though not himself at Oxford, was Trevor Peacock. He was also from Enfield and had been at school with Tod. His acting talents were then already well in evidence, and he and Tod made a very amusing double act. Without Glen to drag me there, I went less frequently to the cinema, but had no difficulty in filling in the time. My chess flourished. I took advantage of my leisure time to make new friends. I met many of these through Neville, whom I now saw more often, though he was diligently preparing for his finals. Several remained close friends after university, some even became clients.

Among these was Clive Labovitch from Leeds. His family owned Darley Mills, a very successful company, and he appeared to be very well off. His passion was publishing. He and Michael Heseltine acquired *Cherwell*, one of the main university magazines. People fought to be mentioned in its columns. Clive and Michael Heseltine revamped the paper, and it became the leading Oxford University journal. When they left Oxford, Clive and Michael established the highly successful Haymarket Press, but Clive was always restless, and seeking new challenges in publishing. He was, surprisingly, in the light of his background, totally uncommercial. He left the very profitable business which he had built up with Michael Heseltine to embark on experimental ventures which tended to be financially calamitous. He had a wealth of ideas, but was never able to exploit them profitably.

After I had established my own firm, Clive consulted me on many occasions. I often felt frustrated at his reluctance – no, refusal – to accept good and practical financial and legal advice. Some years after his divorce from his first wife, a well-known journalist, he married a beautiful and charming lady. I remember that the wedding and reception were most elegant, intimate and convivial with excellent food and wine. Tragically, his wife, Bonnie, soon afterwards developed a brain tumour, from which she died. Not long afterwards Clive himself died following a heart bypass operation. Within two years of their marriage they were both dead, a very sad end to a kind and intelligent man whose later years had been dogged by misfortune.

Among other friends I made through Neville was Bob Gavron. He was to printing what Clive Labovitch was to publishing, and my family to shirts, in the sense that he was totally dedicated to it. The only difference is that Bob, after the usual trials and tribulations attendant upon creating a business, went on to create a major and highly profitable public company, St Ives, and became a big-league player, ending up as a Life Peer. He did it all by himself. The world is small – it turned out that Bob was very good friends with Psiche and Philip Hughes, who became good friends of ours through my wife Evi's academic connections. Dan Lack, who spoke about 13 languages fluently and became an international lawyer of considerable distinction, became another good friend. His talents were sought by many international organisations from the United Nations downwards.

One of the nicest men you could meet was Bill Patterson who later became Dean of Ely. He had a beautiful old Red Label Bentley motorcar, of mid-1920s vintage. It was an open-topped four-seater. Bill and I and anyone else who could get into the car would pile in and we would go on rallies or treasure hunts organised by the University Motor Club – it seemed there was a club for everything you could think of. Navigating for Bill was an adventure in itself.

No one ever questioned how Bill came to own such a car, far less get permission to have it in Oxford. That car came in useful for one of those acts best forgotten, when we rescued an old London cab from some scrapheap (I hope) and painted various rude and puerile slogans on it, including "Lady, don't laugh your daughter may be in here", "Keep out – men at work" and finally, the coup de grace, something really subtle: "Trinity Passion Wagon". To celebrate yet another Eights Week success, we towed it to the front of Trinity College gates, where we abandoned it. To ensure it could not be easily removed, we took off the rear wheels. The pictorial proof is before me even as I write these words. Bill's Bentley came to a sad end, quite inappropriate for such a motor, when he wrote if off in an argument with a public toilet at the end of a continental holiday.

There were also many memorable incidents. I was standing at the door of the Manor on 6 May 1954, just before my finals, when Arthur McClelland, one of the Manor residents, rushed up and almost fell off his bicycle with excitement shouting: "I've just seen the first four-minute mile. Roger Bannister's just done it. He's broken the four-minute mile," or words to that effect. I know that he was almost incoherent and when I expressed total disbelief he managed to catch his breath and give some articulate account of what he had witnessed at the Iffley Road track. It was clear that history had just been made. There was something wonderful about being the immediate recipient of such news at first hand. Arthur, understandably, unable to contain his excitement, got back on his bike and rode around shouting the news at the top of his voice.

Chapter 60 – Finale

I ended my second year with some misgivings about what to expect at home. Though I spoke to my parents on the telephone and wrote several times during the term, I was always assured that all was well. But to speak to my father at any time, even in the direst emergency, was to receive a reassuring answer. My father's middle name was Pangloss.

Me: "How's the House?"

Father: "It burned down last night, but all's well don't worry."

Me: "How is X?"

Father: "OK – he died last week."

Fortunately, these are fictional incidents, but they demonstrate the sort of conversation I could expect to have with my father so, unsurprisingly, I had no idea what had been going on while I was in Oxford.

Before going home I went as an honoured guest of Her Majesty to her Coronation, that is to say that, as a serving (albeit reserve) soldier I was entitled to purchase two tickets for the seats allocated on the route to military personnel. I felt it incumbent on me, having the chance to do so, to witness this historical event and it gave me the opportunity to spend the day with Adrienne whom I invited to come with me. We had to be in our places at some unearthly hour in the morning, when the streets were still being cleaned. It was a typical early June summer's day, cold and wet, with the sun making an occasional desultory attempt to appear and eventually giving up in disgust. We had to sit for hours, in seats incompletely protected from the weather. The procession took some time to pass by, and the Queen of Tonga rather stole the show. She was an enormous woman, and her finery enhanced her size. Seated with her in her carriage was a very small gentleman from some other Pacific Island. Asked who that was, Noel Coward is alleged to have replied "her lunch"! I suppose we enjoyed ourselves as young persons do, but

I have no abiding or affectionate memory of the event, other than of my companion.

I had ended term in high spirits with dances and parties. My days of idleness and irresponsibility would be over after the long vacation, and who knew what that promised? I spent a few days in London staying with Yetti as usual, before going home. When I arrived home, though the ghost of Guisborough still haunted the house, there was almost a feeling of relief that it was all over. The failure of the business was a bitter blow. As proprietors of the Shirt Factory my family had considerable standing in Guisborough and even in Middlesbrough. Overnight, they had been reduced to insignificance. This did not seem to affect my father; his status in the synagogue was not diminished and his personal popularity remained unaffected. My mother took the disaster with considerable fortitude. She was, as I have said, a great pragmatist. She did not believe in looking back. The family had survived greater disasters, and she considered herself lucky to be alive at all. Once the axe had fallen there was nothing to be done but to start again, and that they had done. Her energies were directed to ensuring the future, not to regretting the mistakes of the past. Ideally, she would have liked to have started something new completely on her own, without the involvement of any of the family, even my father. With her skills she would have had no difficulty working from home as a couturier, which in fact, she was already doing as a hobby. I think she felt a responsibility to Max and Jeanne not to abandon them.

Max took the failure very badly. He had no other interests; the factory had been his whole life, the circumference of his world. It wasn't the money, he had never really been interested in money for its own sake. It would have been better for all the family if he had been; the business might have been sold at the peak of its profitability and value. Subject to wise investment, we could all have been financially secure for life. He was the sort of husband who would happily hand over his pay packet to his wife unopened. He enjoyed the good things of life but they were peripheral to his world. He was no spendthrift. Power is, of course, a factor, but he never enjoyed absolute, or indeed sufficient, power, to become addicted to it. His addiction, his opiate, was selling, and, since acting as a salesman for anyone else was unthinkable, he had to provide his own source of supply.

Herman, being in London, had been less dependent on the factory as a source of income or for the good of his ego, and was much less directly affected than the others. With the help and advice of his mother-in-law he had already embarked on various ventures of his own. What they were I do not know, but he seemed to make a decent living.

After Max, the person most affected by the Guisborough debacle was, strangely, Dora. She and Joe had lived in Jersey since 1947. When I asked Joe, "Why Jersey?," he explained that that was the furthest away, within the British Isles, he could get from the rest of the family. He had built up from scratch the only wholesale business in the Channel Islands. He started small at first, with such easily handled items as ladies' stockings. In 1947, nylons were still in short supply, but he found manufacturers in Ireland who were willing to accept comparatively small orders, and the business grew rapidly. Joe was a man of the highest integrity, almost to a fault, and refused to take the easy option. If any of his customers, which in fact meant their customers as they sold direct to the public, claimed goods were faulty, he would readily replace the goods regardless. This was often to Dora's intense annoyance because she knew the claims were false, but his policy paid.

Joe and Dora had no financial investment in Guisborough after they left. Their way of life was not altered by its demise. Yet Dora was the bitterest of all. I do not know why. It may have been due to a feeling of guilt; that by leaving Guisborough, she had betrayed all that her father, her sister (my mother) and she had done to ensure the early success of the business. Also that she had left my mother alone, and that had she stayed the collapse would not have happened. Certainly, she was very attached to both her father and my mother, though she never had much time for her brothers. For the rest of her life, Guisborough was never expunged from her psyche. She always kept looking back and did not forgive Max, whom she held largely responsible, or my father, whom she accused of aiding and abetting Max. Reason rarely played a part in my Aunt Dora's views. Once these had been formed, not a lengthy process based on deep consideration, they were immutable.

After my annual camp I went to Jersey for a holiday, as I had done regularly over the previous years. The obvious advantage was that it cost me only the flight, and I had the free use of a car when I was there. It was a second home for me, and I loved being there. There was invariably a good selection of people my own age, male and female, and I was never short of company when I wanted it. Somehow, the doom and gloom over Guisborough hung more heavily there than at home, and Dora and Joe expressed concern about my future. I was perhaps somewhat ungrateful in my response, because no one had ever expressed any active interest, far less doubt, on that subject, and I felt that I could handle any problems myself, as I had always done.

Chapter 61 – Finals

I arrived back home from Jersey in time for the Jewish High Holy Days. As soon as these were over I returned to college, but Joe and Dora's misgivings had sown doubts in my own mind. There was now, suddenly, an uncertainty about my future for which I was unprepared. However, this was my third year and my first thoughts had to be to ensure that I passed my finals with a good degree. It was more than ever imperative that I did not stumble at that stage, not that I had any doubts, or so I told myself, but however clever, however well prepared, however much the bookies would back you to win, there is still that little niggling feeling. You tell yourself that nothing can go wrong, and then think about that airline joke. [The Captain shortly after the flight has taken off addresses the passengers: "this is a new plane and this is its first flight. Everything is computerised, there is no possibility of human failure. Nothing can go wrong, go wrong, go wrong..."] The only thing that one can do is to work, and I decided it was time I did so. But good intentions give way to temptations; work, you tell yourself, can be postponed: I'll do that tomorrow. And suddenly what could have been done in a timely manner becomes urgent. By December my schedule was a term behind.

Tod and I with our team planned and executed the Manor Christmas Ball, which fully realised the standards of previous years. I decided to work during the vacation, but found it difficult to settle down. The atmosphere at home was as loving and happy as it had always been. My parents expressed no concern about my future. It was not easy to discuss things of that nature with them. They had no real conception or understanding of the legal world, what pupillage or articles meant or the difference between barristers and solicitors. Quite apart from that, however, I found it difficult to cope with their continuing reluctance to talk about money. It would never have occurred to them to say that they were in financial difficulties, or that they would not be able to continue

·to support me. There was nothing in their way of life to suggest otherwise.

The Christmas holidays were spent in the usual joyful fashion and it was only due to Adrienne's presence that some semblance of sobriety was maintained. On New Year's Eve, Adrienne, Martin and his then current girlfriend, a gorgeous black-haired, dark-eyed girl, and I went to Grinkle Park Hotel, which had a fashionable restaurant, in some remote place on the Moors past Guisborough on the Whitby road. The Hillman car which I had virtually run into the ground by driving it at speeds it was never designed to reach, had been replaced by the latest Morris, which was a bigger version of the Morris Minor. On the way through Guisborough, which has, on either side of the main road, a large cobbled market place, which served as a car park and bus stand, the car in front made as if to turn left to park but changed its mind and decided to turn right, just as I was passing. Fortunately, my youthful reflexes managed to avoid a serious accident. Nevertheless, the whole of the near side was damaged, but not sufficient to prevent us continuing the journey, somewhat shaken, but safe. The advantage of having been to the local grammar school became apparent, when one of my old schoolmates, Derek Fawcett, now a policeman, who had been waiting in a bus queue, witnessed the incident. He confirmed that I had not been in any way at fault. The driver of the other car was the father of John (Tommy) Tucker who had also been in the same form at school.

I drove on to our destination very carefully after that. We ate and danced, and everyone else drank, but so far as I was concerned the sparkle had already gone out of the evening. The roads had become icy by the time we left and the journey home was accomplished with caution. When I eventually reached home, I parked the car with its near side hard up against the garage wall so that the damage could not be seen. I said nothing to Mother, but the next morning told my father what had happened. He willingly conspired not to tell Mother. Tessie had to be included in the ring of silence. He arranged to have the car repaired, explaining its absence on the ground that it needed servicing. If my mother suspected anything she never let on. I do not know what happened after that. No more was ever said of the matter. I assume that my father took care of the insurance claim. For some reason, whether it was the after-effects of the accident, or my family's failing fortunes, or just the changes brought by maturity, I do not know, my relationship with Adrienne cooled off, and though we remained good friends, soon after that we went our separate ways.

The accident seemed to me an omen, a warning from above, rather like the Knaresborough one when I was seven, though this time I was wearing my religious accoutrements. I went back to college well before the end of the vacation and got down to some serious work. Had this been simply revision the task may not have been so hard, but so far as I was concerned it involved a considerable amount of new work, which had previously been neglected. As my immediate contemporaries were all in the same boat, that is working hard, my social life became quiet but I did not feel that I was missing anything. Neither did I allow myself to become a drudge. There was no point in peaking too soon; I had to time myself. For once, I attended a complete series of lectures. These were by Professor Warlock on International Law; the concept of whether this existed at all was the sort of jurisprudential argument I lapped up. Though not a charismatic lecturer of the Rupert Cross mould, he made the subject interesting and I had no difficulty in maintaining my concentration. This was one occasion when I found lectures useful.

The Easter vacation came and went uneventfully except for the fact that Dora and Joe acquired a son, Harry, the youngest of my cousins by 23 years. Dora was 40 at the time but she had been beaten to the post, as it were, by Jeanne who had given Max his fourth child and third son shortly before. No one ever really knew how old Jeanne was, but it was rumoured that she was about 45 at the time, more or less my mother's age. Michael Selwyn was conceived and born at the time of the Guisborough decline and fall. My mother was furious at what she considered, perhaps justifiably in the circumstances, an act of gross irresponsibility. Like Dora, she did not consider any matter involving a member of the family as beyond her jurisdiction.

The last few weeks before finals were a period of intense concentration, interrupted only by my self-enforced weekend breaks, which actually helped to keep me on an even keel. I found that these allowed the knowledge, newly acquired or remembered, to settle down in the brain as it were, rather like resting to digest after a heavy meal. At least that is what I told myself, and anyone else who cared to ask. Throughout this time I saw much less of Tod and more of Clive Tayler. Tod had his own finals to worry about, and though he worked conscientiously enough, Music, not English, was where his ambitions lay. I continued to go to London throughout my last year, three nights a term, to eat my dinners at the Middle Temple, where the Queen Mother was the titular head and on special occasions graced us with her company. I met her once on one such occasion, that is to say she bowed her head in greeting in my direction as she was leaving.

I can remember little of the events of my last term before taking my finals, and not much of what occurred immediately afterwards. I recall that the night before the International Law paper I had still not read one of the prescribed textbooks. Fortunately, it was a slim volume and I am a fast reader. The examinations were held in the Schools building where in term time lectures were given. The obligatory dress for exams was dark suits with white shirts and white ties, gowns and mortar boards. This produced an appearance of sartorial uniformity, rather like penguins. Some even had the penguin shape. Each exam took three hours, and there were some seven papers in all, that is 21 hours of regurgitation. Though some may question my taste in such matters I actually enjoyed exams, which is probably why I usually did better than my knowledge deserved. I felt that here was finality; exams marked the end of a chapter and the start of another. There was no more work to be done, no more swotting, no more midnight oil, no more worrying. The die was cast. Barring some cataclysm, you emerged from the exam room with something to show; it might not be as much as you would have liked, but at least there was no more to come.

In the event I surprised myself. Though I disappointed Theo Tylor's original hopes for me, I rehabilitated myself in his eyes and regained some of his respect. He had marked me out as a candidate for a First, but I was not prepared to be as devoted and single-minded as would have been necessary. I had too many other things to do. After four terms of idleness which I could not entirely disguise, he began to have misgivings about my getting even a Second. Oxford at that time did not give Upper and Lower Seconds. It was either a Second or a Third, which seems logical and sensible enough. In the event, I got a very good (Upper) Second, even including some Alphas, one being in International Law, which I argued was a complete chimera; there was no such thing. I don't think I would argue that today. In fact, I thought I had put in a very good all-round performance, coming up on the rails as it were, and was, justifiably, pleased with myself and glad it was all over. Clive, needless to say, got his First, and deservedly so. He had one of the best legal brains – in fact ignore the "legal" – I have known.

There was one big celebration after the exams. Tod had met Barbara Black during his second year. She was an exceptionally fine person. She was tall, dark-haired, slim, beautiful and charming. She had a lovely mellifluous speaking voice, an attraction in itself. She had everything, as they say, looks and beauty, and she loved Tod madly. Tod reciprocated her feelings as much as he was capable of doing. She put aside any ambitions she had had to further his. They had been discreetly living together in the Manor for some time and married immediately after finals. I was best man at their wedding.

Apart from assisting at Tod's wedding, all I did for a few days after the exams was sleep. I was exhausted, the effect of the sudden withdrawal of adrenaline. Once I awoke, I took advantage of my last days at university, not by indulging in one great binge, though there was enough of that, but just relaxing and breathing the air. I was saying farewell to what had been the three happiest years of my life, knowing that that particular happiness could never be repeated. It was like leaving a loved one, with sorrow, sighs and tears where there could not be kisses. I was not only saying goodbye to Oxford, and its life, but to my friends and companions for the last three years, to the Manor, to the Meiggs, the Wards, Theo Tylor, Cyril North, the head porter, Bert who was his deputy, all those with whom my life for three years had been so intimately woven in one way or another; to my tennis and squash, to my football and cricket; to the endless midnight discussions; to all the things in Oxford I so loved. It was a very emotional time, and even its memory still brings tears to my eyes.

I think I cried also for the future which had looked so sure and was now clouded by doubt and uncertainty. And yet, when I had dried my eyes, I was glad to go. However wonderful the experience may be, you can exist in a hothouse for only a limited time. I recalled the words of Ecclesiastes read out on the last day of term at school: "To every thing there is a season...". My season to move on had come. I was actually pleased in retrospect not to have got a First, as I would have been tempted to the academic life, which did appeal to a part of me, but for which I would not have been temperamentally equipped. Clive did stay on an extra year to take a BCL, but that would not have suited me.

I was formally admitted by the Register of Congregation of Doctors and Regent Masters of the University of Oxford "after having, in accordance with the Statutes of the University, kept the prescribed residence and passed all necessary Examinations" to the degree of Bachelor of Arts on the thirtieth day of October 1954. The degree ceremony takes place in the Sheldonian Theatre and is preceded by a long procession led by the chancellor of the university if he or she is around, the vice-chancellor, all the university dignitaries, followed by those to whom degrees are to be awarded in accordance with long-established protocol and ritual. Everyone wears his or her best academic robes according to his or her degree; the occasion is colourful and though some may scorn at the pomp and circumstance, the degree ceremony does bestow an appropriate importance on education. The Oxford Law Degree gown and cloak are black lined with ermine, very dignified, as befits a lawyer.

My parents came to Oxford for the degree ceremony. This was the first time they had been to Oxford. They had not seen my rooms or my college; they had met only such of my friends as I had taken home. It was the first and sadly the last time they came to any prize-giving or similar ceremony during the whole period of my education. How different it was with our own children. My mother was moved to tears; she declared the moment I received my degree to have been the proudest in her life. By the standards of her family she was not a demonstrative person. My father just glowed with pleasure and beamed at everyone. I was happy to have given them something to smile about, some relief from the general gloom, in the difficult period they were experiencing. I asked my mother why they had not come to any of my school prize-givings. She explained that she did not want to embarrass me before my friends with her and Dad's lack of English, and her foreign accent. I received this information with amazement. My father had not been inhibited in his dealings with the world at large or suffered in his popularity, by his lack of English. My mother had run a factory, trained girls, visited other businesses and generally, apart from her business interests, led with my father, a very active social life, in which she had not found her "lack of English" a hindrance. I had regularly brought home friends from school, none of whom had commented on any foreign accent, though once she mentioned it I heard it for the first time; I had never realised that my parents had a "foreign accent". I found her explanation very strange, but I can see that she would not have been comfortable in surroundings to which she could not relate and over which she had no control. She could not articulate the real underlying reason, which was fear of exposure to a totally alien, non-Jewish world. It was a Ghetto mentality, a sort of anti-semitism in reverse, from which, despite appearances, she had not been able to escape. I was greatly saddened by this, because she had denied herself and my father and me moments which would have given us all great pleasure. My father seemed not wholly to share this attitude but he would not have gone without my mother.

Chapter 62 – Farewell

Over my three years at Oxford I had acquired a mass of paraphernalia, and it took some time to pack them all safely in the Morris which I had been allowed to have in Oxford during the last term, fitted with the little green sidelight required by the proctors to identify a student's car. I donated my bicycle, gown and hat to the college porter in accordance with tradition. And so, sitting at the driving wheel of my car packed with luggage, I started the engine and headed north, not knowing what the future would bring.

Balliol was in so many ways the making of me. It restored my confidence, badly shaken by my failure at Exeter College. As I drove home I reflected on what I had learned at Oxford. I thought of the civilising influence it had had on me. I remembered how impressed I had been, at first, with the sophistication of so many of my contemporaries; their knowledge for example of fine wines or their capacity for alcohol. Some of my colleagues seemed to have hollow legs, and while they did not actually drink me under the table, they certainly drank me to sleep. Any occasion started with a sherry or two. I found that by the second sherry I was mumbling and falling asleep. I tried drinking dry sherry rather than the sweet stuff to see whether I could hold out longer, but it made no difference. The one drink which I could not take, and which invariably sent me to sleep, was sherry. Beer or wine were fine, but sherry was death. I therefore eschewed sherry as an aperitif, and stuck to a glass or two of beer. I use that term because that was what the liquid in question purported to be. No one brought up on Newcastle Brown Ale, or John Smith's Magnet Ales, or Vaux's or any of the brews sold in the pubs and working men's clubs of the North East would have recognised the pale yellowy substance as beer. My friend George would have held it up to the light and declared: "This horse was never fit for work!"

I could drink the college, and indeed any southern, beer all night without noticing it. Some time after I was married I brought back a few crates of Newcastle Brown Ale from Middlesbrough, and had left them in my garage, with the door open while I unpacked the car. There was a ring on the door. A passer-by, another lost northern soul, had seen the Newcastle Brown and wanted to know where I got it from as he did not know where it could be had in London, nor could it at that time. I told him that I had personally imported it. I could not deny the disappointed and imploring look on his face, and gave him a bottle out of a charitable heart.

My colleagues, as I have said, would start with a few sherries, then a good white wine would accompany the first course of the dinner. A chateau bottled Burgundy or a decanted claret would follow – nothing much, just a few glasses with the main course – and a sweet white wine – a Sauterne or a Trockenberenaulese (how I love those long German names) – would follow with the sweet. Port would be passed round, to your left. If it got stuck at someone's elbow, as often happened, a few hollers would get it going again. So far, I was still with the room, and just about able to get down from the table and stagger out under my own steam. When the party then repaired to the Buttery or the JCR (or on special occasions the Senior Common Room) for beer – even the virtually non-alcoholic beverage so described – I would surrender. I found the idea of having beer after wine nauseating. I would have a few cups of black coffee, if available, and then crawl to my bed – it would then be about 1 a.m. and the entrance to the Manor still had to be negotiated – to learn that the rest of the party had continued to swig beer into the early hours of the morning. I do not know where they put it all.

I had gone up to Oxford culturally, and certainly viniculturally, ignorant. I learned to tell a Beaujolais from a Burgundy and a Beaune from a Rhone. Those of my colleagues who had been to public school seemed to have a greater awareness of the niceties of wine and food than I had. Whether this was due to their school or their home life I never found out. Most public schoolboys appeared to have had no home life, or if they did, they rarely mentioned it. Not the done thing, I suppose. But I am grateful to them for passing some of their knowledge on to me. My vinous limitations I ascribed to my Jewish upbringing as getting drunk is not something Jews habitually do except to perform a *mitzvah* (that is fulfil a commandment), and this occurs only twice a year: on Purim – which celebrates the downfall of Haman, an early proponent of ethnic cleansing – and on Simchas Torah, which celebrates the giving of the Law – the Torah – to the Jewish people.

I ate my first Indian food in Oxford at the Taj Mahal. It is hard to realise today, when Indian food of every variety is everywhere available, just how exotic that was. Teesside was a gastronomic desert. My own home was no gourmet's paradise – a gourmand's perhaps. Just to have the opportunity of a taste of the Orient was exciting.

I dwell on this subject not because I am one of the world's great topers, but because it is indicative of the cultural divide between my family and myself. Returning home meant a complete change of diet, not simply because my home was kosher. Our staple diet was chicken and eggs, and, a little touch of northern influences, chips with everything. Fish was rarely eaten as a main course, and would usually tend to be of the "gefillte" variety, that is chopped fish, boiled or sometimes fried. Tessie introduced English-style fish and chips, roast beef and Yorkshire puddings into our diet. (Although the best Yorkshire puddings I ever had, as I said earlier, were served by the mother of my school friend, Pete Radford. They were as big as a plate, with high sides, firm and filled with delicious gravy; heavenly!) Though my parents' food was much healthier than that of my grandparents', largely due to my mother's own dietary requirements, it was still essentially European Jewish.

I thought of my memorable contemporaries and wondered what we would all achieve. Some were inevitably marked for success and high positions in the land, others seemed scarcely fit to be let out into the wide world alone.

I thought too of Tod Handley, now a married man, and the many things we had done together, from the early Manor days; the Dances, the dinner parties, the two-man society we had formed with its own tie, a candle burning at both ends; and of Clive Tayler staying on and still to do his army service. I wondered what had become of Glen Petrie, whose disappearance could only be explained by an Alien kidnapping. He was probably on another planet, and so it turned out, metaphorically speaking, he was. They were heady days, and I considered myself fortunate to have experienced them.

"Bliss was it in that day to be alive but to be young was very heaven".

Fortunately, before I succumbed completely to premature nostalgia, I reached home. I was reluctant to let go, but time made me release my grasp. But what now awaited me, I had no idea.

Chapter 63 – A Change Of Direction

After Oxford, I saw my home and parents in a somewhat different light. I realised that the cultural gap between us was not simply due to the differences in our ways of life and our expectations, but had far wider cultural implications. Whereas I had been able to engage in deep and earnest debate with, say, Peter Radford's father, who was a "working" man, as compared to my father's "bourgeois" pretensions, I suddenly understood that with my parents I could not have the type of intellectual discussion, whether on the subject of politics, art, music or anything, that I could with my friends. It was not that they were unintelligent, far from it. It was that they were not interested, which seems strange considering their Berlin and Leipzig origins. Their reading was confined to popular fiction like *Gone with the Wind*, or *Forever Amber*. Their horizons had shrunk and now were limited by their business, first and foremost, the family and, as regards my father, the Middlesbrough Hebrew Congregation, racing and cards. I had nothing to talk about with them, other than the achievements of the Boro', and Mother was not interested in that.

Our lack of communication was not limited to language, and I don't mean to import value judgments, I simply tell it as it was. The only member of the family who had resisted this shrinkage, whose interests and knowledge encompassed wider horizons, and to whom I could relate culturally and intellectually, was Joe Menasche.

When I arrived home, Dora and Joe were there on a visit. I discussed my position with Joe, or more correctly he discussed it with me, because I am a coward in such matters. I also had a genuine reluctance to let any member of my octopus family become involved in my life lest they take it over completely. I took the view that with an Oxford degree I should be able to stand on my own feet, and be financially independent so I refused Joe's offer of financial help. It was still my intention to go to the Bar, but I needed to find chambers where I could obtain pupillage. This is, in effect apprenticeship to a barrister, for which a premium, then around £100, had to be paid. I did not even know of any chambers or counsel, where I would find this, and would have to go to London to look around. In this respect, neither Theo Tylor nor Balliol gave any career advice or assistance. They might have done had I asked, as the college had plenty of contacts, but I did not think to do so, nor had I myself made any enquiries or done anything other than eat my dinners to qualify me for entry to the Middle Temple, one of the four Inns of Court, of which a barrister had to be a member. I was clearly remiss in not making contacts when I could have done, and careless of ensuring my intended career.

I was ready to undertake any legitimate task to earn some money. Joe suggested that I advertise in *The Times*, a sort of "Have Oxford Degree Will Travel" type of thing. I was very loath to do this. To me it was degrading; it was scraping the bottom of the barrel, and an affront to my self-esteem, which was already at a low ebb. This reached an even lower ebb when the only reply I received was a very kindly phrased offer from some old gentleman who required some sort of amanuensis. My sense of humour was becoming seriously depleted by this time but I managed to see the funny side of the situation.

Fortunately, all further decisions had to be postponed as I had to go to my annual army camp. That would at least provide a little ready cash, as in addition to the £90 bonus, I was also paid at the army's rate for a regular sergeant, which was quite generous, as opposed to the national servicemen's rate of pay. The camp was in Ayrshire, just north of Carlisle. I had heard of the state-owned pubs of Carlisle, one of the country's anomalies, like the local authority-owned telephone system in Hull. The government-office colouring of the pubs – a mixture of shades of dull green rather like the pallor of one recovering from a hangover – was not designed to make them appear welcoming, but welcome they were as a refuge from the incessant rain which made the tented camp virtually uninhabitable. It rained and it rained and it rained, 24 hours a day for all the time we were there. We needed Noah's Ark, not tents, and I wondered whether God had forgotten his promise.

When I returned home I was soaked through, cold and thoroughly miserable, and this was in early July! I had a hot bath – the first for two weeks – just to get some warmth back into my bones, and telephoned Dora and Joe in Jersey to ask whether I could go and spend some time with them. I took the train to London and flew out to Jersey the next day. That holiday was to shape the rest of my life.

Jersey was warm and welcoming. I needed a week to thaw and dry out. Jersey's sunshine, sandy beaches and secluded bays were ideal. When some feeling came back into my bones and I was ready to face the world again, I made friends with George, the son of friends of Joe and Dora. He was able to guarantee a regular supply of girls, of whom there were many during the holiday season. Visiting Joe and Dora at the same time were Helen and Hymie (Hyman) Davis. Helen was the daughter of Joe's cousin, Mrs (Gustel) Reiss, who was some years older than Joe. Hymie was a solicitor who had his own firm in London. Helen was a tall handsome woman; Hymie was a dead ringer for David Niven. They were an extremely well-dressed, good-looking couple; a decade or so later they would have been described as "Beautiful People". They were both very charming and pleasant company. I assume that Joe must have spoken to Hymie about my position, and had asked him whether he could help to find me chambers among his friends at the Bar.

One day I found myself walking by Hymie's side, which I am sure was not by accident, and he asked me what my plans were. Though I did not say so, I wished I had the luxury of plans! I explained that I intended to go to the Bar, and was looking for chambers and pupillage. He asked me whether I had considered becoming a solicitor. I had not, because becoming a solicitor was even more forbidding financially than becoming a barrister. A prospective solicitor had to be articled to a solicitor for three years, if he had a Law degree, otherwise it was five years, during which he had to attend an authorised law school and at the end of which he took his solicitors' finals. Solicitors demanded a large premium for giving you articles. The going rate, which my friends up north, Martin Cohen and Brian Levy were paying, was about £300.

A few – and they were very few – firms returned that over the three years of articles by way of a weekly gratuity of £2. In addition, articles attracted a stamp duty of £80, which the articled clerk was expected to pay. The last six months of articles were usually spent attending lectures at a law school and preparing for finals during which you were not paid anything, even if you had been fortunate enough to find a principal who would recognise your efforts by some meagre remuneration. There was no realistic likelihood of any income for at least three years.

I could see no possibility of making a career at the Bar as I had hoped. Even a career in the Law in any form was in doubt. Hymie said "Come and see me when you come to London, and we can have a chat." The only barrister I knew was F. Ashe Lincoln QC, who had stayed several times at our house when visiting Middlesbrough on fundraising visits for Zionist and other Jewish causes in which he was very active. He was a friend of my parents and had suggested that I should go and see him in his chambers when I had finished my degree. I called him and we arranged to meet. It was during the long vacation which lasts all August and September, and I was fortunate to find him in London at the time as most counsel were away on their holidays. Ashe Lincoln was one of the number of memorable people whom I have been fortunate to meet. He was something of a naval hero, very much a public figure, parliamentary candidate and outspoken critic of governments, especially on behalf of Jewish interests, and not always an enemy to controversy. He typified the Jewish Englishman; assimilated, yet conscientious in matters of religious observance; a man who had served his country well while remaining loyal to his Jewish traditions.

He received me in his chambers in a most friendly manner. I discussed my dilemma with him and he explained the facts of life at the Bar. He told me that he could arrange pupillage for me at no cost, and could guarantee me a seat in chambers after my pupillage; what he could not promise me was any income for some time, and he meant years, not weeks or months. There might be some opportunity to do some "devilling", that is researching and preparing papers for other barristers, but that paid very little. Legal aid was not then readily available, nor were there flourishing divorce practices of the sort to which I could have access, even had I wanted to do that kind of work, which I didn't. The Legal Aid and Advice Act was passed only in 1949 and had not yet been assimilated into the system. Things were tough even for established counsel. He told me that unless I knew a number of solicitors prepared to feed me work I had no chance of making a living. Many young barristers made ends meet by living at home with their parents and doing part-time jobs such as teaching. Some sat around the criminal courts hoping to pick up a dock brief, that is, to be instructed by a prisoner in the dock who had no representation. The standard fee on a dock brief at that time was £2.4s.6d. Fees were always quoted in guineas (£1.1.0) and counsel's clerk usually took the shilling, which is five per cent of the fee. In addition, a barrister had to pay chambers rent and the clerk, who is, in effect, the business manager for his chambers. He negotiates counsel's fees, what work they get and their diaries. He can make or break you.

But the worst thing was that even if all went well; if you were highly successful and got loads of briefs marked with high fees, you still had to wait a very long time before those fees were paid. Solicitors were, and still are, very tardy in paying counsel's fees, even though they are personally liable for them, and will wait until they are themselves paid. There can be a gap of 12 months or more between the time the fee note is rendered and it is paid. Barristers, particularly at the start of their career, are in no position to harry recalcitrant solicitors. One of my good friends, Lennie Krikler, now a retired judge, tells how he was constantly being instructed by a solicitor who never paid him. His clerk came in proudly one day stating that he had agreed a brief fee of £100, a large sum then and considerably more than he had been able previously to squeeze out of that solicitor. Lennie told him to reduce the fee to £25; he couldn't afford to lose £100! After a few years when the money does begin to roll in, this gap becomes less worrying, and can sometimes be turned to tax advantage, but it is not very helpful at the start of your career. Some chambers today will assist young barristers during their initial period, but nothing like that existed in 1954. I left Ashe Lincoln with a great deal to consider, and telephoned Hymie Davis.

Chapter 64 – Articles

The offices of H. Davis & Co. were at 42 Brook Street, London W.1, in the centre of Mayfair, opposite Claridge's Hotel. They were on the first floor above what were then the offices of Aerolineas Argentinas, and comprised one large office at the front (which was Hymie's) and two smaller offices at the rear, with a small waiting room in between. Hymie greeted me, and wasted no time. He told me his two partners, Mr Lewinsohn and Mr Fry were leaving to set up on their own and he needed an assistant, particularly to deal with the litigation side of the practice. He explained what was required to qualify as a solicitor, and he was prepared, if I was interested, to give me articles. He was well aware of my financial circumstances, and realised that I needed to be paid a salary on which I could subsist. Did I have any idea what I would need? I had no idea whatsoever, but said I would investigate, and would like to think about the matter. There was no hurry, he said, and suggested I telephone him when I was ready to discuss the matter further.

I relayed the details of the conversation to Dora and Joe whose information seemed to be ahead of mine. I was staying with Yetti at the time and she said that, of course, I must stay there with her. That, I refused, politely I hope, to do. If I were to be independent then I must be free of obligations attendant upon such hospitality, even from my aunt. She knew a Mrs Reckless, who was getting divorced from her doctor husband, who might take me in. She lived in Hodford Road, not more than five minutes walk from my aunt's house in Dunstan Road, and two minutes from Golders Green station, an ideal location. It needed only a telephone call to confirm that Mrs Reckless would be interested. My aunt went round to see her almost immediately to negotiate on my behalf and to ensure that it was good enough for her nephew. After all, I was 23, a senior NCO in Her Majesty's Army, and an Oxford graduate, and such matters as arranging my own living circumstances could not be left to me; who knew where I would end up?

My aunt reported that Mrs Reckless would provide bed and breakfast for 25 shillings per week and the accommodation was satisfactory. Not luxurious, but comfortable and very clean, was the verdict, and would "suit you fine until you can afford something better." It seemed to me that I was in for a long sojourn in Hodford Road.

Herman and Ray, my other London relatives, also became involved. Though there was a distinct disaffection between Herman and Ray on the one hand and his sisters on the other, for some reason, when it came to my welfare, they all worked for my benefit. This all went on over my head, or behind my back, however one cares to look at it. They differed bitterly from time to time as to how my future should best be arranged, and each appeared to resent the involvement of the others. I feel that I did little to deserve such attention, but I was, and am, grateful for all that they did, even if I did not often show this, lest it encouraged them to interfere to a degree beyond that which I could regard as acceptable. My accommodation and morning meal having been taken care of, my meals in the evenings and at weekends had to be organised. They agreed that I would eat at Yetti's Monday to Thursday, and at Herman and Ray's on Friday nights and Saturdays. On Sundays I would be "at liberty". I wasn't consulted but found no particular fault with the arrangements.

I went to see Hymie Davis again, and he calculated my basic living expenses. Mrs Reckless would cost £1.5s.0d. Essential items of expenditure included the bus fare from Golders Green to Oxford Street which was 6d. each way daily (5 shillings per week), and lunches, about 1s.6d. per day (seven shillings and sixpence). He offered me articles without premium, at a salary of £6 per week leaving me with a little spending money for maybe an occasional visit to the cinema; there was not much scope for luxury, but not having to pay for articles was a luxury in itself. Though I appreciated the good fortune facing me, I was still unhappy at this change of course, and felt unable to give a positive answer immediately. Hymie was extremely sympathetic and put no pressure on me at all. That came from Joe and Dora, whose attitude was that I would be mad to refuse. Of course, they were right – and I didn't.

By now it was September. Summer holidays were over and with the Jewish holidays to follow, and allowing time for all necessary arrangements to be made, it was fixed that I would start at H. Davis & Co. on Monday, 18 October 1954, which was during the middle days of the Festival of Tabernacles (Succoth Hol Ha'moed).

My decision to abandon the Bar for what was considered a less prestigious, certainly less glamorous, branch of the Law, caused considerable grief to my parents. They felt they had let me down. It transpired that they had taken out an insurance policy for my education which matured when I reached 21; but they had spent the proceeds, and they felt considerable guilt over this. Whether this money had funded my extravagant 21st birthday party or had just been poured down the Guisborough drain like so much else, I do not know, but frankly I did not care. This was not money I regarded as my own, and though it would have kept me going for a little while at the Bar, the prospects for the foreseeable future were not encouraging. I took the short-term view; I had no other realistic choice. The question of my going to London as opposed to staying in Middlesbrough, where I might have taken articles, was never considered; that was a point on which my mind was fully made up.

There was a great deal to do before I emigrated to London, a move which would inevitably be permanent. I needed to realise some of my assets to raise some capital. I tend to hoard on the basis that whatever you throw out today will be needed tomorrow. I have found this to be true particularly with files. I keep them for months taking up valuable room. The minute I send them to be archived a query arises requiring their immediate production. This invariably occurs when the files are in limbo, making their retrieval inordinately irritating. This is an application of Murphy's First Law. Murphy's Second Law is: If it can go wrong it will, and even if it can't it will.

I had to decide what was dispensable. So far as I was concerned, nothing was. Everything I had had been lovingly, not to say expensively, amassed over the years. To part with anything was like cutting off a finger, but it had to be done.

For a start, I sold my 20-volume edition of the Oxford English Dictionary which had been my pride and joy; I believe I got £21 for it. I also disposed of all my cameras and photographic equipment; the end of my attempts at serious photography, a hobby which I had very much enjoyed. Mr Mather, of whom I had been a good customer, gave me a very fair price and I spent some of the proceeds on a new suit from Montague Burton. I travelled to London on the Sunday with such of my possessions as I could fit into a suitcase, leaving the rest at home, and took up residence with Mrs Reckless at 96 Hodford Road, Golders Green, London NW11.

Mrs Reckless exuded nervous energy. She was thin almost to the point of gauntness and highly strung, a condition not helped by what appeared to be a very traumatic divorce from her husband. She had two sons, John and Paul, aged about 12 and 10, charming and lively boys, the younger of whom would engage me in endless conversations, in the form of question and answer sessions. She also had three white toy poodles.

To my surprise, she woke me up on the Monday morning I was due to start at H. Davis & Co. with breakfast in bed; possibly because it was more convenient for her than having me downstairs when she was trying to get her boys off to school. The same ritual was observed daily. There would be a summary knock at the door which would be flung open by Paul and/or John before I could respond, and three dogs would fling themselves on my bed and give me a preliminary wash or early morning canine kiss. Paul would then sweep them off the bed while Mrs Reckless deposited the breakfast tray on it. I had to be quick to protect my breakfast from the dogs, but soon got the hang of it. Paul would then linger to ensure I ate my breakfast, which was a full English one minus the bacon – none of this continental breakfast nonsense – while his mother would start shouting at the boys to hurry to get ready. The house was rent by screams of "John, eat your breakfast/get ready", "Paul, stop dreaming, put your shoes/jacket/coat/cap on", or screams of "Mum, he's hitting me" (from either or both John and Paul) with variations on that theme.

The hour before they left for school was frenetic, largely due to Mrs Reckless herself being in constant overdrive. When she had eventually got them off to school she would come, out of breath and exhausted, to collect my tray, as ever preceded by her dogs (which were actually quite delightful), and regale me with her woes. It is strange how as soon as someone knows you are a lawyer, even only an embryonic one, they think you know the answers to all their problems, even though they may have lawyers of their own, to whom they are paying substantial fees for the same advice that you would give. And even if it is not, you are best advised to keep silent. But I saw her point about giving me breakfast in bed. I do not like having breakfast in bed but there was nowhere else to eat it.

And so, on Monday, 18 October 1954, all expectancy, I took the number 13 bus from Golders Green station, which was so near that I practically fell out of bed into it, and arrived at the offices of H. Davis & Co. shortly before 9.30 a.m. when, I was told, they opened. I went to the first floor, but all was dead. There was no sign of life. I was somewhat nonplussed. There I was, with shining morning face, hair Brylcreemed into some sort of discipline, newly suited with Montague Burton's best, and no one to greet me. I wondered whether I might have made a mistake, but no, the name was on the door. I waited for some 15 minutes, and thought that I might as well go and have a coffee. When I returned there was still no one there. I walked up and down outside and was about to go off to telephone Hymie to see whether I had the date wrong or something, when a very pretty girl, who would have given the lie to Dorothy Parker's aphorism that no one made passes at girls who wear glasses, arrived. She introduced herself as Rosemary Noel.

"You must be Freddy," she said. "Mr Davis said you were coming. I'm your secretary. This is your office." She showed me into the smaller of the rear rooms which contained a desk, a desk chair, two chairs for visitors, and a four-drawer steel filing cabinet full of files. "Mr Davis said would you please start with the files in the cabinet. I'll bring you a coffee in a minute. Just let me know if you need anything."

She was well-spoken in a London sort of way. Though not what could be described as sophisticated, she had an air of self-confidence and poise about her which you would not find in secretaries at home. I found that girls in London – even if they were not necessarily Londoners – generally had an air of self-confidence, an assuredness, which girls from my part of the north lacked. This had nothing to do with charm or competence. They earned more, and usually lived away from their parents; this independence made them more self-assertive.

I looked around me. The room was adequate. It was quiet except for the noise of the secretaries' typewriters and the telephone switchboard next door. My door led into their room and from there into the hallway, lift and stairs. Hymie's office, which was the size of the two rear offices together, was at the front of the building. There were two secretaries, Hymie's and mine, and a copy typist. The switchboard was the type which seemed to be strangled by wires. When the telephones were in use it looked rather like a cat's cradle. The typewriters were big heavy Imperials and Remingtons like those on which I had trained as a clerk in the army. There were no such things then as copying machines, dictating machines or any of the equipment and technology to be found in a modern office. Even an internal call from one office to another had to go through the switchboard. For calls outside the London area you still needed to go through an operator. Everything was done by hand. The secretaries took down dictation by shorthand. The copy typist copied letters and typed out leases, agreements and any sort of document which merely needed to be copied. She did not have shorthand. Particularly long documents, such as leases, might be sent to a law stationer for engrossment, and if the lease was for a long term, say 99 years, it might even be engrossed in manuscript on parchment. The Prudential Assurance Company produced handwritten engrossments as late as the end of the 1960s. They looked beautiful but were the very devil to read. The copying machine put an end to them even before more modern technology took over, as they were impossible to photocopy. As there was no automatic duplication – carbon copies could not be used for documents for court for example – everything had to be checked against the original, and this took two people a very long time. Hymie and I would usually do this. It was intensely tedious, but I did learn the nature and contents of leases and other commonly used documents. As I had not actually seen a lease before (even during my Oxford days) this had some advantage and it was not long before I came to know the standard part of legal documents by heart.

I thought that I might as well look at the files which had been left by Mr Lewinsohn and Mr Fry on their departure from the firm so I started with the first file in the top drawer and went through them until I found something interesting. They were all litigation matters. That they had been neglected was obvious even to me from the first file I picked up, and confirmed by a random check of the others. I had no idea what to do. The best thing it seemed to me, was to write to the solicitors on the other side, apologising for any delay where this was appropriate, and ensuring them that the matter would be receiving the writer's earliest possible attention. Procrastination was the first thing I learned. I became an expert. At about 11 o'clock, Hymie put his head round the door.

"Everything all right? Miss Noel looking after you? I'm sure she has told you what to do."

We were very formal: the secretaries were called "Miss" or "Mrs" according to their status. I was called "Mr Fishburn", except by Hymie. Only the office boy was called by his first name. I called Hymie "Mr Davis" till the day I left, even after we had been partners for some years. It was a habit which I could not break. It might have had something to do with the fact that I thought Hymie a totally inappropriate name for him. He didn't look a Hymie. Had his name been Henry or James or something similar and English, I might not have felt so inhibited. His looks, dress and deportment were those of an English gentleman.

I told him that I was afraid I didn't know where to start and I really had no idea what to do.

"Why?" he retorted. "You've got a Law degree, haven't you? I'm sure you'll manage. You said you wanted to do litigation so get on with it. By the way, I'm off on a couple of weeks holiday at the end of next week. Look after the office while I'm away." And then, like the Cheshire cat in *Alice in Wonderland*, he disappeared, and I was left wondering what sort of Wonderland I had stumbled into. That was the sum of the tuition and training I received from my principal during my articles.

Hymie Davis was one of that strange breed – at least I thought them strange – who were very "English" in their speech, their deportment and their dress, but who remained "frum", that is religiously observant; they kept kosher when they ate out as well as at home, they did not drive on Shabbat, they went to synagogue every Saturday, and on all the Jewish holidays. So far as I am aware, Hymie and Helen mixed only in Jewish circles, lived in a Jewish enclave and had only Jewish friends. The great majority of our clients were Jewish, most of them friends of Hymie and Helen. Paradoxically, and in this respect they differed from the traditional Orthodox Jewry, this was accompanied neither by any great Jewish learning nor "Yiddishkeit", which, like the elephant, is easier to recognise than to describe. It is, I suppose, the antithesis to English sophistication. It has nothing to do with being religious, and everything to do with a feeling of Jewishness, a consciousness, an awareness of one's cultural Jewish heritage, a love of things Jewish, an identification with one's past. Above all, a warmth, a homeliness, a self-deprecating sense of humour. Helen's brother Joe Reiss had all these qualities. Hymie did not.

Hymie was a cultured man; he was well read, and had a great love of music and opera in particular. To me, he seemed a man of the world, the acme of urbanity and city polish. He was well dressed and well groomed, at all times. Cleanliness and tidiness were almost a fetish with both Hymie and Helen, which was a contrast to my anarchic hair and clothing unamenable to discipline. For many years I stood in awe of him, looked upon him as a role model and could see no fault in him. And indeed fault was difficult to find, because he did everything well. He was an excellent commercial lawyer, one of the best I have known. He had enormous self-assurance, impeccable manners and great charm. I never knew him overtly angry or saw him lose his temper; in fact I never saw any display of emotion from him at any time: he was a cold fish. You did not know what he was really thinking and he rarely opened up or gave of himself. He was kind to me, but always reserved, and even when I became a partner in the firm we never sat down and discussed anything. He was not given to gossip and rarely talked about people. When he thought it professionally necessary for me to know, he would give me a brief rundown on a client.

As regards work and the running of the office, he dealt with the administration so far as it was dealt with at all. He went his own way and did not interfere with me, and I therefore did my own thing. I was effectively my own boss from the day I started. As a result, regarding the profession of solicitor, I had all the advantages and failings of the autodidact. Much as I enjoyed the freedom given to me, I think it was something of a poisoned chalice. Such legal discipline as I acquired was of my own devising, and it became very difficult for me later in my career to work as part of a team. I had never been subject to any third-party discipline or rules made by others, and though I was usually instrumental in the making of such rules, I found it unduly restrictive having to abide even by them.

Over the next few weeks I continued to work my way through the files, archiving those which were effectively finished, settling those matters which had been so long outstanding that everyone had forgotten what they were all about, and trying to come to grips with those that needed serious attention. I attended the compulsory interview at the Law Society who decided that I was fit to join their august ranks, and became duly enrolled as an articled clerk.

Hymie went off on holiday as planned, leaving me alone in charge. I did not think so much of the matter then, but looking back now, it seems to me to have been the height of irresponsibility. But as I was to learn, that was typical of Hymie, he went his own way regardless. I coped in his absence with the bliss of ignorance. When he returned and we completed the necessary documentation for my articles, he wished me good luck, and almost as a joke in passing said to me: "If you bring in any work I'll give you a third of the fee as a commission." Although he couldn't formally share the fee with me, he could pay me a percentage. "Fat chance," I thought to myself, but thanked him graciously anyway.

My first two months in London passed quickly. I was settling into a new life, and enjoying it. I had been away from home long enough not to feel homesick, despite my somewhat less than luxurious surroundings. Though I knew Mother was not well, and my parents had been having a difficult time, there was no obvious change in their living standards and there seemed nothing unduly to worry about.

I loved London. It has always been one of my favourite cities in the world – indeed possibly *the* favourite. I loved the bustle and excitement. The people I mixed with, the people I came across on the buses and on the Underground, were different from those in the North. They were much more cosmopolitan but, by and large, very much less friendly, but then how friendly do you need strangers to be? Travelling by the number 13 bus to the West End was, in a short space, to go through several different worlds. Golders Green was always a largely Jewish area, but the Jewish population was more inhibited than it is today, and it was very unusual to see men wearing yarmulkes or kippahs, that is skull caps, in the street. They did wear hats, usually the heavy black Homburg type. In those days, Golders Green Road was still a proper suburban shopping centre before its local community shops were destroyed by the shopping complex at Brent Cross and it had to reinvent itself. It was a shopping street with its own character and soul, and a very much sought-after location. Golders Green was a village in itself. I learned that London consists of a series of little villages side by side, each with its own character.

Travelling down the Finchley Road, the bus went through the margins of Hampstead and West Hampstead, on either side of the road, to the Finchley Road station and Swiss Cottage, an area which had attracted a large number of German-speaking Jewish refugees. Little English was spoken in that area, and the restaurants along the Finchley Road, particularly the Cosmos, catered for the European ladies used to their "Kaffee schlag" and torte from Vienna or Berlin. The cafes provided newspapers and allowed their customers to stay for hours over a cup of coffee, in true European fashion. The standing joke was that you needed a passport to drive through Swiss Cottage and bus conductors had to be fluent in German. They did actually seem to achieve an understanding of the garbled English spoken by their passengers, many of whom never mastered the indigenous language. Cosmopolitanism is taken for granted today, and Swiss Cottage was an example of the tolerance shown by Londoners, who may seem not to be the most courteous or outgoing of people, but they go about their business minding their own, and are tolerant of the peculiarities of others. In London, you may not be able to leave your front door open, but you can, by and large, walk the streets dressed as you like without attracting attention.

The number 13 bus passes St John's Wood, goes past Lord's Cricket Ground, by Regent's Park, down Baker Street and into Oxford Street. I never tired of watching the passing scene from the top of the bus. Oxford Street was a world apart. I realised what a country mouse I was. Binns and Dickson & Benson, Middlesbrough's emporia, were very small fry compared with Selfridges, John Lewis and the great Oxford Street stores, to say nothing of Harrods and Harvey Nichols in Knightsbridge and Kensington. I was fascinated and excited; I greeted every day with enthusiasm. The buzz was very different from that of Oxford, to say nothing of Middlesbrough; great cities have a spirit and momentum of their own and I found it exhilarating to be part of London's. This was another new and wonderful world.

The office was in the heart of Mayfair. Just how much of a village it was soon became clear as you came across the same people in the restaurants, shops and the streets themselves, day after day, and you soon came to know and become one of the locals. We were just off New Bond Street, which I still think of as one of the greatest select shopping streets anywhere. Whenever I felt a little down and depressed, a walk along Bond Street (New and Old) would assure me that if there could still be such a display of ostentatious luxury, all was right in the world. Claridge's Hotel was just opposite and its Buttery became a favourite place for entertaining clients and occasionally family and friends when funds permitted it. Lunch could be had for a guinea (£1.1.0) and I doubt whether better value has ever been available in London. Just to be across the road from Claridge's created a feeling of opulence and luxury which were not matched by my pocket, but if I was poor, I was so, at least, in beautiful surroundings. Brook

Street itself, leading from Park Lane to Hanover Square, Grosvenor Square (before the new American Embassy was built), and all the surrounding streets and squares consisted of wonderful houses and buildings. Just to take a walk around that area is always a pleasure, and I considered myself fortunate to be able to spend most of my time there.

Chapter 65 – A Change Of Circumstances

Over the next few weeks a routine developed; as agreed, I had my evening meals from Monday to Friday at Yetti's and on Friday nights and for Saturday lunch would go to Herman and Ray's in Hampstead Garden Suburb, which was rather less easily accessible by public transport than Golders Green. On Sundays I went to Neville's. He was now in the army, a second lieutenant in the RASC. Being the perfectionist he was, he had been the top cadet in his intake and been awarded the Sword of Honour. His military service was nearly as exacting as mine as he was stationed at Stanmore, only about ten minutes drive from his home, to which he returned nearly every weekend. I had always been made most welcome at Neville's home, and I became part of the family, spending most weekends with them over the next three years.

Neville's home was the meeting place for many of his friends, who seemed to congregate there whether or not Neville was home. There was a nucleus of four: Alan Miller, Norman Nathan, Godfrey Raivid and Tony Jaffe (the Cohen's doctor's son), whom I had already met at Oxford where he was at St Catherines' College (or more correctly Society as it had not yet received collegiate status). They welcomed me into their circle and as Neville had three siblings, two sisters and a brother, with friends of their own, the house was always full of young people. Mavis, the elder of the two sisters, had grown from a beautiful child into a very pretty young woman, although she rather distanced herself from Neville's friends. Rosalind, the younger sister, was full of fun, and happy to engage in adolescent banter with the boys, and she usually managed to have the last word. Brian, who was twelve years younger than Neville, having been born in 1944 just at the time the V-bombs caused his family to seek the safety of Middlesbrough, was too young to be part of our world. Presiding over this happiest of homes, which was to become such an integral part of my life over the next few years were Alec and Bessie, whom I always addressed as "uncle" and "aunt", as one did to older people who were family or virtually so.

Bessie was, even later in her eighties, a most beautiful woman. She never lost her north country accent, or robustness of approach. She reminded me of my own mother, with whom she got on very well and had much in common. To her no-nonsense approach, in keeping with her northern background, she allied a warm, open-hearted and generous disposition and, like Dora, never hesitated to tell me what she thought I should do, and give me a piece of her mind when she felt it appropriate, which seemed to me at times rather frequently. I felt very much at home.

I had – still have – the greatest respect and admiration for Alec, probably more than for anyone else I have known. I cannot write of him dispassionately. What he lacked in height, he made up for in the strength of his character. He had a big and outgoing personality, an insatiable curiosity, a zest for life, and an innate kindness. He was a very rare breed, a man without vanity, not altered or spoiled by success; one of nature's gentlemen. With his younger brother Morris, he built up Victor Value, the business which had been started in the 1920s by his father, to become one of the major supermarket groups in the country, rivalling Sainsbury's and Tesco, his greatest competitor. Alec truly had the ability to "walk with kings yet keep the common touch". For all his success and financial standing, he had no side. He treated everyone in the same way.

Though business matters did not dominate his life (as they did Max's), after his family, Victor Value was his main interest. He had a hands-on management style and most Saturday afternoons he would visit various shops. Neville and I would often go with him and I learned my way round London as a result. I was able to observe Alec at work at close quarters, and the more I saw of him the more I admired him. He seemed to know the name and family details of every shop manager. He would show the same courtesy to every junior shop assistant as to senior executives; in fact, in some respects more so, as the juniors would not be subject to the stern criticism he would hand out to anyone who failed to meet the very high standards he expected. He did not suffer fools gladly.

But I noticed that even in his – often very severe – strictures of staff he was never personal or impolite. He was constructive, and though some of the objects of his ire may have felt that they had been through a mill after he had finished with them, there was no resentment or bad feeling. He had not criticised them in any personal manner, but had focused on what they had done wrong; he had explained his reasons and told them what they should be doing.

And, having once or twice been at the receiving end of Alec's advice, I know whereof I write. But I have always been grateful for that advice, which, unpalatable as it may have seemed at the time, I knew to be correct. Alec was not a man given to expediency or to mincing his words. If he thought a thing was wrong, he said so in no uncertain terms.

In due course, I joined a chess club and began to play for London County, but apart from that, the society in which I now mixed was wholly Jewish. I had not yet met any girls in London. Strangely, neither Neville nor his friends seemed to know any girls. I do not know why. Perhaps because they had been away for so long, what with army service and university, they had lost touch. Relationships with the opposite sex were, even in London and certainly in the London Jewish circles in which I found myself, not as relaxed and informal as today. At the age of 25 or so, taking girls out carried with it the risk of matrimony, and, if not careful, paternity. None of us wished to incur either risk! Whatever the reason, it was a very masculine set, but no one seemed to mind. We played bridge instead.

I became part of Yetti's immediate family over the next few years, a fact which Harold (who was born in 1945) welcomed more than Sarah (born in 1947). My first memories of them are two large pairs of eyes peering at me when I first stayed on the put-you-up in their lounge, a stranger being on weekend leave from the army or a large figure passing through on his way to somewhere.

Though Karl's father also lived with Yetti, she had little discourse with him. She was starved of adult company. By the time I came home for dinner, usually at about 7 p.m., she had already packed the kids off to bed. Usually, she had eaten by the time I got to her house but she would sit over me watching me eat, her face cupped in her hands, eagerly awaiting my reaction to every mouthful. I know it may sound ungrateful, but I found this off-putting. Her cooking, though wholesome and welcome, was hardly gourmet and lacked variety. When hungry and tired I am not naturally communicative, so I was not generally in a mood for conversation. She would regale me with tales of the children and her own day, and question me in great detail about everything I had done. My answers tended to be monosyllabic, and the less I spoke the more she probed. She was a voluble lady, and needed little inspiration from me, so I developed a method of feeding her little snippets which set her off, and let me get on with my meal. I am afraid that in some respects I was a disappointment to my aunt, but she never let it show. She remained attentive and inquisitive throughout my time at Dunstan Road.

My parents' silver wedding, at Christmas 1954, was celebrated – as were all "simchas" –with a huge party. Its munificence, though not perhaps quite up to that of my 21st (but it was wintertime), gave no indication of the family's financial difficulties. There was the usual influx of family and friends from London and elsewhere to Middlesbrough. It was, like all my mother's parties, a wonderful affair. It was also her swansong. She died three weeks later, aged 45.

I stayed at home over the Christmas period, and returned to London for the new year. I was horrified to learn that New Year's Day was not a public holiday in the South, as it has since become, but an ordinary working day, and Hymie was not overgenerous in terms of giving time off, which statement is not a criticism or a complaint, merely a fact of life. About three weeks later my mother sent Tessie down to London for a few days, ostensibly to ensure that my things were in order, but more I think as a token of appreciation for Tessie's work in connection with the silver wedding. On the Sunday afternoon I took Tessie to King's Cross and saw her on the train back to Teesside. I telephoned my mother to let her know when Tessie would be home, and I chatted to her for some time. She had a cold, was tired and in bed, but was well otherwise. That was the last time I spoke to her.

During that night at about 3 a.m. there was a huge banging on the door at my Hodford Road digs. It was freezing cold and there was a heavy layer of snow all round. I got up to see what all the noise was about and opened the door. Karl stood there. I looked at him in astonishment. "What's up?" I asked.

He could not speak. I was quite befuddled myself, but had no inkling of why he was there. Obviously, something untoward had happened but I had no idea of what it was.

Eventually, he said: "Your mother has had a car accident and is ill in hospital."

I replied: "That's nonsense. She was in bed with a cold when I spoke to her only a few hours ago. She would not have got up and gone out."

He stammered something more completely unintelligible, but I got the gist that I must hurry as we had to catch the first train up North. I dressed as quickly and warmly as I could and we went back to Dunstan Road, where Yetti was sitting crying. I cannot recall who else was there, but Herman and Ray soon appeared. Karl then told me that my mother had had a heart attack and was in hospital, very ill. He still could not tell me the whole truth, and I chose not to contemplate it, but I knew in my heart that my mother was dead.

The journey in the dark early hours of a January morning first to King's Cross and then home is just a blur in my memory. On the train Karl told me the truth I already knew. We arrived at a deeply grieving Brierfield. My father was totally lost. Tessie, through her tears, had managed to achieve some sort of organisation and had brought her sisters in to help. My mother had had a heart attack around midnight and died almost instantly. Tessie was with her, giving an account of her visit to London. Dad was out playing cards only a matter of some minutes away. Mother was dead by the time he got home. I asked to see her but both Dad and Tessie were very anxious that I should not do so.

"Remember her as she was when she was alive," they both urged.

As I am by nature cowardly, I accepted their advice, and did not see my mother. My memory of her is that of a living, vibrant, life-loving personality, and I have no regrets about my decision. In Jewish tradition funerals take place as soon as possible. As the winter day was very short in the North the latest time the funeral could take place was at 2 p.m.

We tried to eat something warm, but no one was in a mood for food. We had to get ready for the funeral. The rending of my clothes, which involves a garment being cut or torn, a ritual of funerals, the process of getting into the leading mourners' car, the journey to the cemetery in the cortege, which as a mark of honour to my mother went past the synagogue, the great number of cars which followed the hearse, the large crowd of people at the funeral, all appeared to me as if in a dream. I had still not woken up. The snow at the cemetery was four feet deep. Luckily, I had put on Wellington boots. I could not understand how it had been possible to prepare the grave in time. The lack of sleep, the shock, the cold, all combined to leave me feeling numb. I had no feelings. I could not weep. As the only son, I had to say the Kaddish, a special prayer for the dead, several times during the course of the funeral service. I did this as if in a trance; I had no idea of what I was saying.

After the service at the cemetery we went back home to sit *shiva*, as had been done when my grandparents died. Those who had to sit *shiva* were my father, my mother's brothers and sisters, and me, as her son, the main mourner. I remained in a state of shock throughout the seven days of the *shiva*.

Shivas are never happy occasions. This one was particularly unhappy. It is not unusual for family dissensions to become evident during the *shiva*. There is little else to do but dwell on grievances, real or imagined, or take the opportunity to pay off some old scores, trade a few insults or lay claim to what you consider is due to you. Dora, in her special grief, as she was the closest of all the siblings to my mother, took the opportunity to lay into Max and my father, blaming them for the demise of the factory which she saw as the cause of my mother's death. She also took it upon herself to fight for what she considered to be my rights and my entitlement to my share of my mother's estate. My mother had left no will and her whole estate devolved upon my father on her intestacy. I resented this uncalled for and unwanted championship of my cause. While I could understand that Dora was anxious that certain items which had been in my mother's family should stay in the family, these had been part of my parents' home. They were now my father's and I did not consider that I had any right to anything other than my own personal possessions. Dora's suspicion that these would all simply disappear may have been fully justified, and was, as it turned out, but the matter was none of her business. However, as I have several times indicated, in my family this was not a consideration which ever entered her mind and it did not inhibit her. Sadly, her misguided intervention proved counterproductive. My father, never one for an argument, just put up the shutters and refused to discuss anything. I can't say that I blamed him, but this caused a rift between him and Dora and I was the battleground.

After the *shiva* everyone went back to their homes. I stayed at home, as I continued to think of Brierfield, another week. I hoped, I suppose, that my mother's death might bring my father and me closer together. We were not estranged, we had just grown increasingly apart. My father must also have been in a traumatic state. He avoided any discussion about his future intentions: about the house, its contents, the business, anything. I became increasingly frustrated. This was his typical fudge and this time there was no Mother to step in and force the issue.

I had no objections to whatever my father decided to do, nor could I have had. I would not have thought it any more acceptable for me to interfere in his life than for him to do so in mine. This made my father's attitude all the more difficult to understand. All I wanted was that he should sit down and talk to me, confide in me, treat me like a son. I was his only relative, apart from his brother in America, with whom he very rarely communicated. But he was simply not capable of doing so. Whether 25 years of Schmulewitsch domination had destroyed any capacity he had had for expressing himself, or indeed, making up his own mind, I do not know. I do know that during their marriage, Mother made all the relevant decisions; now she was no longer around to do so. He may have needed time to adjust. I do not know what he felt because he would not talk. I found this very distressing, and the months following my mother's death was a difficult period for us both.

My father made no difficulties about my taking those items I wanted back to London with me after the funeral period or later. There was obviously little room at Hodford Road and Dora and Joe suggested, or rather, insisted, that I took a bigger room, so that I could accommodate more of my belongings. Mrs Reckless was willing to let me have a larger room for an extra ten shillings a week which was beyond my financial range at the time so Dora and Joe offered to pay the extra. I accepted on the basis that this would only be a loan. With the luxury of more space I was able therefore to bring to London all the contents of my own room at Brierfield: chairs, settee, bookcase and contents, which were actually a very great comfort to me, as I now lived among my own things, and it felt rather like being at home. The bookcase was to remain with me, almost as a talisman, for many years. But the greatest asset was the car. I was aware that I could not afford to run it, but I knew that if I did not take it back with me to London, my father would sell it and I would see nothing of the proceeds. I only used it at weekends but having a car again made life easier for me, as getting around by public transport was not conducive to having a social life.

My other great comfort at that difficult time was my dog, Peggy. As I could not have her with me at Hodford Road, she came to live with Yetti where she had a very happy home, adored and spoiled by Harold and Sarah (who loved animals), my aunt and even by old Father Katz, to whom she was a companion on his otherwise lonely walks. Peggy was a remarkable animal. She learned her way around Golders Green in no time at all, despite the fact that she was in entirely new surroundings with much heavier traffic both on and off the road than she had been used to.

It was a welcome relief to return to London and work although my life was also affected in other ways. From her grave, my mother effectively ensured that I kept faithful to my Judaism. In accordance with Jewish tradition I had to go to synagogue twice daily to say Kaddish. I did this faithfully for eleven months after my mother's death; it never occurred to me not to do so. Admittedly, any dereliction of duty in this respect would have distressed my family and brought severe criticism down on me, but that possibility or threat never entered my thinking. I was fortunate that the Dunstan Road synagogue was only about 5 minutes' walk away. Evening service was usually at 7.30 p.m., which could be difficult to get to if I had to work late, so I found out the times of other synagogues where I could go if necessary. As a mourner, I was often invited to take the service. The laity are very much involved in the running of synagogues, which includes taking the daily services, and I became fairly proficient at taking both the morning and evening services.

Saying Kaddish also has an inhibiting effect on your social life. During the period of mourning, going to the cinema or listening to music are prohibited. I spent much of my free time playing chess, and increasingly bridge, although I gave up chess when the standard – County – at which I was playing became too professional and too time-consuming to maintain.

The exigencies of attending services made it difficult for me to spend the day with Neville's family, and during this time I was usually there only on Sundays. Through my regular attendance at the Dunstan Road synagogue I began to know some of the older members. One, a Mr Epstein, an accountant, would invite me to lunch and tea on Saturdays with his family, to fill in the time between the morning and afternoon services. Whether this was out of a spirit of charity or because they saw in me an eligible bachelor I do not know, but it widened my circle of acquaintances and made a change from my meals with the various members of my family, and a budding solicitor needs as wide a circle of potential clients as he can get. Being Saturday, you walked everywhere, and Mr Epstein and his family would drag me with them from one house to another. By the time we had to return to the synagogue for the afternoon service, I would be quite exhausted. I decided then that this sort of restrictive and restricted religiously observant life was not for me, but it did have certain attractions. It is very relaxing not to have to drive, not to answer a telephone, to have no radio or television, to be undisturbed by the world outside and to be at peace with your surroundings. It is also intensely boring when you are young with no proper home of your own, and no one to go to bed with and make love to, which is another traditional Saturday afternoon sport indulged in by observant Jews in fulfilment of God's commandment to "go forth and multiply".

One Saturday, Mr Epstein was not in synagogue, but he was in the newspaper headlines for having disappeared, at the same time as a great deal of his clients' money, only to turn up soon after in Israel; just shows!

Chapter 66 – Sad Cases

By going so early in the morning to synagogue, I arrived at work before anyone else and before the telephone calls started, so I had more time to get to grips with what I had to do. I gained confidence, and felt able to deal properly with the cases in hand and those coming in. But I was still learning as I went along.

The aftermath of the war had produced several new trades, even industries, one of which was trading in army surplus. This included military vehicles and equipment and above all spare parts, largely of British and American army origins. Much of this was virtually new, having arrived shortly before the war ended. The armies had no further need for it and it would have been too expensive to repatriate it. At a time when there were great shortages of materials, vehicles and spare parts, there was a ready market for such goods. There were great profits to be made. It was a trade which provided great scope for fraud and other forms of criminal activity. Many who dealt in those commodities were untrustworthy, no better than and direct descendants of horse thieves and forerunners of some of today's second-hand car dealers. This is not to say that everyone in the business was crooked. Some very large and reputable companies were properly set up and run with integrity but the lower end of the market was not altogether savoury, and the small man who wished to keep out of trouble had to be very careful. Many cases arose from claims that the goods sold were not of merchantable quality pursuant to section 14 of the Sale of Goods Act 1894, or that the goods had been falsely described, and many implied or openly alleged fraud. Two of my earliest cases arose from this background.

One concerned a civil action which was not particularly noteworthy from a legal aspect but which taught me an important lesson, namely that time was money.

The first of these concerned goods which it was alleged were not fit for the purpose intended. I spent many hours researching this matter; getting expert evidence and considering it, seeing counsel in conference both with and without the client, preparing the papers for the hearing and preparing the brief to counsel. After two years, the case came to trial. Following a three-day hearing, we lost, and my client had to pay the plaintiff's costs as well as his own. I was surprised when he came out of court smiling and was astonished when he shook me warmly by the hand.

"Well done, very well done," he exclaimed with delight.

"Well done?" I said. "What do you mean? We lost. How can you say well done?"

"Two years ago I couldn't afford to pay the claim," he told me. "I would have been bankrupt. Today I can afford to pay. I've bought two years. I've done well in that time and paying now means little."

"So why didn't we settle the matter before we delivered the brief to counsel and incurred the costs of the hearing?" I asked him.

"You were so persuasive in your arguments and presentation of the case, I thought we had a chance and might as well take it all the way," was the reply.

Because of the nature of our clientele, we had very little criminal work experience but one of my first cases involved a visit to Wormwood Scrubs Prison to interview a man for whom Joe Reiss, Hymie's brother-in-law, asked us to act. It was a sad story.

When the war ended, Albert Wenlock was just one of millions of displaced persons trying to find a refuge. He had somehow survived the war in hiding, moving from one place to another. Being a man of some resource, he had learned to survive, but his terrible experiences had left him distrustful of others, and afraid of anyone in uniform. He had had to scramble and fight for every crust of bread and he bore the marks of the beatings he had received. He was an astute man and began to earn a living in buying and selling goods, among them army surplus both here in England and on the continent where he had started his business. He came to England, and married a charming lady who had also survived the war in hiding. She had relatives in Buenos Aires, who knew of Joe Reiss's business connections in London. She appealed to her family for help, which is how we came to be instructed in the matter. Wenlock had just been convicted of conspiracy to defraud, together with

George Dawson, and had been sentenced to two years imprisonment.

George Dawson, then known as "The Cockney Millionaire", was reputed to have made a large fortune through dealing in army surplus. In doing so he had often sailed very close to the wind; the police had been "gunning" for him for some time. Eventually, they thought they had caught him. He and five others, including Mr Wenlock, were accused of conspiring to sell goods which did not exist. That there was a crooked deal of some sort was not, I think, disputed.

At the trial, which was at the Old Bailey as I recall (though we did not act for Mr Wenlock at the trial), four of the defendants elected not to give evidence. George Dawson, a very cocky cockney, thinking that no London jury would convict him, did give evidence. I think that he rather misjudged the esteem in which he was held. Mr Wenlock was also advised not to give evidence, but certain in his mind of his innocence and that he would be able to convince a jury of it, he too chose to give evidence. A lawyer can do no more than advise. He cannot oblige a client to accept this advice although in extreme cases the lawyer can withdraw from the case. It will come as no surprise that both Dawson and Wenlock were convicted. The other defendants were all acquitted.

Whether Hymie so intended I doubt, but my first visit to the prison ensured that I stayed honest. Nothing in my experience before or since so depressed me as going through the prison gates. I immediately felt dehumanised. I was treated with the utmost courtesy, and so, as far as I could judge, was my client, but the whole place reeked of hopelessness and failure. I had not yet seen the transcript of the trial. I took a full statement from Mr Wenlock who was in a pitiable state. He simply could not understand what had happened to him, or why he was in jail. Like so many who have had no experience of it, he had a blind faith in British justice. He just could not believe that it had treated him so shabbily.

His knowledge of English was limited, though he did not appreciate that. He thought he spoke perfectly. He had a very strong Middle-European accent, a mixture of Polish and Hungarian. In his dealings he had somehow become involved with George

Dawson, not directly but through several intermediaries including some of his co-defendants. He himself was only an intermediary. He was not simply an agent, because he dealt for himself, buying and selling back to back. He would take an option on goods which he would only exercise after he had managed to sell them. Others would buy from him on a similar basis, and chains with many links of buyers and sellers developed. It was very complicated. He was in a very small and insecure way of business in a highly competitive and unreliable market. He was anxious to conceal his sources from any prospective buyer, because if his buyer found out from whom he was getting the goods, the buyer would go direct to his seller cutting out the middleman. This was not a business for the unwary or overscrupulous. He therefore kept two distinct sets of books, one for buying and one for selling, and the right hand was never allowed to see what the left hand was doing.

Wenlock was only a very small cog; in this particular case, George Dawson was the key figure at the end of the line. It did not require any great exercise of the imagination to see how an English jury would react to a description of such working methods by a witness who had the misfortune to look shifty, whose English was broken, and who was quite unable to give a straight answer to any question. His experiences had taught him to be careful how he responded to interrogation. He would repeat sotto voce any question put to him, searching for any hidden meaning, and seeking to give the answer that he thought his interrogator required. It never occurred to him to give even me a simple truthful answer though I was there to help him. I found it impossible to get direct and simple answers. He trusted no one and even less so after his conviction. I could see that before a xenophobic, middle-class jury and a very unfriendly judge, he had no chance at all. As I left to go, Mr Wenlock took hold of my arm: "Please help me," he said. "I shall die in here. Please believe me that I am innocent in this case. I may have been guilty of many things in my time, but of this charge I am entirely innocent." I believed him.

I instructed James Burge, one of the top criminal barristers, and an immediate appeal was lodged, coupled with an application for bail pending the appeal. We had to wait a little while to obtain a transcript of the trial. When I read this, it became immediately clear how Wenlock had come to be found guilty. The charge was that of conspiracy, i.e. conspiring with others to defraud and cheat. The evidence against him was circumstantial and very thin. The police were out to get George Dawson, who had eluded them for some time. It was possible, of course, that he had committed no crime but the police thought otherwise. In this case, they simply arrested all those who had been associated with Dawson in the transactions which gave rise to the charges. The weakness of their case was evident from the fact that they relied on the conspiracy charge. What one person may do legally can, when done in concert with others, become a conspiracy, and hence illegal. Wenlock was guilty by association. As so often happens, the judge, in his desire to ensure that the jury convicted the defendants, became very tendentious in his summing-up. In the course of the appeal it also became clear that the police had withheld evidence which could well have been helpful to the defendants. Mr Wenlock's application for bail was granted, pending hearing of the appeal, very unusual in such cases particularly where the conviction was by a jury.

I often wished, rather unkindly, that we had been less successful in that respect because he began to make a nuisance of himself. He would drop in to the office unannounced, to see me on almost a daily basis, asking to see papers, wanting to take copies and insisting on speaking to me, regardless of any other commitments I may have had. If I did see him, and I found it hard to refuse, he engaged me in endless and repetitive discussions. I had every sympathy with him, but I had other work to do and there was nothing more we could do until the hearing of the appeal. This had to await the convenience of the Court of Criminal Appeal and its own workload of cases. Wenlock was becoming increasingly obsessive. He claimed that the police had deliberately persecuted him, and he was going to get justice from them.

His appeal succeeded. The Appeal Court found that there was no evidence against him to sustain a conviction, and that he should never have been prosecuted. He was awarded all his costs from the outset of the trial to the appeal out of public funds, and walked out of court with a clean name. James Burge had pleaded the case superbly well. The irony was that though Dawson had no real grounds of appeal, once the last of his alleged co-conspirators had been found not guilty there was no longer any conspiracy and Dawson also had to be released. The tragedy of the situation was that Wenlock would not let matters rest there. He insisted on suing the police, which was very much harder then than now. Thanks to the *Dixon of Dock Green* image of the policeman, the force had a squeaky clean reputation. It was a brave counsel who would attack the police head-on. To do so could harm his client's case and would undoubtedly lead to a longer sentence if he or she were found guilty. No one would then have believed the corruption, brutality and racial prejudice of which some police officers have since been shown to be capable. Wenlock pursued a personal vendetta against the police superintendent in charge of the prosecution.

I refused to act for him on what I considered to be a hopeless case, so he became that scourge of the law courts, a litigant in person. He lost his house and all he owned. His long-suffering wife, who had stood by him and supported him with undiminished faith throughout his trials and tribulations, could take no more and left him, taking their children, and went to her family in Israel. He took on odd jobs to keep going. He was offered financial help and practical assistance to make a new start in life, which he refused, but no one in his family would or could help him as long as he retained this obsession. Nothing would move him. He was addicted to his search for vengeance. He may have been released from jail, but he found no freedom. He remained imprisoned in his obsession. I do not know what became of him. This was my saddest case.

Another sad case but in a different sense was that of Mr Dvoriansky. He was another refugee from Poland, a survivor of the war, who had come to London and was trying to make a living by, among other things, buying and selling diamonds. He had a small flat in Endsleigh Court, Bloomsbury. At about six one morning, he was raided by the police. The police found some diamonds which they alleged had been stolen. Mr Dvoriansky was hauled before the magistrate, charged with being in possession of stolen goods, and granted bail. He had been recommended to us by another client, a Mr Katz, for whom we were acting at the time on a tax case. Mr Dvoriansky insisted that Mr Davis dealt with his matter. He was a rather pathetic character, afraid of his shadow, who would have had neither the nous nor the courage deliberately to undertake any criminal act. He needed some convincing that I was perfectly capable of dealing with the matter. So did I, but I was consoled by the fact that Hymie knew even less about criminal law than I did.

I took a full statement from the client. He had acquired the diamonds the previous day in Hatton Garden for about £200 and actually (and unusually) had a piece of paper – it was no more than that – to prove it. Buying and selling diamonds on the pavement is, or was then, a common way of doing business in the diamond trade. He was caught literally with his pants down. I was hard put not to show my amusement at the mental picture of this fat little man being surprised by a police raid in that state but it was not at all funny to Mr Dvoriansky. The charge was that of handling stolen goods, i.e. being a "fence". The police case was based on the assertion that the diamonds were worth considerably more than that and that the defendant, being a diamond merchant, as he claimed to be, must have known or "had reason to believe" that the goods were stolen by the fact that he was obtaining them at an undervalue. I cannot recall that the owner, from whom they were supposed to have been stolen, was ever established. I again instructed James Burge. On his advice we asked a firm called Antrobus & Co. who specialised in valuations for insurance purposes, to value the diamonds. Their valuer, a woman (to my surprise as I had thought the diamond trade to be wholly male), explained that these were not white diamonds but Brazilian yellow diamonds; not of any great quality or value and that, if anything, our client had overpaid for them. One thing about being a solicitor is that you learn a good deal about various trades and industries. I had become quite an expert on army surplus and now, for a short time, became one on diamonds. The stipendiary magistrate who heard the case had little difficulty in throwing it out and awarding costs against the police.

These two cases tended to influence my views as to the relative merits of trial by jury and stipendiary magistrate. Juries are just as likely to convict wrongly as to find defendants innocent wrongly, and a judge is not always able properly to instruct a jury nor does a jury always understand what a case is about. In order to ensure a conviction, a judge may well go beyond the mark, and thus afford grounds for what would otherwise be an unmeritorious appeal. A stipendiary magistrate has sufficient experience to see through totally spurious defences on the one hand and suspect prosecutions on the other.

We had another big case involving diamonds, not a criminal matter but a back-duty case, that is a claim by the Inland Revenue for unpaid tax. Our client was the said Mr Katz, a Czech diamond merchant who had managed to escape from Czechoslovakia, just before the war started, with (he claimed) a large fortune in diamonds, which formed the basis of his business here. Like many businessmen, he had a determined reluctance to pay tax, and eventually the Revenue caught up with him. I have always wondered how they manage so often to establish tax defalcations, particularly when they are simply non-payment of tax on transactions of which there is no official record, and do not appear in the books shown to the Revenue. Often their investigations arise solely from routine spot checks. The Inland Revenue have the right to inspect the books and accounts of any taxpayer and are gentlemen by comparison with Customs & Excise and usually give notice of their intentions. At that time the two departments were separate. In this case, their inspection started as a routine matter, but their suspicions were soon aroused by the unsatisfactory nature of the information given, and the fact that the profits shown were inadequate to support the taxpayer's (our client) lifestyle. He maintained that his wealth was merely the result of the realisation of his assets, namely the diamonds he had brought with him, not from trading.

The Revenue had heard this argument before. They assessed him on the basis of his lifestyle, and demanded payment of tax accordingly, simply asking Mr Katz to disprove their assessment. This he was unable to do. In order to avoid a prosecution for fraud, an agreement was reached whereby he agreed to pay a sum in respect of tax and penalties, some £10,000, and to provide by way of disclosure a full statement of assets. This would form the basis of his future taxation. This was a very fair deal by the Revenue, who realised that it would be difficult and lengthy to bring a case against Mr Katz. From Mr Katz's point of view he had the opportunity at a fairly low cost to "kosher", or launder, a considerable amount of money. He was advised – badly as it turned out – to maximise the amount of his disclosure but when the Revenue saw what he disclosed, they felt they had been deceived and reopened the case. It is at that point that we came into the picture. We were instructed to deal with the appeal against the fresh assessment to be heard before the Special Commissioners for Tax. Up to then, Mr Katz had been advised by another firm of solicitors and his own accountants.

The value of assets disclosed by Mr Katz was £120,000. That was a large amount; today's equivalent would be about £8,000,000. As the Revenue's counsel said to me later, the Revenue had only expected a disclosure of some £30,000. They would have smiled to themselves had the figure been £60,000, raised an eyebrow or two at £90,000, but £120,000 was so far beyond their expectations, and so inconsistent with the information on which they had agreed the original settlement, that they felt they were being made to look foolish. To put the matter more technically, they felt that the information now produced was so far from what they had been led to believe that it amounted to a "new discovery", entitling them as a matter of law to raise a fresh assessment.

Recently down from Oxford, with the notions of various equitable remedies still fresh in my mind, I suggested that we might argue that the Revenue was estopped from reopening the case because Mr Katz had only made his disclosure on the basis that the Revenue had agreed not to do so. I could see no other argument succeeding. It had been thought that the doctrine of estoppel did not affect the Crown, that such an issue could not be raised against the Revenue, but there had recently been a case – Robertson vs Minister of Pensions – where the issue had been successfully argued against the Crown. Our counsel agreed to run this argument. Estoppel, briefly, means that if you agree to a certain course of action or make certain representations on which another person has relied and acted to his detriment, the court will not let you renege on your promise. This is an inadequate and somewhat crude summary of the matter; volumes have been written on the subject, but this will suffice for the present purposes. The Revenue were somewhat taken aback at this argument, but rather than have the point litigated which might set an unhappy precedent took the view that while reserving their rights they would accept the point, if it were established that they had, in fact, agreed to the terms as we asserted. In short, they denied that there had ever been any such agreement, or that they had ever given any promise or made any representation as alleged.

The deal had been struck by Mr Katz's accountants (a highly reputable firm) in a telephone conversation with the tax inspector sometime after working hours on a Friday night, and though an internal memorandum was made by the accountant at the time, this was never confirmed in writing. The tax inspector said that while he did not deny that there had been a conversation, he had no note of it, and was not aware that there had been an agreement. In the face of the Revenue's categorical denial, and it was hard to establish that they were lying through their teeth, the commissioners found that though they accepted that there had been a conversation, its terms were unclear; there had obviously been a misunderstanding – they did not say on whose part – but they could not conclude that there had been an agreement as alleged. They allowed the case to continue but two days later, while being cross-examined by counsel for the Revenue, Mr Katz had a major heart attack and died in hospital a few hours later. He was buried the next day, and his widow, against whom there was no case, took all the diamonds and other portable items she could find, and departed for Israel. So Mr Katz finally defeated the Revenue, though in a somewhat drastic fashion.

This case made an impression on me for two other reasons, apart from Mr Katz's fate. The first was the utter courtesy with which the case was conducted by Crown counsel; there were no theatricals, no harrying or bullying of witnesses, just clever examination and cross-examination. Every question was carefully phrased, every answer carefully probed and tested. Mr Katz, like Mr Wenlock, though considerably more intelligent and shrewder, was unable to give a straight answer. He could not give a simple "yes" or "no" to a question. He tried to anticipate the response his adversary was trying to elicit and framed his replies accordingly, that is, he avoided answering. This gave the same impression of shiftiness as Mr Wenlock. The other point was that no matter whom you deal with, you cannot rely on the spoken word; everything must be confirmed in writing. This is not simply due to suspicion or fear of dishonesty, but because memory is fallible. Being able to refer to a contemporaneous document can save considerable doubt and distress. This was an important lesson, which I carried with me throughout my career.

Chapter 67 – Consequences

Mother's death was followed by two unhappy events, one trivial the other tragic. Whether they were a direct result of Mother's death I cannot say but the coincidence is too close to disregard any suggestion of a link. The trivial matter was that for the first and only time in my life I failed an exam. To become a solicitor, a knowledge of trust accounts and bookkeeping was required. The study of this was usually kept separate from the main body of studies, such as tort, contract and property law, which occupied the last six months of articles. The trust accounts and bookkeeping exam was usually taken after six months. Though there were live courses and good correspondence courses I thought I could manage without any of these and go it alone. Perhaps under normal circumstances I might have been able to, but my mother's death upset my equilibrium and I was not able to settle down for any period of study. I think in retrospect that my attitude was more than somewhat arrogant, and I doubt whether I could have managed these subjects alone in any event, as they were very different from anything else I had done. The result was dismal failure. Chastened, I took a course at Gibson & Weldons, the law tutors, and passed the next time I sat some months later.

The sad and tragic event was the serious stroke suffered by Max only a few weeks after Mother's death. He was in hospital for some six months, much of the time in intensive care. Medical opinion was that he would not survive. But my family are nothing if not fighters. Max refused to give up the struggle. Sheer willpower carried him through, but he was never able to work or walk properly again. One side of his body remained paralysed, and his speech, though it improved over the years, remained slow and slurred, a far cry from the voluble, excitable and fast-talking Max we had known. Strangely, however, his voice, though weakened, never lost its fine tone or musicality. His illness put paid to any hopes which might have remained after Mother's death of continuing the business, in whatever reduced circumstances.

He required full-time nursing for a long time. When after some months he was able to return home, his needs and those of her four children took up all Jeanne's time, and things were very hard for them. It would be an exaggeration to say that Max, even when he was as fully recovered as he could be, was more than a memory of his former self. But he fought his disability and achieved a certain serenity with the passing years. He had looked death in the face, though he probably never realised it, and he set about rehabilitating himself physically with the same determination he had always shown.

This double blow virtually destroyed the Schmulewitsch family as an independent commercial entity. Apart from Joe and Dora, who after some struggles had made their own financial success in Jersey, only Herman and Yetti were left. Neither of them had any financial strength, nor were they able to assist Max and his family financially. Only Joe and Dora had the means to do so. As some of Jeanne's family were well off, Joe took the initiative in arranging some financial support for Max and Jeanne to give them some independence.

Max's illness seemed to increase my father's loneliness and sense of isolation. Whatever arguments there may have been over business matters, there were rarely any over private ones, and the family relationship remained close, even after Mother died. My father had always got on well with Max and Jeanne, and he was deeply affected by Max's condition. I cannot say that I did much to help my father; indeed I probably contributed to his sense of abandonment. I was too concerned with my own pain, and sense of loss, and with trying to establish my life in London, to try to understand his problems. I was also subject to pressure from Dora to protect my "rights", which would never have occurred to me, as I did not think I had any, nor did I and the pressure created an unnecessary and unhappy conflict. I began to suffer from a sense of injustice and I must have made some comment or said something to Uncle Alec (Cohen) one day, because he took me aside, and in the nicest possible way gave me the dressing-down of my life. And yet he did so with such sympathy, warmth, understanding and affection, that I was grateful to him then and have been ever since. He did not lay blame, he did not take sides, he just pointed out that whatever grievances I imagined I had suffered, my father was my father, and whatever decisions he made I had to accept. He made me see matters from an entirely different point of view from that to which my own morbid introspection at that time had led me.

Morbidity and introspection do not come naturally to me, but I do occasionally suffer from a form of paranoia which my family was prone to. My Aunt Yetti was particularly susceptible to this. "Everything happens to me" she would cry. One sad day I had an anguished telephone call from her. Could I come at once. She never phoned me at work so I knew this must be serious. When I got there she was sobbing bitterly, "Everything happens to me." Once I managed to get some sense out of her I learned that her son, Harold, had had a very serious car accident, and had nearly been killed, but apart from a serious injury was in no danger. It was bad, and her concern was natural and well justified, but I was never able to convince her that what had happened had actually happened to Harold.

Alec's wise strictures restored in me a sense of balance and a proper perspective. The year of mourning for my mother ended and I went home again for the stone-setting. Though my father did not discuss or indeed even make mention of his plans, it was clear to me that what had been my home would soon be so no longer.

I came back to London deracinated, as it were. Though I had made my room at Mrs Reckless's as comfortable as possible it could not be regarded as any sort of home. It was not a homely room in which I could spend any length of time, or to which I could invite friends, as my room in Oxford had been. This was not due to my landlady who was only too anxious that I should feel at home, but to the limitations of the accommodation itself. I would take my turn in hosting our regular bridge game but that exhausted the room's possibilities. A large bed, an armchair, the bookcase and settee, all from my old home, left little room for people. Such time as I did spend in my room, other than for sleeping, or entertaining the odd girl, was for studying, of which, after my initial debacle with Bookkeeping and Trust Accounts, I did a considerable amount. My studying had to be done at night but after I got that first hurdle out of the way I had no further studying to do until the last six months of my articles.

Before returning to London after the memorial service for my mother, I went through such of my belongings as I had not already taken to London. It took a considerable amount of emotional soul-searching to decide what I had to discard, over and above what I had already disposed of. I am by nature a hoarder, as I have said. I collect things. Clothes were not a problem but my stamp collection and my records were sacrosanct.

Shortly after I returned to London, my father telephoned to say that he and Yenty Kersh were to be married. It was to be a private and quiet wedding. He did not invite me to attend and I didn't. I sent him a greetings telegram wishing them "mazeltov". He decided to sell Brierfield, and move to Yenty's house in Sunderland.

When he gave Tessie notice she was devastated. She had served my parents well for over eight years, and thought that she would grow old under their roof. Though she was often too free with her views and opinions (generally unasked), she was loyal and totally trustworthy. I think she deserved rather more consideration than was shown to her but my father could not afford her, and had no further need of her. Dora offered to take her on as her housekeeper in Jersey. It was a big move for Tessie, who had lived in Middlesbrough all her life and rarely been out of the town and she was very close to her sisters. It is hard to say what motivated either Dora to offer the job or Tessie to accept it. Dora, I think, acted out of a spirit of loyalty to my mother on the one hand and perhaps to spite my father on the other. She wanted, as it were, to express her appreciation for Tessie's care of my mother, which went far beyond the call of duty. Tessie's motivation is perhaps easier to understand; she was out of a job and was unlikely to find another one like it in Middlesbrough. The sort of position where she virtually ran the household was very rare in the mid-1950s. I imagine that another major factor was that she thought she would see much more of me as, after my mother's death, I had become the unhealthy focus of her affection. In this respect she was correct because although my visits to Jersey were rare, I did go there. In fact, until I became engaged to be married, I did not go back to Middlesbrough at all.

The tennis court at Brierfield had been sold some time before, while Mother was still alive, to Philip Niman, a local solicitor and friend of the family. He was a charming man and one of the few genuinely cultured members of the Jewish community in Middlesbrough. He and his wife Judy were among the few people in the town for whom I had any great respect and affection. The rest of the house and gardens at Brierfield were sold to Leeds University for what I thought was a derisory sum of £5,000. There was little interest in the house from private buyers as houses of the size of Brierfield did not sell easily in that part of the world. They were too large for the small bourgeois nuclear family and needed staff to maintain them. Domestic labour, which only a few years before had been one of the largest sources of work for women and girls, had become rare: factories and shops offered far better rates, and fewer restrictions. The same house in one of the more fashionable parts of London would have fetched ten times as much. The small three-bedroom house in a pleasant but modest crescent which, following our marriage, Evi and I bought only three years later in Hampstead Garden Suburb, cost just under £5,000, and by the time it was modernised was worth much more.

I do not know what happened to the contents of Brierfield, the beautiful silver cutlery, the crystal glasses, the art deco and Bauhaus furniture which would have graced any museum of applied arts. The tablecloths and bed linen, much of which had been my mother's trousseau, and the many other items, were all of exceptionally fine quality. There was her Bechstein Baby Grand, and my billiard table. We had lived in great style and luxury, which were a tribute to my mother's taste. Tessie managed to rescue a few tablecloths which we use even today when we have guests for dinner, though they must be at least 100 years old, and they are still much admired. I assume that my father sold everything. Yenty had her own fully furnished home, which was too small to accommodate my parents' furniture, and she would not wish to have anything which reminded my father of my mother.

My father had no other means of support or of raising money. There was no business to produce an income, and no job that he could or would have found it within his dignity to take. He had to keep up appearances, to say nothing of the wolf from the door. He neither told me what he had done nor how much he had raised. When I asked him point blank he didn't reply, as I might have done, that it was none of my business; typically, he totally avoided the issue. When I said, after it was much too late, that he might have given me the opportunity to buy some items which were of particularly sentimental value to me, he replied vaguely that he had sold everything as a job lot. I suspect that he took the easiest option, and failed to obtain anything like a proper price.

There was soon nothing left of my home. My father moved to Sunderland where Yenty had her own fur business. Though he had no experience in the fur trade, she took him in and I think he helped with the books, to keep him occupied. Within a short time there was nothing but a grave to draw me back to what had been (and to me always was) my home town, and I am not given to visiting graves.

Troubled though I was at the way he had dealt with matters, I was greatly relieved that my father had been able to reshape his life so soon. He was not a man who could live alone. He was quite incapable of looking after himself. He could not mend a fuse, change a plug or boil a kettle. For twenty-five years he had had everything done for him, and he needed a companion, someone who would go on looking after him. Yenty, in her competence and business acumen, was not unlike my mother. She adored my father, and not only did she in effect keep him, she tended to his every wish and gave him the stability and warm home he so badly needed. She also made it her business to get on well with me, and to ease the relationship between my father and me. I liked Yenty, and for my part got on well with her. I appreciated all that she did for my father, perhaps even more than he did. I regarded my father fortunate to have found someone with so many of the qualities he had become used to in my mother, and who put him first in everything. In the fullness of time, she became an excellent and affectionate grandmother to our children.

Chapter 68 – A Change In Fortune

Not long after my mother died, when my life was still constricted by the need to go to synagogue daily, I was at Neville's home when Uncle Alec started to cross-examine me rather closely about my work, my firm and above all my principal, Hymie Davis. What sort of lawyer was he? Did I think he was any good? I gave him a clean bill of health and said that I thought he was a first-rate commercial lawyer, a view I never altered. Alec wanted to know if he gave my firm any work would I receive any benefit from it? I told him what Hymie had said about giving me one third of all fees I brought in. I had better make sure, Alec said, because he was thinking of changing his solicitors. For years he had been dealing with a firm called Teff & Teff in Bishopsgate, who were no longer giving Alec the service he had been used to. As usually happens in small firms, the senior partners with whom Alec was familiar were getting older and less efficient, and handing over to new faces in whom the older client had little confidence. I benefited from this attitude many times in the early years of my career and suffered from it in my later years.

The next day I feigned indifference and asked Hymie whether he had meant what he had said about any fees I introduced. He said he did, and I reported back to Alec. Alec said no more to me at the time but some days later we received a letter from another firm with draft documents for our approval. The letter began: "We understand that you will be acting for London Grocers Ltd". The matter concerned a new shop lease. Hymie was somewhat puzzled, and asked me whether I knew anything of the matter. I didn't, but I assumed that Alec had decided to try us out.

Charming as he was, Alec was a very tough and demanding client. If we failed to satisfy him, no closeness of connection or charitable impulse would have caused him to use my firm. In fact, when I saw him at the weekend and thanked him for sending me some work he replied: "If you make a mess of it you won't get any more work." But behind his occasionally gruff exterior and no-nonsense attitude there was a man of great generosity of pocket as well as spirit.

London Grocers Ltd. was the parent company of a number of companies trading under the name of Victor Value, the largest of which was Victor Value & Co. Ltd. London Grocers, which later changed its name to Victor Value so as to reflect the trading name by which it was better known, had grown, and continued to grow not only naturally by the acquisition of new stores but also by taking over other multiple companies. It competed with companies such as Sainsbury's and Tesco. Sainsbury's was regarded, even by its competitors, as the Rolls Royce of grocers. Tesco was at the bottom end of the market. "Pile it high and sell it cheap" was their yardstick. Victor Value came in somewhere in between. These three were at that time the major grocery chains in London and the Home Counties. Marks and Spencer had not yet entered the food business and Waitrose were not regarded as competition.

A supermarket was then considered to be a shop of more than 1,000 sq. ft., a double unit, in other words. So rapidly did the industry grow that within a period of two to three years a supermarket would have an area of 10,000 sq. ft. and before long 50,000 sq. ft. and more. Alec must have been satisfied because work started to pour in, and in my first year I earned over £1,000, riches then beyond the dreams of avarice. I must have been the best-paid articled clerk in the country!

I learned much from acting for London Grocers Ltd., and it was the beginning of a very happy and satisfying period as regards my work. However, it could have been a disaster as the first matter we dealt with was very nearly the last. Hymie, who had dealt with the matter, had sent the lease to Alec for sealing with a covering letter asking him to check that the lease met his requirements. The lease came back, unsigned, with a terse note to the effect that that was what we were paid to do; Alec had no intention of reading the lease and expected that whatever documents he was asked to execute conformed with his instructions to us. I fully agreed with his comments, but of course I was still a rookie, and in no position to criticise Hymie. Though I always provided a short resume of its contents I never again made the error of asking a client to check a document sent to him for signing, other than perhaps to confirm that a plan or drawing was correct as sometimes these had gone through several versions and you could never be sure that you had been supplied with the correct one, particularly when they came direct from the architects.

Though my main obligation was to deal with my firm's litigation I also made sure that I myself dealt with as much of Victor Value's work as I could. I have no doubt that Alec or his brother Morris, and later Neville when he came into the business, read every document very carefully, but no document sent by me to a client for signature was ever returned unsigned by them or any other client.

The relationship one had with one's clients was very different then from what it is today. The notion of client/solicitor loyalty has virtually disappeared, certainly as regards the corporate client and the big commercial client. Clients today follow the unfortunate lead set by American institutions in such matters, and adopt the consumerist policies advocated by such prophets as Ralph Nader. They have no compunction in suing their advisers at the drop of a hat, especially when they themselves are at fault. Of course, they react differently when their clients or customers complain. I recall an occasion when Hymie Davis had made a mistake in a lease for one of his major clients, Maurice Wingate, a very successful businessman and property developer for whom he had acted for some time. The error became manifest as I was reading through a lease with which I was dealing while Hymie was on holiday, and I was in sole charge of the office. When Mr Wingate came into the office on another matter I told him that I thought he should take independent advice.

"For what?" he asked.

"I think there may be a problem with a lease," I replied.

"And why should I take independent advice?" he asked again.

"Because there may be a conflict of interest," I said as non-committally as I could.

"If you mean because Hymie buggered up the lease, forget it. Don't be daft (what he actually said was in Yiddish: "sei nich kein naar"), I know all about that. I wouldn't dream of suing. We all make mistakes and this is not the first, and probably won't be the last, and it's not very serious. Hymie has given me much good advice over the years and I wouldn't be where I am today without him. Just get the matter sorted out as quickly as you can."

I said nothing of this conversation to Hymie when he returned from his holiday.

I had great respect for Maurice Wingate. I learned a good deal from him. Like Alec Cohen, he was a very exacting client, but he was fair. He expected a good service but he appreciated the contribution he had to make to get it. Like Alec, he let you know what he wanted and then let you get on with your job, while he ensured that you had the information and backup you needed. Like Alec, he never talked down to anyone. From the day I started he accorded me the same respect as he did Hymie. If he lacked confidence in my experience or abilities he never showed it, which of itself created confidence. Mr Dvoriansky may have treated me, at first, as an inexperienced underling, not fit to take his case and may well have been right, but Maurice Wingate never did. He and Alec Cohen effectively provided the bulk of our work.

The quality of the work we had was remarkable for so small a firm. At one time we acted for six public companies. It was also my good fortune to be acting for Victor Value at a time when they were undertaking their biggest period of expansion. Not long after I first became the happy object of Alec's welcome nepotism, which aided my morale no less than my pocket, at a time when my usually ebullient optimism was at a very low ebb, it was decided that in order to finance their expansion Victor Value should issue some debenture stock. This is one way for a company in effect to print its own money. A great deal of work is involved as the stock has to be underwritten by the City. All this involves a large number of meetings with the merchant bankers who arrange these matters, lawyers, and accountants. Reports on title for the company's (and its subsidiaries') properties have to be prepared, but there is a sizeable fee at the end. The amount of the proposed loan stock was £200,000, a laughable amount when looked back on from today's perspective, but much anguished heart-searching took place in the company's boardroom, that is, in the Cohen household.

Alec's brother Morris, who had equal status in the business, lived in the same road, Cedars Close, immediately opposite Alec. Morris and Betty, his wife, treated me (as did Alec) more like another son than an adoptive "nephew" – and I was even less of a relation to him. Bessie Cohen was at least my aunt's sister; there was no such connection with Betty and Morris.

Several weekends on both sides of Cedars Close were taken up with the debate: "Should we; shouldn't we?" do the deal. The debate moved from house to house and back again. They had never borrowed money before; they had never needed to. Expansion was paid for out of existing resources. Gearing – borrowing money to finance development on the basis that the income generated would pay the interest charges while the capital value of the property rose – was still an engineering term and had not become a financial philosophy. As far as they were concerned, they were sailing into uncharted seas. A very considerable mind shift, a culture change, was needed. I don't think that the amount was an issue; it was the principle of the thing. In the end, their first venture into the money market proved so successful that all their inhibitions disappeared and they embraced the new financial world with great enthusiasm and success. I was involved closely with the debate, not that I could make any useful contribution to it other than to look wise by saying nothing.

Though my professional life was developing very nicely, my unexpected increase in income, welcome though it was, did not allow me to wallow in comfort. I was able to rely less on my aunts and uncles for nutrition, and was able to eat out a little more often. A favoured place at the time was Schmidt's Restaurant in Charlotte Street. As its name implies, Schmidt's served German and Austrian food at prices so low they seemed to be giving it away. The service was Teutonically efficient and graceless but the food was plentiful, wholesome and sometimes even tasty, if your predilections were for Bratwurst, red cabbage with raisins, sauerkraut, stuffed cabbage, steamed potatoes and a variety of soups. It was the sort of food my grandmother used to produce, and my uneducated palate lapped it up.

There was also Bloom's kosher restaurant in Whitechapel, sadly no longer there, which for many years rated a Michelin star. It was a little less accessible than Schmidt's (which was still within the W.1. area and easily walkable from my office), but I could eat at Bloom's without having to worry about the contents of my plate. It was not that I was particularly concerned about eating non-kosher food, but I tried to avoid "forbidden" foods, such as pork and seafood. I had not yet developed a taste for fish, so was very much a meat eater and Bloom's was cheap and good of its kind. Their idea of service was non-existent. I believe they had a strange system of paying their waiters. Whether for tax or other reasons – I do not know why they did it – apparently the waiters were not employees but self-employed. They bought the food you ordered from Bloom's and sold it on to you! The net result of this was that they were anxious to get you in and out again as quickly as possible. This seems to be typical of Jewish restaurants, although they are certainly now more aware that they live in a competitive world. I remember in New York once with Evi and the children we decided to eat at a Jewish Chinese restaurant on the East Side. It was a hot day and we were all very thirsty. I was dying for a nice cold beer, and Evi and the kids wanted Cokes. The waiter came over and I asked him for a beer. "Foist," came the response, "foist, we'll deal with the food; then the drink." I am still waiting for that beer.

At the other end of the luxury scale was the Buttery at Claridge's. For a guinea you could get a glass of champagne and a variety of open sandwiches, or a plate of smoked salmon or other delicacies. I enjoyed being able to invite a client "across the road for a snack" and lead them into Claridge's, particularly as I could charge it up to expenses. I am afraid that when I had to pay, it would more often be at Schmidt's than Claridge's.

Having a little more money in my pocket meant that I no longer had to feel like a *schnorrer* or a beggar at the feast. I could afford to run my car and get around more, although my limitations came home to me much later. The art dealers, Gimpel Fils, had a gallery at the corner of South Molton Street, where they always had exquisite items on display. For some time they had a sculptured head by Jean Arp, and though my artistic tastes still remained to be shaped and honed, I was enchanted by its simple beauty. It cost £600 which doesn't sound much but it represented my basic salary for two years. I should have sold my car and begged, borrowed or stolen the money to buy it, but I lacked the imagination, the vision and the confidence. The investment would have paid handsomely. On another occasion, a friend was trying to raise money from acquaintances for his new business. An investment of £500 would have secured me financially for life! Missed chances, which is not to say that my investment record when I had the money is much to write home about.

My social life at that time was fairly stagnant. I began to miss the company of girls. I have not only enjoyed, but needed, female company. I felt the need but saw no easy solution. My closest friends, my bridge partners, Neville and his friends, either had girls quietly tucked away somewhere, or had no need of them. They were certainly absent from our gatherings. I missed the easy access afforded by the Saltburn Spa but knew of no London equivalent. It was difficult to break into a settled crowd, where you never knew who was not spoken for. I was 24, too old for youth clubs, too old for the Hammersmith Palais, and of an age when fathers would look suspiciously at me and mothers start planning weddings. Yetti had no friends with suitable daughters; Uncle Herman had all sorts of ambitious ideas for me, all involving instant matrimony, but I steered well clear of them. There were charity dances but I met no one I fancied, nor so far as I could tell, was I the object of anyone's wild and passionate dreams. It was an arid time.

Helen Davis's brother, Joe Reiss, who had the office floor above ours, would have been happy to help. He had many female friends, but they were of an age, beauty and expectations far beyond my reach. If I couldn't afford an Arp I certainly couldn't afford one of his female friends. Not even a lunch at Claridge's would have tempted them, even had they been up in time for lunch. Helen and Hymie then introduced me to one of Hymie's oldest friends, Len Bluston. Len was the key to the solution of my problem.

Len Bluston was one of those people who could well have featured in the *Readers' Digest* series of "Notable Characters I have Met". He was a true eccentric. How he came to be friendly with Hymie remains a mystery because two more different personalities it would be hard to find, and it is to Hymie's, and even more so Helen's, credit that the friendship persisted, because no one could have more affronted Helen's ideas of social propriety and formality than Len. Where Helen would carefully put out cocktail sticks for olives or the like, Len would grab at them with his hands; where Helen put out forks for some delicacies in a jar, Len would fish for them with his own used spoon. Yet it would be wrong to describe him as a boor. He was never that. It was just that he had no table manners and hated any sort of show or formality. He liked to puncture egos and one of his missions in life was to *épater les bourgeois*.

Len trampled through life like the bear he resembled, an impression aided by the fact that he always wore brown. His suits hung loosely on him as if his relationship with them was purely coincidental. He claimed that he never wore underwear on the grounds that underwear adversely affected a man's sexual prowess. Such reports as I ever received – not from him I hasten to add

– did nothing to support his theory. He never untied the laces of his shoes which were also always some shade of brown. His height, well over six feet, was disguised by his slovenly walk, not so much a stoop as giving the impression that he was about to fall apart. Everything about him was big, particularly his nose and moustache. He drove a large 1938 Rolls Royce; a beautiful car, black with the traditional winged lady mascot, gold lines, white leather interior, headlamps the size of dinner plates and running plates (which modern cars do not have), on which you had to step to climb gracefully into the car.

Though it was his great joy, his pride in it was such that he allowed others, whom he considered sufficiently competent, to drive it. When I first saw it and expressed my admiration in wildly enthusiastic terms, he invited me to drive it. "You start in second gear and as soon as the wheels turn you put it into top, and you leave it there. Don't make any further gear changes. Remember that this is a Rolls Royce – you drive it like a gentleman. You NEVER use the horn; you do not overtake in town and you do not exceed the speed limit. You're not driving your jalopy!"

I did exactly as instructed. I was amazed at the power of the engine, which virtually noiselessly, picked up the weight of that heavy vehicle when it was barely moving in top gear without any strain. I was never allowed to find out its top speed. I would have loved to have done so, but it was not a car made for speed; it was designed for comfort and dignity. Sitting in the driving seat and enjoying the sheer luxury of the vehicle, which sat so high on the road and gave excellent visibility, I did not understand why rich folk paid drivers when they could drive such a car themselves. He kept that car until he died; in fact, effectively he died while driving it, but that came much later.

Len was self-made and self-taught. He had all the faults of the autodidact; strong opinions not always well founded. He was from the East End of London, and had been financially successful. His core business was screws. He had a shop in Clerkenwell Road which sold screws of all sizes and for all purposes. He used to claim that screws were the only commodity that once used, could not be reused, and hence needed a never-ending supply. I pointed out that there were many other commodities of which the same could be said more correctly. It was not true of screws. He would call me a "Bloody Peruvian", his favourite form of abuse. I never did find out what he had against Peruvians.

His wealth came not from screws but from a very specialised type of property development. He would drive around London in his Rolls, looking for small sites, usually in mews or side streets, often bomb sites, on which one or two small houses could be built. These were not sites which would attract a big developer, and were not usually advertised. Len would find out who owned them, not as easy then as today, buy the land, then build and sell the finished product. He had an eye for this; he could spot a potential site which others would pass by. He ended up buying such a site for himself in Boyne Terrace Mews, just off Ladbroke Grove, where he created his own dream house on an empty plot between two existing mews houses. This was like Len himself, out of the ordinary. Typically, he named it "Mortgaged".

It was attractive but not particularly remarkable from the outside, apart from its very large windows. Internally was another matter. The living area on the ground floor was overlooked by a minstrel gallery, which took the place of a first floor landing, so there was nothing between the roof and the ground floor, and the whole wall was taken up by a huge window. The effect was stunning if you liked that sort of thing. His bedroom, off the gallery, appeared to be his idea of a Turkish harem, though it looked more like a brothel. There were great drapes and crown-shaped net curtains surrounding the bed. The colour theme was a pastel shade of blue. It was a monument to bad taste; it was awful. Len satisfied another ambition; he had a sauna fitted. Although these are now quite common, he was one of the first people I knew to have one. He would spend hours in it, far longer than was good for his health, and I have always suspected that this must have contributed to his early death.

Len was divorced. He had one son. He had a bad relationship with both his ex-wife and his son, that is to say he never saw either of them, and when they spoke, which was hardly ever, it was to row over some financial issue. In the divorce his son had taken his mother's part, understandably I would have thought, as Len must have been impossible to live with. His relationship with his son replicated that which he had had with his own father. If this did not actually amount to hatred, it came very near it. The only time I met his son was at Len's cremation. I was astonished by their resemblance to each other. To compensate for the loss, as he saw it, of his son, he surrounded himself with young people, the children of friends or relations. There was not the slightest impropriety in this, but he was a Peter Pan, and sought in this way to retain his youth. He was very generous to anyone he liked.

Following my introduction to him at the Davis's, I became a member of his "club". Other "members" included Simon Goldblatt, whose father David was a member of the Liberal Party, a close associate of Lord Beveridge, and Marion, the daughter of one of Len's cousins, a most attractive girl. She was a model, tall with, as might be expected, a wonderful figure. Though I was very anxious to become better acquainted with her, she was not very forthcoming, which I found strange. Without being conceited, I had never had any problems before when asking a girl out. When I explained my dilemma to Len, he said, "You're too fat," in his usual diplomatic style. "She doesn't like fat men." I was completely taken aback, but I took the matter seriously.

I had always been a little self-conscious about my tendency to put on weight but it had never before been a problem. I had not done any real exercise for some time. The most serious exercise, apart from shuffling cards, was the occasional run for the bus or train and I could hardly say that I did this very often. I did not even take my dog Peggy out for walks. She was quite capable of taking herself out but Aunt Yetti and her family ensured that Peggy was adequately exercised because she went everywhere with them. I found a weighing machine, put in my penny and was horrified to see that I was approaching 16 stone in weight. In fact, "approaching" is putting an optimistic gloss on it. I had got there, and more. I had let myself go. I tried a few other machines just in case the first was wrong, as I thought it must have been, but they all told the same sad tale. Lack of exercise and an unhealthy diet had contributed to my bloated appearance. As this came about by a gradual process, no one mentioned it to me. Perhaps it was simply strangers being tactful. My family would consider it normal. It took an objective bystander to bring home to me the extent of my self-indulgence. It has only just occurred to me that I never saw myself in a full-length mirror, or indeed other than a shaving mirror, as I had none at my digs, and I wasn't the type to be self-consciously or conceitedly looking into mirrors. I immediately resolved to do something about this and started what was to be the first of my periodical diets. I took soundings from Len from time to time, as to the progress I was making with the object of my desire.

Anyway, it did the trick, and when I had reached a suitable svelteness, Marion consented to go out with me. She really was very attractive – she always looked a million dollars – undemanding, uncomplicated and good company, and I very much enjoyed our time together. I rarely discussed my private life with my aunts or any of my family, however, Yetti was horrified when she heard – not from me I hasten to add – that I was going out with a model. Even worse, her mother was a model. This was true; she modelled for the older and fuller figure. I don't know what my aunt had in mind, but my model was a nice Jewish girl from a nice Jewish family. I was, I suppose, in modern terms a serial monogamist. I rarely had more than one girlfriend at a time, and Marion was the last before I married.

Chapter 70 – Vacations

My increased income made me think of holidays. I was officially entitled to 14 days holiday each year and I construed this so as to exclude the Jewish holidays. During my first years in articles I still had to attend my annual army camp, the income from which augmented my annual stipend from Hymie by nearly 30%; it was as much as fifteen weeks' pay, and was not a sum which I could easily forego, even if it meant that I had to spend my vacation in the army. Foreign holidays were not commonplace in those days. Under exchange control regulations, there was a limit of £50 holiday spending abroad. This did not present a problem to me and in the summer of 1956, Neville Cohen and I decided to take a holiday on the continent, in the cheapest way available. We would end the holiday in Rome where we would meet his parents and Morris and Betty.

We went by train, third class only because there was no fourth class, breaking the journey at Paris for a few days to renew acquaintance with the city, an old love not seen since I left school. We stayed at the most modest establishments we could find. We then went on to the French Riviera. I always envy those who visit a beautiful place for the first time. Though familiarity brings its own pleasures, there remains something special about the first time you see somewhere breathtaking. I am essentially an urban creature, but the conjunction of land, sea and mountains gave Nice an extra dimension shared by few other European cities. To explore the Riviera, about which I had heard and read so much, we decided to be extravagant and hired a Vespa scooter. I had no idea how to drive this and had no wish to learn. Neville, on the basis of his national service in the Royal Army Service Corps, claimed expertise in the field. Whether he had it or not my eyes were never open long enough to see, but we did negotiate safely all three corniches, and such of the Route Napoleon as could be covered in a day. The sight of the two of us, particularly the rather oversized and terrified me riding pillion, must have been amusing for any onlooker. But as in all things, it became easier with practice, my terror abated, and we soon enjoyed our outings. The great advantage of a scooter was that you could hire it by the day or even the hour, and it was cheap on fuel.

When we were not exploring the Riviera, we sat on the beach. Neville did not like sitting in the sun, I do. So we had to find somewhere which provided sunshine for me and shade for Neville. Usually, this meant that Neville and I would be some distance apart. I don't know what it was about Neville. There were myriads of mermaids where I sat, but Neville seemed to attract the older women, whose grandmotherly instincts were aroused by him. Whereas I found myself surrounded by the Demoiselles d'Avignon, Neville found himself imprisoned by ladies who brought to my mind the image of the Three Fat Women of Antibes. They must have thought he was some sort of invalid sitting alone in the shade with a book, and thought it only kind of them to take him under their wing. And they were clingy. Neville has always been a gentleman and did not have it in his heart to be unkind to them. I, of course, was operating in different territory. We met from time to time to compare notes, though Neville was somehow rather reserved about his doings.

After travelling overnight we arrived in Rome hot, dishevelled and hungry. With our limited baggage we went to the Excelsior Hotel in the Via Veneto where Neville's family were staying. How they allowed tramps like us to enter the Via Veneto, far less the hotel itself, I do not know, but as we entered its magnificent halls, Alec and Morris were just leaving. We went up to their rooms where the ladies were still breakfasting. Dirty, tired and hungry, we made a beeline for the bathroom. After we were clean and refreshed we sat down to breakfast, wearing the bathrobes supplied by the hotel. We ignored the quizzical looks from the waiter. We then decided to take a quick look around the Via Veneto before meeting for lunch. As we came down from the bedroom, and left the hotel, so Alec and Morris came back. Both Bessie and Betty were extremely attractive and certainly did not look old enough to be our parents. We noticed the odd raised eyebrow among the hotel staff to whom doubtless such comings and goings

(with less innocent connotations) were neither unknown nor surprising – shades of *The Roman Spring of Mrs Stone*. Their reputations were rescued when all six of us lunched together though
Auntie Bessie was at great pains to say to all and sundry: "This is
my son," and as an afterthought, rather lamely, pointing to me,
"and this is my nephew."

So much has been spoken and written about Rome that it is
hard to say anything novel, but all I had read was true. Rome
exceeded my expectations. As I have said before, I fall in love with
cities. It is not that I am fickle, as in each case it is an undying
affection, but every city has its own mystique. Rome is very different from Paris. It is smaller and easier to explore on foot. In fact,
there is no other way to see any city. I enjoyed the statues, foun-
tains, columns and arches, many of which had figured in my Latin
lessons and which I had only seen on film or in pictures. I found
the pace frenetic. There was a buzz and excitement which I found
exhausting. I could very happily live in Paris, but not in Rome.
The traffic alone would deter me. One thing I did notice about the
traffic was the almost complete monopoly of Fiat vehicles. It is not
so today but then, in 1956, you might see the odd Lancia or Alfa
Romeo but everything else was Fiat.

But Rome is our history. Its effect is somehow more immediate and certainly more enchanting than modern Athens. As I
walked from the Forum, where I could not avoid the words of
Mark Anthony ringing in my ears, past columns, ruined temples
and arches, to the Colosseum, I became increasingly moved. By
the time I reached the Colosseum, walked round its arena, and
looked up to the top of its enormous walls, trying to imagine what
it must have looked like before it fell prey to plunder, I was over-
whelmed by an emotion which I cannot really explain or describe.
I burst into a flood of tears which I could not stem. This was so
very un-British, not at all how I expected myself to react. I felt the
same emotion and had the same tears when I first stood at the
Temple Wall in Jerusalem. I felt the passage of time, a strange connection across the centuries, an invisible umbilical cord. I was
deeply affected by its grandeur, and overawed by the knowledge
that I was standing in the very place where Roman legions had

marched, where Nero provided his bread and circuses, where gladiators had fought and killed to amuse the multitudes, and people had been martyred for their faith. I felt this to some extent throughout all the ancient parts of Rome, and on seeing the Vatican, the Sistine Chapel and the other great statues and paintings of the city, but nothing affected me as much as the Colosseum.

Two weeks went quickly and reality beckoned. We travelled home by train and ferry. Adrenalin had kept us going on our journey, when sleep seemed unnecessary and was taken when we could. It took me some days to recover and this was before the days of jet lag. Life resumed its normal course, but the experience had moved me deeply and left me, not discontented perhaps, but certainly with a greater appreciation of how little we counted, how unimportant we were individually, when compared with the grandeur of the past. My feelings for Europe, that is to say, the part we used to call The Continent, were also reawakened, and I began to feel that that was part of my cultural inheritance, not so much the Roman past but the continental connection. I do not know why I should have felt this more in Rome than Paris. It may be that I was older, but it did change my way of thinking. I began to see life on a more cosmopolitan scale; culturally, I had left Teesside.

There was not much time for leisure in my early days in London. Learning my job took up most of my time, but I enjoyed it, so that was no hardship. I played tennis occasionally. My enthusiasm for football was satisfied by Tony Jaffe's father providing me with a season ticket for Tottenham Hotspur matches, so every other Saturday afternoon during the football season was spent at White Hart Lane watching Spurs. However, it wasn't the same as supporting my home team, the Boro'. I always felt like a guest at a wedding: enjoying the occasion but indifferent as to the outcome. Apart from chess and bridge I played few sports or games. During the week much of my spare time was spent listening to my records of opera and classical music, and occasionally going to the cinema. Basically, I led a lonely existence, certainly, while I was still in mourning, but things got better as I found my feet and started knowing girls again, though most of such activities were limited to the weekend. But solitude has never troubled me, I was used to it.

Chapter 72 – Jersey Comes To Town

Dora decided that as it was not easy for me to visit Jersey for my holidays, now I was working, she and Joe should come and spend some time in London. They rented a magnificent house in Stormont Road, Highgate (where all the houses are magnificent) opposite Kenwood House, on the edge of Hampstead Heath for a whole month so that they could be with me.

Through Len I had become very friendly with Simon Goldblatt, another in my gallery of eccentrics. He was a barrister by profession from a politically well-connected family. He dressed formally and seemed to wear his working clothes of black jacket and pinstriped trousers at all times, and from their appearance, he must have slept in them too. Simon had a brilliant mind, and it was hard to keep up with him. He was a much better bridge player than any of us, but then he was better at any intellectual pursuit than we were, and did not hesitate to display his talents. There was something charming and youthful about his eccentricities.

He too drove a Rolls Royce. It was about ten years older than Len's, which would have made it a 1928 model, which I think it was. It was big and black, the sort of car used for funerals. One day when Simon came to Stormont Road for dinner, Dora happened to be looking out of the window and saw what she took to be a hearse arriving. A man in black jacket and pinstriped trousers, the traditional undertaker's uniform, got out and came up the drive. She was mad with worry. She was sure that something had happened to Joe. Though he looked robust, Joe had always ailed with one thing or another, and she and Joe were terrible hypochondriacs and worriers for each other. A typical telephone conversation between them would run as follows:

Dora: Hello! Is that you Joe? (Who else could it have been?) How are you feeling?

Joe: I'm well dear, how are you?

Dora: I'm alright but are you well?

Joe: Yes dear, I'm alright, but is all well with you?

Dora: Joe, you're not well; I can hear it in your voice!

Joe: Dora, I am perfectly well. Have you a cold? Your voice seems hoarse.

Dora: Never mind about me. I don't believe you Joe, you're hiding something from me.

And so the illness ball would be thrown to and fro for what seemed like hours. When she had eventually hung up, Dora would turn to me, or whoever was there, and say: "He's not well, but he's so stubborn he won't admit it. He doesn't want to worry me."

It was totally in character, therefore, that she should have mistaken Simon's car for a hearse. But she had a wonderful sense of humour and wit and she saw the comedy of the situation. It was a tale she never tired of telling and it became embellished over the years.

Stormont Road for a short time became the nearest thing to a home I had had since coming to London. While Dora and Joe were here I regarded that as my home, and I spent most of my time there. I was able, for the short time the house was available, to entertain all my (male) friends in style and reciprocate their hospitality. I only ever inflicted my family on one girl, and that was the one I married.

This is not to criticise or diminish all that Yetti did for me; no one could have put herself out more, but somehow Dunstan Road was not a home for me. I was not part of the furniture. I was conscious of the trouble she was going to, and felt guilty that I was not sufficiently grateful. It was not that she asked for thanks but I think she would have appreciated more input from me. She was tired of childish needs, and geriatric demands, and looked to me for company when I arrived for my evening meal. Never at my best when hungry, I was in no mood for idle chit-chat and by the time I had eaten was usually ready to embark on the evening's activities.

The demands made on Yetti by her children, her father-in-law and her husband made me feel that I was simply adding to her burdens, without giving her any corresponding benefit. The tensions between her and Karl which had begun to manifest themselves not long after they married were beginning to become more obvious. Karl was usually away at his factory in Lancashire during the week, and when he came home at the weekends he was anything but a loving husband. Though he was never less than warm and welcoming to me, I could not bear the way he spoke to Yetti, and indeed to his children. He was unbelievably mean. On one particular occasion, I saw him deduct a few pence from her housekeeping money for a box of matches which he had bought himself. I know things were financially tight, and that Yetti had for some time been subsidised, without Karl's knowledge, by Oma and later my mother, but they were not so tight that a few pence would have made the difference between penury and abundance. I don't think it was about the money; the intention was to humiliate Yetti and this he did continually. I think it was his way of repaying the humiliation he felt the family had subjected him to.

Whatever the reason, theirs was not a happy household, such as I had seen at my own home. The matrimonial storm clouds were brewing. They took a long time to break but break they did eventually, and in a big way.

Dora and Joe's return to Jersey left me rather sad and lonely for a while. My own clients were feeding me an increasing amount of work, and my practice was expanding. Though most of the work by now was commercial, there were still the odd interludes of crime, divorce, personal injuries and wills. I turned nothing away. I loved the work and my confidence increased with experience. I like to think that I was, in all modesty, a good lawyer, and my family business background had given me some insight into and understanding of how business works. Perhaps I was too cautious in my approach in the light of my family's business history, but lawyers are not paid to take risks or advise that risks be taken. Yet I had, I think, an innate sense of what pitfalls there might be. In this respect, I could not have had a better tutor than Alec Cohen, who managed to strike the balance between risk and caution.

One of my criminal diversions concerned the secretary of one of the gentlemen's clubs not far from my office. I was telephoned by a very well-spoken man who said that he had been recommended by a client of ours, who was one of his members. He said it was a confidential matter which he could not discuss over the telephone so I made an appointment to see him. I checked with our client who confirmed that he had given our name although he had no knowledge of the nature of the matter. A few days later, a very dapper-looking gentleman wearing a smart blue blazer with a badge on the pocket, which I assumed was that of some regiment, and military twill trousers, presented himself in our general office promptly for his appointment.

He told me that he had been unjustly accused of embezzling the funds of a club he had worked for previously, not the one by which he was presently employed. Innocent and unwilling to believe ill of any client or potential client as I was, I still sensed something wrong. His story was too glib, and for some reason I could not put my finger on, not entirely convincing. Reluctant to take on what could be a losing case, I asked for what was then a large sum, £500 on account of costs, before I would take on the matter. He readily agreed this, but asked for a few days' time to arrange payment. I thought that would be the end of the matter but a few days later he duly arrived at the office with a cheque in our favour and when it had cleared I took on the case. The facts were simple. His previous employers had, he claimed, charged him with stealing funds which were under his control. This was quite unjustified; he was a military man, he had been a captain in the army and would not stoop to such a thing. He was very convincing and as he was then in employment, and had paid us a cheque for his fees in advance without demur, I accepted his tale as he told it. There was no suggestion that he had borrowed the money alleged stolen intending to repay it, and that things had gone sour, which is the usual sort of defence. He was quite categorical. He completely denied the charge.

When we came to the Magistrates' Court at Great Marlborough Street, prosecuting counsel took ours aside for a quick word. This often happens and I resented this code of secrecy, the private discussion between opposing counsel. After all, I was the client and the paying party; there may have been matters which they might wish to discuss away from the lay client but why exclude the solicitors instructing them, their bread and butter? However, when our counsel came back he had with him a paper, which he then showed me, containing a long list of previous convictions. Our man was a confidence trickster of many years standing. He had been in the army, but his highest rank was corporal. He had obtained positions of trust on the basis of forged references. He was very good. Had he used his talents more honestly he might well have secured a better living than he did, but I think he enjoyed making fools of people. He pleaded "Guilty" and was sent to prison for two years. Had he tried to defend the charge he would have gone down for much longer.

Some months later, Hymie was by chance invited to lunch at the club where our villain had been employed by the member who had recommended us. He was introduced to one of the directors, who recognised Hymie's name. "Tell me," he asked Hymie. "Did you do some legal work for X some time ago?" Hymie said guardedly that his colleague (me) might have done, but he was not sure. "Was your fee by any chance £500?" Hymie again answered as guardedly as he could. "Oh, don't worry," said his interlocutor, "I won't ask you to break any confidentiality, but, you see, that amount is missing from our accounts at about the time he suddenly left our employment without notice. There is a note of a payment to you which we cannot account for. By the way, what happened to him?"

I felt professional satisfaction whenever we won a case, because it meant that my advice had been vindicated, sometimes in the face of contrary advice the client had received, and sometimes even against counsel's inclination. There have been occasions when I have had to persuade counsel to adopt a certain line about which he was doubtful. It needs a great deal of confidence to do this, and mine often came under great strain. Such talent as I had, I felt, lay in being able to get to the real nub of a matter, and cut away all the surrounding persiflage. A client can rarely identify the real issues. Often personal feelings, antagonism, ambition, vanity or jealousy cloud his views, and it is not easy to persuade a client that he is not seeing straight.

Advising clients is often rather like giving directions to someone hopelessly lost. This is where Hymie was so good; he could find ways and means of doing things which others failed to find. Not every wall can be breached; many have to be circumvented.

Chapter 73 – Love…

As Joe Reiss was not much older than myself, and good company, I became very friendly with him. I was regularly invited to dinner on Friday nights at his mother's flat, only a few minutes walk from my digs. Joe and his elder brother Mannie were usually there with their guests, often friends or business acquaintances from abroad. Their mother, Golda, always known as Gustel, Reiss was Joe Menasche's cousin. She was a lovable, grandmotherly figure and the kindest and most hospitable of people. Small, round, white-haired, gentle, with delicate hands and features, it was easy to recognise her youthful beauty which even in her later years had not deserted her. She was deeply religious. Beneath her sweetness and kindness lay an iron will, and no amount of cold or rain would stop her from walking on the Sabbath or during festivals to her synagogue over a mile away. She was not a great cook, but the company was generally good and the conversation usually witty and interesting. Mrs Reiss presided over the evening rather as one imagines a 1920s hostess might have done.

Joe Reiss was fairly small, about 5' 6" tall, with a round face and fairish curly hair which was rapidly receding. He was very quietly-spoken. His business was ostensibly importing and export-ing mainly electrical equipment but no one ever really knew what he was doing. He seemed to know and be known by everyone. He had some involvement in finance but I never managed to find out what, as he tended to be reticent about his activities. All I knew was that he had fingers in many pies.

As a result of one transaction which had gone wrong, he was given a very expensive Maserati sports saloon car in settlement of a debt. It was a beautiful vehicle, capable of some 170 mph. It was quite wasted on him; he was once stopped for driving that car at only 30 mph on the motorway. He was an "angel" who invested in shows, plays and films. Sadly for him, his judgment in these ventures was questionable. Joe told the story against himself of how Cubby Broccoli, the film producer who was ever seeking finance, approached him for an investment of £5,000 for the filming of *Casino Royale*, the first Bond film. He even offered him a share of the action. Joe read the book and said, "Cubby, I'll gladly give you £5,000, but please leave me alone. Don't bother me with such rubbish." This was clearly one of the great commercial decisions of the century.

I will always be grateful for my friendship with Joe. One Friday evening in mid-June, the 14th to be exact, a week before my birthday, Joe said he couldn't give me the usual lift as he had to pick up a business visitor and would meet me at his mother's flat. They were also expecting a young lady from Buenos Aires. I stopped off at my digs for a quick wash and brush-up and as I was rather late, I took my car. When I arrived at the flat, a vapidly pretty, young blonde girl was sitting on the settee, rather giggly, and with only a fleeting grasp of English, holding a drink. I found it hard to believe that this was the girl from Argentina. A few minutes later there was a ring at the door. Suddenly the blonde, who it appeared had come for an interview for a job as an au pair, disappeared and there came into the room a most attractive, elegant young woman, dressed in a Givenchy suit. She was beautifully groomed, charming and spoke perfect English. Her name was Evelyn Politzer. She had been given Joe's telephone number by a very close mutual friend of her mother (the same friend who had asked us to act for Mr Wenlock) to call when in London, and as she was staying in London before going to Cambridge for a May Ball, she did, and Joe had invited her for dinner.

I looked at her admiringly as she sat gracefully on the sofa and I thought to myself: "That is the sort of girl I would like to marry." All of ten seconds later I thought again, "No! That is the girl I am going to marry!" And nine months later I did. It was clear to us both from the moment we met that that would be the outcome even though we did not then put it into words. We might have been married much sooner, had my future mother-in-law not had to return to Buenos Aires for the birth of her first grandchild in November.

I doubt whether I made the best of impressions on that first evening. By the time all the introductions had been made and the pre-prandial drinks had been consumed it was nearly nine o'clock and I was very hungry. Another guest, also Argentinian, was engaged on an inordinately lengthy telephone conversation. Increasingly weak from lack of nourishment, I may have become somewhat impatient and been less than diplomatic. Evi later told me that she thought I was the rudest person she had ever met. After dinner I was better able to concentrate on the matter in hand, which was to get her away from the rest of the company and to be on our own. It did not occur to me that meeting me had not been the mutual friend's intention when giving her Joe's telephone number, but had it been I would still not have been deterred.

The gentleman who had been on the telephone earlier, whose name perhaps appropriately was Dr Begleiter (accompanist), offered to escort her home. I would have none of it. Fortunately, I had my car, and Evi accepted my offer to show her London night-life. This turned out to be a Horlicks at one of the Fleet Street all-night caffs, frequented by noisy journalists and inky printers. However, the next evening we went for dinner at the Compleat Angler in Marlow, then very fashionable and expensive, a fact which, again according to Evi, I kept mentioning throughout the evening. Asked by her friends, "Are you going to marry him?" she replied, "I'm afraid I am." The next day she went off to the May Ball with her friend from L'Ecole D'Interpretes in Geneva. When she came back to London we went out to dinner again, this time somewhat more modestly at Schmidt's, before she returned to Geneva to finish her term. We knew we would marry, but when?

Evi's background was similar to mine, except that she came from Vienna, and not Leipzig, as different in sophistication as Paris and Marseille, or London and Leeds. Her father Sandor, a very successful businessman came from Miklos in Hungary. They left Vienna in late 1939 for Buenos Aires, when she was nine months old. Tragically, her father had died when she was twelve. Some years later her mother married Martin Gronich, strangely also from Leipzig, who had actually been at school with Uncle Max. Evi's family retained their European cultural roots. Evi brought with her not only beauty, and elegance, a sense of what fitted and what did not, what was right and what was not but also

Viennese charm, a sense of class, self-assurance, a strong personality and great intelligence, and appreciation of the arts, in which she educated me in the years to come.

In the next few months there was a lot to be done, and we had no idea of the logistics involved. I had just started studying for my Law finals at Gibson & Weldon's premises at 27 Chancery Lane, where, some years later, I was to have my own offices. I had to attend lectures for three hours every morning, then go to the office, do a full day's work and study in the evening. The course lasted six months, ending about three weeks before finals to allow time for revision. Articled clerks were usually given leave during this period, which was recognised by the Law Society as time spent in articles for the purpose of qualifying for the necessary three years. As I was getting paid, and doing a full-time job, I could not expect time off work, nor could I be spared, and indeed, I now had a lively practice of my own which needed tending. I found the course of lectures very difficult to adjust to at first. These were not like Oxford lectures or tutorials. There was nothing academic about them, no questions, no debates, just force-feeding of facts. The lecturers lectured and we wrote it down. The methodology was simple: "write it down and memorise it" by rote, rather like times tables at school. To digest information in this way required a complete change of mindset.

There were textbooks, but reference to them was unnecessary; all we needed to know was in the notes which were dictated to us at what often seemed breakneck speed. There was no time for discussion and questions were discouraged. I cannot say other than that it was hard work, and there were no shortcuts. The forthcoming papers allowed no room for waffle. You either knew the answers or you did not. The questions were somewhat like case studies: a set of facts was given and you were asked to advise your client, giving chapter and verse. Having had charge of cases for nearly three years did help me, but in the office I had time to look things up, and ask others. In the finals due in November, we would be on our own.

I said nothing to any of my London family at that time of the great event which had occurred in my life. There would be time

CHAPTER 73 – LOVE...

enough to expose Evi to my family; I did not want her put off, and our parents had to be told first. Neville was the only person I took into my confidence, and I knew that he was discretion itself.

Evi had to finish her term at Geneva. She postponed her return to Buenos Aires, for a very long time – eleven years as it turned out – and decided to come back to London, just as I had arranged to go to Jersey for my holiday. I had now finished my five-year stint with the Army Emergency Reserve, and was released after an unusually easy 14 days camp. I was unsure what to do because I felt it was too soon to introduce Evi to my family, but on Neville's instigation, I asked Dora and Joe whether I could bring a "friend". It was arranged that Evi should come to Jersey and she duly arrived a day or so after me. Though I had given her no description or other means of identification, Dora, who had come with me to the airport to meet Evi, anxious to meet my "friend" as soon as possible, identified her as soon as she saw her: "That's the girl," she said. "Isn't she? She looks lovely." She was right on both counts.

Evi was given my usual room, which Tessie appeared to guard with her life. I slept on a camp bed in Joe and Dora's bedroom. On the second night we were there, as I lay in my uncomfortable berth, during the course of the inevitable discussion about my future, Dora turned on me wagging an angry finger – I don't know what triggered her off – and said: "If you don't marry that girl, I'll break every bone in your body."

Dora was given to hyperbole but her intention was serious and she would have been justified in carrying out her threat, so I couldn't risk that. We returned to London together, where Evi found very nice rooms in Montague Square. I now had to telephone my father. He should have been the first to be told, but I knew that he was not likely to be critical of any girl who was kind enough to agree to marry me, whereas Dora was unlikely to be uncritical. He sounded pleased and we went up to Sunderland where he was then living. Yenti made us very welcome and was anxious that we should feel at home. I'm glad to say that this visit ended the coolness which had existed for some time between my father and myself, and the occasion was a joyful one.

I can only guess at what was happening across the Atlantic. I know that suddenly Mrs Reiss found it necessary to visit the

Lichtman family, Joe Reiss's friends who were inadvertently responsible for the introduction, in Buenos Aires, where – surprise! – she accidentally met Evi's mother. Whether the visit was to get the low-down on Evi's family or to blow the gaff about me and mine, and at whose behest it was made – Dora's hand may not have been absent – I do not know, but I do know that it was supremely well intentioned. Apparently I was given glowing and not entirely truthful reports. Evi's mother was assured by Mrs Reiss, oblivious of the fact that I had not yet qualified, that I was "both a solicitor and a barrister". None of this was of the slightest relevance so far as Evi and I were concerned but it was nice to know that others were concerned on our behalf, and this was symptomatic of the kindness I have always been shown. The upshot of this was that Evi's mother decided she had to come and see for herself, and it was not long before she came to London.

Meeting Evi's mother was as nerve-wracking as any test I have had. Happily, I passed that test and she became one of the most loved, respected and admired people in my life. I could see at once where Evi had obtained her sense of style, humour, wit, charm and grace. My mother-in-law was a great lady, and became as dear to me as my own mother had been. It cannot have been at all easy for her, having sent her daughter to university in Geneva at the age of 17, expecting her back home in due course, now to find that she would not be returning at all and would instead be entrusting her future to an entirely unknown man whose own future was far from guaranteed. True, it was not difficult at that time for anyone with an Oxford degree and professional qualification to find employment. The demand for such people was great but the rewards were not assured and could be small, at least initially. It was also difficult at that time for anyone Jewish to get into the top City firms. Most had their statutory Jew, but just as the only way of getting into some golf clubs, which de facto excluded Jews, was to have a single figure handicap, so to get into a City firm you needed exceptional qualifications, and as yet I had none at all. I knew I could stay with H. Davis & Co. and from that aspect my future was secure, but what I would earn and how well a small firm like that would fare was anyone's guess. Hymie was by his own admission professionally unambitious. He more than once gave me clearly to understand that he was not interested in expansion or growth, and was happy with things as they were. Not for him were the long working days, and the strains and stresses of partnerships which might wrest control from him. None of this worried me the slightest at that time, though it came to do so later.

My mother-in-law knew none of this but regardless of the assurances as to my brilliance and genius and ability to do and be all things she received from Mrs Reiss and my family, she must have known in her heart that her daughter's journey into matrimony, so far from home, was not entirely free from risk, and she would not be there to help in case of need. All other considerations apart she would be missing a much loved daughter. Yet not once did she raise the slightest objection or seek to put any obstacle, even that of reality, in our way. She had raised her daughter to be independent and had to respect her decisions.

When at last I broke the news to Yetti and Herman, there was a furore. Dora, in an exceptional exercise of restraint, doubtless under Joe's influence, had said nothing to anyone. As she rarely spoke to Herman this was unremarkable in his case, but she spoke regularly to Yetti, and yet remained silent on this subject. Yetti was totally taken aback. Her first reaction was "Am I the first to know?" followed by great joy for my happiness; then doubt – who was the girl, what did I know about her, how could I make such a decision without first consulting her? – then tears, recollection of my mother – "Berta would have been so happy" – indeed she would have been – then her usual all-encompassing embrace. She was a big woman and you knew about it when she embraced you – then more tears, and laughter. My cousin Harold, who was about 12 at the time, burst into tears. Sarah, his sister, seeing everyone else cry thought she should join in. It was a scene worthy of Dickens.

"I must tell Herman," Yetti suddenly remembered. "No," I said, "I'll go round and tell him myself." But she couldn't resist the triumph of knowing before at least one other person and she telephoned him. How he came so quickly I do not know. The telephone had hardly been put down when the doorbell rang and Herman ran in: "What do you mean he's getting married?" he said to Yetti, then he addressed the same question to me.

"How could you do this to me?" he asked. Loving and generous as my family were, they had a strange idea of what was due to them in return.

"Do what?" I asked.

"Get engaged without telling your aunt and me."

"I'm telling you now."

"But you should have told us earlier."

"Earlier than when?"

No answer.

"But I had plans for you. I had a nice girl I wanted to introduce you to, pots of money, good family, you would have been made for life."

"You never said a word to me about it. Anyway I've found all that on my own."

To be honest, I wasn't sure about the money because that was the last thing on my mind and in any event I would never have expected a dowry. Dowries were still common among Jewish families of the sort Herman mixed with, not those I did.

"A solicitor is worth a lot of money you know," he replied.

"To whom?" I said. "I have no intention of selling myself. You both married for love not entirely with your family's blessing."

That was a little below the belt and not entirely called for, but I was getting a little cross at the concentration on economics. I thought it strange that Herman, who had married a penniless girl, for which he had not been forgiven, should be making such a fuss about matters which were really not his concern, but it was not out of self-interest.

"But how will you live? Where will you live?" asked Yetti.

As to the first question, I replied that I expected to qualify shortly and become a partner. As to the second, I had no idea.

"But what will you do if you fail your exams?" Yetti persisted.

I acknowledged that that was a possibility that I had not contemplated.

After the initial excitement subsided, more telephone calls were made to Ray, to Karl, to Jersey, and *mazeltov* was wished all round. The only thing left was to meet the bride.

As for the bride, when I actually formally proposed, as lawyers say, "for the avoidance of doubt", splitting an infinitive in my ardour, so that I could safely ask her mother for her hand, she replied: "Don't be silly. Greta (her mother's couturier) is already making the dress!"

Evi has always anticipated me.

When they met Evi, all objections, voiced and silent, were unreservedly withdrawn, and they were generous enough to admit I could not have found a better bride. In fact, they made a complete *volte face* and the general view was that she was far too good for me. Evi became part of the fabric of my life as if she had always been there. She joined in all my activities, she became part of Len's entourage, and a regular at the Cohens. At the time, she was living in a very pleasant flat in Montague Square in London's West End but Bessie Cohen got busy and declared that it was not right for a young girl to be living in a flat in the West End and that she should be where she could be properly looked after. It so happened, she said, that an old employee of hers had opened a small hotel in Golders Green Road, and she arranged terms for Evi to move there. I certainly welcomed the move; she was now only a block or so away from me. Her mother, however, decided that it was not seemly for a young girl to be alone in London with her boyfriend, even her fiancé, despite the number of family watchdogs and that she had to have some better ostensible reason for being here. "What will I tell my friends?" she said, "It would be different if you were studying."

So Evi enrolled on a Pitman's typing and shorthand course and acquired skills which were to serve her well later in her academic career. I still do not understand why we allowed ourselves to be organised like this, but in a way, we were both strangers in the land.

Herman and Ray insisted on making an engagement party for us in their flat. It was a kind and loving gesture, even if the guests were mainly their own friends and family. The party took place on 18 October, coincidentally the same date as I started at H. Davis & Co; much had happened in the three years since then. Herman took the opportunity to say a few words. He had become very religious and liked to quote from biblical and rabbinical sources.

"The word *Mazel* (the Hebrew word for good fortune)," he said in his speech at our wedding, "is made up of three letters: mem, zayin and lamed. Mem stands for mokom (place), zayin is Hebrew for time, and lamed for learning, or wisdom." "Mazel," he went on, "means the combination of the right time and the right place and the wisdom to recognise it." Not, I think, a bad definition, and one particularly appropriate in the circumstances, though I make little claim to the "lamed" part.

We now had to fix the wedding date. There was then a considerable tax advantage in marrying before 5 April, the end of the tax year; you would be entitled to the married man's allowance for the whole tax year. It was not as easy as it might sound to arrange this. We wanted a Sunday wedding to maximise the number of guests and the synagogues were already fully booked, to say nothing of the hotels, caterers and the like, as there was no question of anything other than a fully kosher and Beth Din-supervised reception and meal. The nearest date we could get to 5 April was 16 March 1958.

Before that however, my immediate attention was on the impending finals. Maybe Yetti's doubts helped to concentrate my mind. When I received the application papers for the exams I saw that you could take Honours papers separately, for an extra £5 fee. The main examinations were held Wednesday to Friday, and the Honours the following Monday and Tuesday. I told Hymie that I would like to take the Honours papers, which were more like those which I had taken at Oxford. Though I had done no work on their subjects since coming down I wanted, as a last fling, to have a go at these. I had made a private vow with myself never to take another examination after these were over; 15 years of taking exams was enough. Hymie demurred; he would pay the fee for the normal exams but not the Honours papers and was reluctant to give me the extra time off to take them. But when he saw that I was determined, he relented, and he both paid the fee and gave me the time off.

I remember little of the main exams. I regurgitated what had been force-fed into me and I came out feeling generally dissatisfied and unhappy, though I was confident that I had passed. I enjoyed the Honours papers; these were more my cup of tea. Many years later some of my colleagues criticised me for being too academic. They did not mean it as a compliment, though I took it as such.

The results were not due for some weeks. When they came out, on a Saturday morning in December, many of my co-students went down to Fleet Street to get the first edition of the Saturday *Times*. I did not think it necessary, nor did Evi fancy another visit to the high spots of Fleet Street. Mrs Reckless brought in *The Times* with my breakfast as usual the next morning. She knew the results were due and stood and waited while feigning indifference.

I turned to the inside page bearing the results and looked among the passes but to my absolute horror, I could not find my name. I looked again at the various potential misprints my simple name might have suffered. Nothing there. Mrs Reckless saw my distress, but remained waiting patiently, her faith undiminished. I was just getting ready to sue the Law Society for something or other when I noticed that above the passes there was a small column saying "Honours". I thought I would look at that to see who among those I knew had distinguished themselves. There were two names in the First Class list, I knew them both; then there I saw my name nestling among some five or six others under "Second Class Honours". Rarely, if ever, has utter despair turned into instant delight so quickly.

"I've done it," I shouted, "I've done it. Come and see, my name's here!"

I was less concerned about the Honours, pleasing as that was, than about having passed. I felt that I had justified myself in taking the Honours papers, which I still feel was one of my better academic achievements, and I thought that for once I could be immodestly pleased with myself. Evi was equally happy, not she said, that she had ever had the slightest doubt. Next I had the pleasure of assuring Yetti that her doubts had been unwarranted – little did she know for how long I thought they had not been – and Hymie congratulated me warmly. His first words were, "Now we can get some work out of you!" but he always had a somewhat wry sense of humour.

The next stage was the wedding itself, now that my mother-in-law had survived the birth of her first grandchild (a son to Evi's brother's wife). We had to make all the arrangements ourselves, not so much because family help was denied us, but because we wanted to make it our wedding, not theirs, though to what extent we succeeded in achieving this is questionable. The chosen venue for the reception was the Dorchester Hotel, which had a room just the right size for a small wedding. I recall that I had to disguise the fact, from the banqueting manager responsible, that I was acting for his Savile Row tailor who was suing him for unpaid bills, it being an old British tradition, I believe, not to pay your tailor.

My father was so pleased at the way things were turning out that he offered to pay for a new suit for me to get married in, in his usual money-no-object approach. I thought I might try our Savile Row clients. When I found the courage to climb the few stairs and enter the forbidding establishment, I was passed down from one person to another until they found someone sufficiently lowly to deal with me – I was still an articled clerk, not yet a partner. The assistant greeted me in the manner peculiar to English servitors with that sort of unctuous insolence which puts you firmly in your place from the outset. He didn't quite wring his hands and profess his humility, though I expected him to do so at any moment. He started to take my measurements. After he had finished with the neck, shoulder, arm, sleeve, chest and waist (which all provided pretty grim evidence of being overweight), he continued:

"How does Sir dress?"

"What do you mean how do I dress?"

"How does Sir dress?" he repeated the question with a vague flap of his hands which meant nothing to me.

"Well, I usually start with my socks and work my way up," I replied totally puzzled.

"No, Sir, how do you *dress*?" he asked me with a desperate appeal in his eyes and another twitch of his hands, this time somewhat lower down the body.

"Does Sir dress left or right?"

I thought I got his meaning this time, but no one had ever asked me that before. This seems not to be a problem affecting Jewish tailors. But I still wasn't entirely sure.

"What do you mean, left or right?"

"How does Sir HANG?" he almost shouted. Ah, I had it now.

"I don't know," I replied, "shall we look and see?"

By this time I was almost ill trying to conceal my laughter, and it took me some moments to recover what was left of my aplomb, which had taken something of a battering. This, I thought, was not my kind of tailor. I had not yet reached either that level of pocket or sophistication which could justify the expense, even if it was Dad's expense, of Savile Row with its technical details. I went to a traditional little Jewish tailor, who did not worry about dressing or hanging, but just got on with the job. Admittedly, it was not as good a job, and the finished product might have looked better on a hunchback, but no one noticed. It may be that cutting a bit off creates an even hang, but I doubt whether there has been any serious research on the subject.

The next step was to find somewhere to live. House-hunting is wearying and often depressing. If you find a house you really like there is usually something wrong with it; it is either too expensive or in the wrong place, or impracticable. We found a house in Hampstead which we both loved. It was just off Hollybush Hill; one of those old houses on four floors. Surprisingly, it was within our price range but unfortunately, we took Yetti to see it. She took one look at it:

"You'll need four Hoovers," she boomed in her manly voice.

"Why?"

"Who's going to schlepp your Hoovers up all those stairs? We'll all get heart attacks just climbing the stairs. You'll have no visitors, and where are you going to eat – the bedroom?" The kitchen was on the lower ground floor, or the basement, the dining room on the ground floor, the living room on the first floor and so on.

"You'll get no sleep," she went on, "there's a pub just across the road. They'll all be drunk and never go home."

And so step by step, floor by floor, she demolished our dream. There was truth in her comments, and the practical objections she raised convinced us, but she lacked poetry in her soul, and I often wonder how different our lives would have been had we listened to our hearts and not our heads.

Although we were in no hurry, we spent most weekends house-hunting and saw nothing we liked until one day I had an excited telephone call from Yetti. She had chanced to meet a Mrs Weinberger, an old friend of my mother's, and in the course of their long chat over coffee it transpired that her son, Bernt, was in the throes of a divorce and anxious to sell his house. He had not yet put it in the hands of agents. She gave me the details and I got in touch with him. Evi and I went to see the house, at 13 Howard Walk, in Hampstead Garden Suburb. It was perfect. The number,

13, did not put me off one bit, rather the contrary. We did a quick deal at £4,875, I got a mortgage, and we had our home. All that was left now was the wedding itself.

A problem arose a few days before the wedding which was to be held in the Hampstead Garden Suburb Synagogue, Norrice Lea. All marriages in synagogues under its jurisdiction have to be approved by the Beth Din. They wanted to see my mother-in-law's *Ketuba*, or Jewish marriage certificate, to establish her Jewish credentials. Whether she had forgotten to bring it or whether she had been unable to find it I cannot recall, but my mother-in-law did not have hers with her. So she had to go before the Beth Din to be interviewed. She was not best pleased at this, but putting her daughter's happiness first, she agreed. My mother-in-law's generally benign appearance and Viennese charm cloaked a formidable lady. She was no pushover. She became increasingly angry at what she considered to be foolish and personal questions delivered in a rude and offensive manner, as if she was being cross-examined in court, which of course is exactly what it was. Satisfying the rabbis with an arcane point of law, and having obtained their irrevocable sanction to the wedding, she said to them: "Gentlemen, had you asked me I could have given you even better proof of my origins," and proceeded to reel off a list of relatives who had perished in the Holocaust. She then said: "Goodbye, gentlemen!" and left the room to a stunned silence.

It was very sunny but bitterly cold on 16 March 1958, our wedding day. Neville was my best man, and Evi surrendered to my aunts' pleas to let their daughters be bridesmaids. She exercised the bride's prerogative to be late, but I had already learned that Evi had an Argentinian sense of time.

Despite my mother-in-law's attack on our clergy, one of the dayanim, Dayan Lew, who was on the Beth Din and was our rabbi, performed the ceremony, spoke kindly to us under the *chupah*, and gave a speech at the reception. The ceremony itself was made beautiful by the glorious singing of our cantor, Rev. Freilich, the best in England, who was over the next several decades to perform the same ceremony for each of our three daughters. The guest list was very one-sided. We had our own friends, of course, but there were not many of them. Evi's family was small, and the newly born nephew prevented the attendance of his parents. Few of Evi's and her mother's friends were there, but my numerous family, Dad's coachload from the North and Herman's friends, as well as the Davises and the Reiss family filled the room. I have often regretted that we did not have the wedding in Buenos Aires, but our home was to be here and in a way I felt an obligation to thank those who had helped me to this point and amongst whom our future would be spent.

We were not able to go away on honeymoon as we wanted to see my mother-in-law, and her husband Martin, off back home. Instead, we spent a few days in the Chilterns, along the Thames, The Compleat Angler, which we thought deserved a revisit, and the Mitre at Oxford, as I had not yet shown Evi my old stamping ground. We wandered into Balliol, and almost the first person I saw was Theo Tylor. Proudly, I introduced my bride to him:

"It's Fishburn. Let me introduce you to my wife, we're on our honeymoon. Darling this is Mr Tylor whom you've heard so much about."

Evi, offering her hand: "Delighted to meet you."

Theo Tylor: "Oh, yes; how nice. Peggy (his sister) has just bought a new car."

We had a much warmer welcome at Holywell Manor from the Meiggs and the Wards, who always expressed delight at the return of any of their men, and regarded marriage as a proper institution. Our short honeymoon was over. Work called and we were off to married life together.

I had, on 1 March 1958, been duly admitted as a Solicitor of the Supreme Court and was now officially the "& Co" of H. Davis & Co: my name appeared on the firm's notepaper. I wondered just how much control we have over our destinies. Had my family not lost their money, I would have gone to the Bar. Had I not gone to Jersey, I should not have met Hymie Davis; had I not been with H. Davis, I would not have gone to dinner at Mrs Reiss's, had Evi not come to Cambridge for a May Ball and had I not gone to dinner there that night we would not have met, and I would not have been the luckiest of men.

I had not until then appreciated what a wandering Jew I was and how rootless I had been. Though I had had great help from my family and friends, it had never been help I had actively sought. It had been generously offered, but I was anxious to retain my independence and freedom of choice. Now I had a wife, a very exceptional person who was prepared to start a new life with a comparative stranger, far from her own backyard, and from the surroundings and culture familiar to her, with the attendant responsibilities, and I could not be happier.

THE END OF THE BEGINNING.